2001

Books by W. S. Merwin

POEMS

The River Sound, 1999

The Folding Cliffs: A Narrative, 1998

Flower & Hand, 1997

The Vixen, 1996

The Second Four Books, 1993

Travels, 1993

Selected Poems, 1988

The Rain in the Trees, 1988

Opening the Hand, 1983

Finding the Islands, 1982

The Compass Flower, 1977

Writings to an Unfinished Accompaniment, 1973

The Carrier of Ladders, 1970

The Lice, 1967

The Moving Target, 1963

The Drunk in the Furnace, 1960

Green with Beasts, 1956

The Dancing Bears, 1954

A Mask for Janus, 1952

PROSE

The Lost Upland, 1992

Unframed Originals, 1982

Houses and Travellers, 1977

The Miner's Pale Children, 1970

PURGATORIO

NEW YORK

ALFRED A. KNOPF

2000

Dante Alighieri

PURGATORIO

A NEW VERSE TRANSLATION BY W. S. MERWIN

Sections of *Purgatorio* previously appeared, sometimes in slightly different form, in the following publications:

Foreword: *American Poetry Review;* Canto I: *Colorado Review;* II: *Ohio Review;* III: *Grand Street;* IV: *The Formalist;* V: *Poetry;* VI: *Salt Hill Journal;* VII: *Shenandoah;* VIII: *Ohio Review;* IX: *Metamorphosis;* X: *Kenyon Review;* XI: *Slate;* XII: *Seneca Review;* XIII: *Antioch Review;* XIV: *Five Points;* XV: *Brick;* XVI: *American Poetry Review;* XVII: *Ploughshares;* XVIII: *Southern California Anthology;* XIX: *Arts and Letters;* XX: *Pequod;* XXI: *The Tampa Review;* XXII: *American Poetry Review;* XXIII: *Tri-Quarterly;* XXIV: *American Poetry Review;* XXV: *Thumbscrew;* XXVI: *The Yale Review;* XXVII: *Poetry International;* XXVIII: *Washington Square;* XXIX: *The Boston Review;* XXX: *Osiris;* XXXI: *The Cortland Review;* XXXII: *The Bitter Oleander;* XXXIII: *Manoa*

Library of Congress Cataloging-in-Publication Data
Dante Alighieri, 1265–1321.
   [Purgatorio. English & Italian]
   Purgatorio / Dante Alighieri : a new verse translation by
W. S. Merwin.
        p.   cm.
ISBN 0-375-40921-1
I. Merwin, W. S. (William Stanley).   II. Title.
PQ4315.3.M47   2000
851'.1—dc21   99-40708
                   CIP

Manufactured in the United States of America
First Edition

CONTENTS |

FOREWORD | IF A POEM is not forgotten as

soon as the circumstances of its origin, it begins at once to evolve an existence of its own, in minds and lives, and then even in words, that its singular maker could never have imagined. The poem that survives the receding particulars of a given age and place soon becomes a shifting kaleidoscope of perceptions, each of them in turn provisional and subject to time and change, and increasingly foreign to those horizons of human history that fostered the original images and references.

Over the years of trying to approach Dante through the words he left and some of those written about him, I have come to wonder what his very name means now, and to whom. Toward the end of the *Purgatorio,* in which the journey repeatedly brings the pilgrim to reunions with poets, memories and projections of poets, the recurring names of poets, Beatrice, at a moment of unfathomable loss and exposure, calls the poem's narrator and protagonist by name, "Dante," and the utterance of it is unaccountably startling and humbling. Even though it is spoken by that Beatrice who has been the sense and magnet of the whole poem and, as he has come to imagine it, of his life, and though it is heard at the top of the mountain of Purgatory, with the terrible journey done and the prospect of eternal joy ahead, the sound of his name at that moment is not at all reassuring. Would it ever be? And who would it reassure? There was, and there is, first of all, Dante the narrator. And there was Dante the man living and suffering in time, and at once we can see that there is a distinction, a division, between them. And then there was, and there is, Dante the representation of Everyman, of a brief period in the history of Italy and of Florence, of a philosophical position, a political allegiance—the list is indeterminate. Sometimes he seems to be all of them at once, and sometimes particular aspects occupy the foreground.

The commentaries date back into his own lifetime—indeed, he begins them himself, with the *Vita Nuova*—and the exegetes recognized from the beginning, whether they approved or not, the importance of the poem, the work, the vision, as they tried to arrive at some fixed significance in those words, in a later time when the words themselves were not quite the same.

Any reader of Dante now is in debt to generations of scholars working for centuries to illuminate the unknown by means of the known. Any translator shares that enormous debt. A translation, on the other hand, is seldom likely to be of much interest to scholars, who presumably sustain themselves directly upon the inexhaustible original. A translation is made for the general reader of its own time and language, a person who, it is presumed, cannot read, or is certainly not on familiar terms with, the original, and may scarcely know it except by reputation.

It is hazardous to generalize even about the general reader, who is nobody in particular and is encountered only as an exception. But my impression is that most readers at present whose first language is English probably think of Dante as the author of one work, *The Divine Comedy*, of a date vaguely medieval, its subject a journey through Hell. The whole poem, for many, has come to be known by the *Inferno* alone, the first of the three utterly distinct sections of the work, the first of the three states of the psyche that Dante set himself to explore and portray.

There are surely many reasons for this predilection, if that is the word, for the *Inferno*. Some of them must come from the human sensibility's immediate recognition of perennial aspects of its own nature. In the language of modern psychology the *Inferno* portrays the locked, unalterable ego, form after form of it, the self and its despair forever inseparable. The terrors and pain, the absence of any hope, are the ground of the drama of the *Inferno*, its nightmare grip upon the reader, its awful authority, and the feeling, even among the secular, that it is depicting something in the human makeup that cannot, with real assurance, be denied. That authority, with the assistance of a succession of haunting illustrations of the *Inferno*, has made moments and elements of that part of the journey familiar and disturbing images which remain current even in our scattered and evanescent culture.

The literary presence of the *Inferno* in English has been renewed in recent years. In 1991 Daniel Halpern asked a number of contemporary poets to provide translations of cantos of the *Inferno* which would eventually comprise a complete translation of the first part of the *Commedia*. Seamus Heaney had already published fine versions of sections from several of the cantos, including part of canto 3 in *Seeing Things* (1991), and he ended up doing the opening cantos. When Halpern asked me to contribute to the project, I replied chiefly with misgivings, to begin with. I had been trying to read Dante, and reading about him, since I was a student, carrying one volume or another of the bilingual Temple Classics edition—pocket-sized books—with me wherever I went. I had read parts, at least, of the best-known translations of the *Commedia:* Henry Francis Cary's because it came with the Gustave Doré illustrations and was in the house when I was a child; Longfellow's despite a late-adolescent resistance to nineteenth-century poetic conventions; Laurence Binyon's at the recommendation of Ezra Pound, although he seemed to me terribly tangled; John Ciardi's toward which I had other reservations. The closer I got to feeling that I was beginning to "know" a line or a passage, having the words by memory, repeating some stumbling approximation of the sounds and cadence, pondering what I had been able to glimpse of the rings of sense, the more certain I became that—beyond the ordinary and obvious impossibility of translating poetry or anything else—the translation of Dante had a dimension of impossibility of its own. I had even lectured on Dante and demonstrated the impossibility of translating him, taking a single line from the introductory first canto, examining it word by word:

Tant' è amara che poco è più morte

indicating the sounds of the words, their primary meanings, implications in the context of the poem and in the circumstances and life of the narrator, the sound of the line insofar as I could simulate it and those present could repeat it aloud and begin to hear its disturbing mantric tone. How could that, then, *really* be translated? It could not, of course. It could not be anything else. It could not be the original in other words, in another language. I presented the classical objection to translation with multiplied emphasis. Translation of poetry is an enterprise that is always in certain respects impossible, and yet on occasion it has produced something new, something else, of value, and sometimes, on the other side of a sea change, it has brought up poetry again.

Halpern did not dispute my objections, but he told me which poets he was asking to contribute to the project. He asked me which cantos I would like to do if I decided to try any myself. I thought, in spite of what I had said, of the passage at the end of canto 26, where Odysseus, adrift in a two-pointed flame in the abyss of Hell, tells Virgil "where he went to die" after his return to Ithaca. Odysseus recounts his own speech to "that small company by whom I had not been deserted," exhorting them to sail with him past the horizons of the known world to the unpeopled side of the earth, in order not to live "like brutes, but in pursuit of virtue and knowledge," and of their sailing, finally, so far that they saw the summit of Mount Purgatory rising from the sea, before a wave came out from its shore and overwhelmed them. It was the passage of the *Commedia* that had first caught me by the hair when I was a student, and it had gone on ringing in my head as I read commentaries and essays about it, and about Dante's figure of Odysseus. Odysseus says to Virgil:

Io e i compagni eravam vecchi e tardi

In the Temple Classics edition, where I first read it, or remember first reading it, the translation by John Aitken Carlyle, originally published in 1849, reads

I and my companions were old and tardy

and it was the word "tardy" that seemed to me not quite right, from the start. While I was still a student, I read the John D. Sinclair translation (Oxford), originally published in 1939, where the words read

I and my companions were old and slow

"Slow," I realized, must have been part of the original meaning, of the intent of the phrase, but I could not believe that it was the sense that had determined its being there.

The Charles S. Singleton translation, published in 1970, a masterful piece of scholarly summary, once again says

I and my companions were old and slow

That amounts to considerable authority, and it was, after all, technically correct, the dictionary meaning, and the companions surely must have been slowed down by age when Odysseus spoke to them. But I kept the original in my mind: "*tardi,*" the principal sense of which, in that passage, I thought had not been conveyed by any of the translations.

When I told Halpern that I would see whether I could provide anything of use to him, I thought of that word, "*tardi.*" It had never occurred to me to try to translate it myself, and I suppose I believed that right there I would have all my reservations about translating Dante confirmed beyond further discussion. As I considered the word in that speech it seemed to me that the most important meaning of *"tardi"* was not "tardy," although it had taken them all many years to sail from Troy. And not "slow," despite the fact that the quickness of youth must have been diminished in them. Nor "late," which I had seen in other versions, and certainly not "late" in the sense of being late for dinner. I thought the point was that they were late in the sense that an hour of the day may be late, or a day of a season or a year or a destiny: "late" meaning not having much time left. And I considered

> *I and my companions were old and near*
> *the end*

and how that went with what we knew of those lines, how it bore upon the lines that followed. Without realizing it I was already caught.

That canto had always been for me one of the most magnetic sections of the *Inferno,* and among the reasons for that was the figure of Dante's Odysseus, the voice in the flame, very far from Homer's hero, whom Dante is believed to have known only at second hand, from Virgil and other Latin classics and translations. Apparently Odysseus' final voyage is at least in part Dante's invention, and it allows him to make of Odysseus in some sense a "modern" figure, pursuing knowledge for its own sake. In Dante's own eagerness to learn about the flames floating like fireflies in the abyss he risks falling into the dark chasm himself.

That final voyage in the story of Odysseus is one of the links, within the ultimate metaphor of the poem, between the closed, immutable world of the *Inferno* and Mount Purgatory. It represents Odysseus' attempt to break out of the limitations of his own time and place by the exercise of intelligence and audacity alone. In the poem, Mount Purgatory had been formed out of the abyss of Hell when the fall of Lucifer hollowed out the center of the earth and the displaced earth erupted on the other side of the globe and became the great mountain, its opposite. And canto 26 of the *Inferno* bears several suggestive parallels to the canto of the same number in the *Purgatorio.* In the latter once again there is fire, a ring of it encircling the mountain, and again with spirits in the flames. This time some of the spirits whom Dante meets are poets. They refer to each other in sequence with an unqualified generosity born of love of each other's talents and accomplishments (this is where the phrase *"il miglior fabbro"* comes from, as one of Dante's predecessors refers to another) and their fault is love, presumably worldly love, and no doubt for its own sake. The end of that canto is one of Dante's many moving tributes to other poets and to the poetry of others. When at last he addresses the great Provençal troubadour Arnaut Daniel, the troubadour generously refers to

Dante's question as "courteous"—a word that, within decades of the great days of the troubadours and the courts of love, and then the vicious devastations of the Albigensian Crusade, evoked an entire code of behavior and view of the world. And in Dante's poem, Daniel's reply, eight lines of it that are among the most beautiful lines in the poem, is in Daniel's own Provençal, and it echoes one of Daniel's own most personal and compelling poems with an affectionate, eloquent closeness like that of Mozart's quartets dedicated to Haydn.

The *Commedia* must be one of the most carefully planned poems ever written. Everything in it seems to have been thought out beforehand, and yet such is the integrity of Dante's gift that the intricate consistency of the design is finally inseparable from the passion of the narrative and the power of the poetry. His interest in numerology, as in virtually every other field of thought or speculation in his time, was clearly part of the design at every other point, and the burning in the two cantos numbered twenty-six is unlikely to have come about without numerological consideration. His own evident attraction to the conditions of the soul, the "faults," in each canto, is a further connection.

The link between the Odysseus passage and Mount Purgatory was one of the things that impelled me to go on trying to translate that canto for Halpern's project. (I eventually sent him the result, along with a translation of the following canto.) Those two cantos which I contributed to his proposed *Inferno* I include here even though Robert Pinsky has since published his own translation of the whole of the *Inferno*—a clear, powerful, masterful gift not only to Dante translation in our language but to the poetry of our time. I am beginning with my own translations of these cantos partly because they are where I started, and because they provide the first glimpse in the poem of Mount Purgatory, seen only once, at a great distance, and fatally, at the end of the mortal life of someone who was trying to break out of the laws of creation of Dante's moral universe.

For in the years of my reading Dante, after the first overwhelming, reverberating spell of the *Inferno*, which I think never leaves one afterward, it was the *Purgatorio* that I had found myself returning to with a different, deepening attachment, until I reached a point when it was never far from me; I always had a copy within reach, and often seemed to be trying to recall part of a line, like some half-remembered song. One of the wonders of the *Commedia* is that, within its single coherent vision, each of the three sections is distinct, even to the sensibility, the tone, the feeling of existence. The difference begins at once in the *Purgatorio*, after the opening lines of invocation where Dante addresses the holy Muses (associated with their own Mount Helicon) to ask that poetry rise from the dead—literally, "dead poetry [*la morta poesì*] rise up again." Suddenly there is the word *"dolce"*—sweet, tender, or all that is to be desired in that word in Italian and in the word's siblings in Provençal and French—and then "color," and there has been nothing like that before. Where are we?

We—the reader on this pilgrimage, with the narrator and his guide, Virgil—have plunged upside down into the dark frozen depths of Hell through the bowels of the Evil One, at the center of the earth, and have made our way through the tunnel of another birth to arrive utterly undone at a sight of the stars again. And we are standing on a shore seeing the first light before dawn seep into the sky, and the morning star, *"lo bel pianeta che d'amar conforta"* "The beautiful planet that to love inclines us," with all the suggestions of consolation after the horrors of the infernal world. We are seeing the sky, our sky, the sky to which we wake in our days. There is no sky in Hell. There are no stars there, no hours of daylight, no colors of sky and sea. One of the first vast differences between Hell, the region of immutable despair, and Purgatory is that the latter place, when we step out on it, is earth again, the ground of our waking lives. We are standing on the earth under the sky, and Purgatory begins with a great welling of recognition and relief.

Of the three sections of the poem, only *Purgatory* happens *on* the earth, as our lives do, with our feet on the ground, crossing a beach, climbing a mountain. All three parts of the poem are images of our lives, of our life, but there is an intimacy peculiar to the *Purgatorio*. Here the times of day recur with all the sensations and associations that the hours bring with them, the hours of the world we are living in as we read the poem. Tenderness, affection, poignancy, the enchantment of music, the feeling of the evanescence of the moment in a context beyond time, occur in the *Purgatorio* as they do in few other places in the poem. And hope, as it is experienced nowhere else in the poem, for there is none in Hell, and Paradise is fulfilment itself. Hope is central to the *Purgatorio* and is there from the moment we stand on the shore at the foot of the mountain, before the stars fade. To the very top of the mountain hope is mixed with pain, which brings it still closer to the living present.

When I had sent the two cantos of the *Inferno* to Halpern, I was curious to see what I could make of canto 26 of the *Purgatorio*, which had captivated me for so long, and also of the lovely poem of Arnaut Daniel's which Dante echoed in that canto, and of at least one of the poems of Guido Guinizzelli, to whom he spoke with such reverence, as to a forebear.

Other moments in the *Purgatorio* had held me repeatedly. Almost thirty years earlier, on the tube in London, I had been reading canto 5, which was already familiar ground. It was like listening to a much-loved piece of music, hearing a whole current in it that had never before seemed so clear. I rode three stops past my destination and had to get off and go back and be late. And here once again, trying vainly to find equivalents for words and phrases, I was in the grip of the *Purgatorio*. After canto 26 I went back to the beginning.

The opening cantos that comprise the section known as the "Antepurgatorio" are among the most beautiful in the whole poem. I thought of trying to make something in English just of those, the first six in particular. I turned them over slowly, line by line, lingering over treasures such as La Pia's few lines at the end of canto 5, hoping that I was not betraying them by suggesting any other words for them (though Clarence Brown once said to me, to reassure me about another translation of mine, "Don't worry, no translation ever harmed the original") or at any rate betraying my relation to them. There were lines that had run in my head for years, their beauty inexhaustible. The morning of the first day, looking out to sea, in canto I:

> *L'alba vinceva l'ora mattutina*
> *che fuggia innanzi, sì che di lontano*
> *conobbi il tremolar della marina.*

What could anyone do? My attempt ran:

> *The dawn was overcoming the pallor of daybreak*
> *which fled before it, so that I could see*
> *off in the distance the trembling of the sea.*

It was, I kept saying, *some* indication of what was there, what was worth trying to suggest, at least, in English. I wanted to keep whatever I made by way of translation as close to the meaning of the Italian words as I could make it, taking no liberties, so that someone with no Italian would not be misled. And I hoped to make the translation a poem in English, for if it were not that it would have failed to indicate what gave the original its memorable power.

The *Purgatorio* is the section of the poem in which poets, poetry, and music recur with fond vividness and intimacy. The meetings between poets—Virgil's with his fellow Mantuan Sordello, over twelve hundred years after Virgil's own life on earth; his meeting with the Roman poet Statius; Dante's with Guido Guinizzelli and with Arnaut Daniel and the singer Casella—are cherished and moving moments. It is worth noting something about the current of poetic tradition that Dante had come to in his youth.

Of course there was Virgil, to whose *Aeneid* he alludes with such familiarity that he must have long known many parts of it by heart. And Statius and other Latin poets whose work was available in late-thirteenth-century Florence.

Another dominant lineage of poetic tradition which Dante inherited and felt around him as he reached maturity, that of the troubadours and their own antecedents, was at once closer to him and more complex, but it gathers into one strand the poetic conventions that were available to him, and some essentials of his thinking about love, and a crucial directive in the development of the figure of Beatrice in the *Commedia*.

The three currents, and Dante's ideas about them, merge inextricably in the poem, as they seem to have done in the mind of its author. Beatrice, in the story as he finally made it, is the origin of the great journey itself, sending the poet Virgil to guide the lost Dante through the vast metaphor: the world of the dead which is the world of life, the world of eternity which is the world of time. The principle that binds the metaphor in all of its aspects, as we are told in one way after another, is love. After the passage around the beclouded terrace of anger, and Virgil's statement that "neither creator nor creature was ever without love," Dante asks, with considerable hesitation, for Virgil to explain (indeed to *demonstrate*, "*dimostri*") to him what love is. Virgil's presence there itself, as a guide on this unprecedented journey with nothing to gain for himself in all eternity, and the watchful provision of Beatrice that had sent him, and is waiting for Dante the pilgrim at the top of Mount Purgatory, are of course, both of them, dramatic *demonstrations* of love; but Virgil proceeds to expound, to explain, the origins and evolution of love according to Aristotle, whose work he might have known in his lifetime, and Aquinas, whose work he could only have encountered posthumously somewhere between his own day and Dante's. In due course Beatrice speaks on the subject, and some of her sources are the same. But quite aside from the explications of the scholastics, the subject of love, including aspects of it that were being purged in canto 26 of the *Purgatorio,* was the central theme of the great flowering of troubadour poetry in the twelfth and thirteenth centuries. In that surge of new poetry and feeling, the forms of love ranged from the openly sensual to the unattainably ethereal, and from such familiar treatment as may have verged upon folk poetry of the time (and is still to be found in the popular culture of our own time) to courtly, allusive, highly stylized poetry that seemed to treat love on many planes at once.

In its rapid development the tradition of troubadour poetry evolved the convention of a beloved to whom, and about whom, for whom the poems were written. Of course love poetry, both erotic and idealized in one way or another, had existed and had been important in other ages and in many—perhaps in most—cultures. And the figure of the beloved who is the subject of the poems and to whom they are addressed had often been evoked, whether idealized or not. But the theme and elevation of a beloved emerged with particular intensity in the tenth-century Arabic poetry of the Omayyad Moorish kingdoms of southern Spain. In the highly cultivated poetry and culture that had evolved there, a code of attitudes, behavior, gestures developed, a stylized choreography, that were clearly the matured result of an ancient tradition. Early in the eleventh century Ali ibn-Hazm of Cordova, a philosopher and literary theoretician, produced a work entitled *On Love* in thirty chapters. In the chapter "Love at First Sight" he tells of the poet Ibn-Harûn al-Ramadi, who met his beloved only once, at a gate in Cordova, and wrote all his poems for the rest of his life to her. Love in that tradition is spoken of as the greatest of inspirations and the ultimate happiness. In Spain, Arabic philosophy absorbed the work of Plato, which the Provençal poets and then their Italian successors drew upon in turn. The forms of the Andalusian Arabic poetry were developed from, or in accord with, the songs of the folk tradition. A stanza was evolved, its measure strictly marked for chanting, and it made important use of something that had not been part of the classical languages of Europe and their Latinate descendants—rhyme. One form in particular, the *zajal*, or "song," became the most common one in Spanish-Arabic poetry in the tenth and eleventh centuries. Out of the eleven surviving poems of the first Provençal poet whose works have come down to us, the one who is generally referred to as the first of the troubadours, Guilhem de Peitau, or Guillaume de Poitiers, three are in the form of the Hispano-Arabic *zajal*. And Count Guilhem, one of the most powerful men in Europe in his generation, was at least as familiar, and probably as sympathetic, with the courts of Arabic Spain as he was with much of northern France. So were the troubadours who were his immediate successors; and the brief-lived courts of love of Guilhem's granddaughter Eleanor of Aquitaine continued a brilliant kinship with the Moorish kingdoms to the south.

The rhymed and highly stylized poetry of the troubadours, with its allegiance to music, the codes of the courts of love, the Hispano-Arabic assimilation of the philosophy of classical Greece, were essentials of the great Provençal civilization of the twelfth and early thirteenth centuries. The secular splendor of that culture and its relative indifference to the tedious imperium of the Church were in the end (1209) barbarously and viciously ruined by the wave of political ruthlessness and deadly self-righteousness known as the Albigensian Crusade, one of the great atrocities of European history. (It was a bishop, Arnaud de Cîteaux, who gave the order, at the sack of Beziers, "Kill them all. God will know His own." And they did.) Both that rich, generous, brilliant tradition and the devastation that had been visited upon it were part of Dante's heritage. The latter had taken place less than half a century before he was born; the Mantuan poet Sordello, for one, had spent a major part of his life at the court of Toulouse. The legacy of the troubadours survived even beyond Dante. Petrarch is sometimes described as the last of the troubadours. And the attention given to the manners, the psychic states, the perspectives, the ultimate power of love, the exalted beloved, the forms of verse, including rhyme, all come from the culture of Provence either directly or via the court of Frederick II of Sicily.

But Dante's beloved, Beatrice, did have an earthly original in his own life and youth. From what can be known at present she was named Bice, daughter of Folio Portinari. Dante describes his first sight of her, in 1284, when he was nineteen. She eventually married, and then died in 1290, when he was twenty-five, ten years before the ideal date of the *Commedia*. In *La Vita Nuova*, finished in the years just after Bice's death, Dante vows to leave her a literary monument such as no woman had ever had. So she led him, he tells us, to the journey that becomes the *Commedia* and his own salvation.

That love, and that representation of it, took place in a life of enormous political turmoil and intellectual ferment. Dante, as his words and the passions in them make clear, was from Florence, where he was born in May 1265. His family believed themselves to be descended from the original Roman founders of the city. An ancestor, Dante's great-great-grandfather, had died, Dante tells us, on the second crusade. But his family ranked among the lesser nobility of the city and was not wealthy.

The Florence into which Dante was born was deeply divided into political factions. Principally, there were the Ghibellines, who were in effect the feudal aristocracy and, with the backing of the Empire, the holders of most power; and the Guelphs, the party of the lesser nobles and the artisans, bitterly opposed to the principles and conduct, the heedless self-interest of the Ghibellines. Dante was educated in Franciscan schools and at an early age began to write poetry. There were troubadours in Florence in his youth, and apparently he knew them, knew their poems, learned from them. His early friendship with the aristocrat Guido Cavalcanti led them both to develop a style and art which distinguished them from their predecessors and most of their contemporaries. Cavalcanti too had a literary beloved, named Mandetta, in his poems; he tells how he caught sight of her once in a church in Toulouse.

In his mid-twenties Dante served the commune of Florence in the cavalry. He was at the battle of Campaldino, and scenes of the battle return in the *Purgatorio*. And his studies—the Latin classics, philosophy, and the sciences—continued. Within the circle of those who read poetry in Florence, his poems became well known, and after the death of the woman he called Beatrice he assembled a group of them, embedded in a highly stylized narrative—*La Vita Nuova* (1292–93). At a date now unknown he was married to Gemma di Manetta Donati, and they had at least three children, two sons and a daughter.

In 1295, in order to participate in municipal government, Dante became a member of the guild of physicians and apothecaries, and he came to serve in electoral and administrative councils, and as an ambassador of his city on a number of missions. He engaged in a Guelph campaign of opposition to Pope Boniface VIII, who had a plan to place all of Tuscany under the rule of the Church. The conflict became prolonged, bitter, and dangerous, with warnings of worse to come. The Pope's cynical proceedings became more ruthless and ominous. The opposition was no less determined. In 1301, on the occasion of Charles de Valois's meeting in Rome with the Pope, Dante was sent by the commune of Florence as one of three emissaries to the Pope to try to exact from the moment something that would help to maintain the independence of Florence. The Pope dismissed the other two emissaries and held Dante in Rome. There, and then in Siena shortly afterward, Dante learned of the triumph of his opponents, the "Blacks," in Florence, and then of their sentencing him to a heavy fine and two years' banishment, besides a perpetual ban on his holding any further public office, and charges of graft, embezzlement, opposition to papal and secular authority, disturbance of the peace, etc. Just over a month later, when he had not paid the fine, he was sentenced a second time. The new sentence stated that if ever he should come within reach of the representatives of the commune of Florence he was to be burned alive. He was then thirty-seven. There is no evidence that he ever saw Florence again.

In the subsequent years of exile he found lodging and employment in other city-states. He served as aide, courtier, and secretary to various men of power, lived for a time with the great lords of Verona. He wrote, in *De Vulgare Eloquentia,* that the world was his fatherland, as the whole sea is the country of the fish; but he complained of having to wander as a pilgrim, almost a beggar, through all the regions where Italian was spoken.

At some point during those years in exile he conceived and began the work which, because of the plainness of its style and the fact that it moves from hopeless anguish to joy, he called the *Commedia*. It was written not in Latin, nor in the Provençal that was the literary language of his immediate forebears—a language that he certainly knew very well—but in his own vernacular. And the subject of most poetry in the vernacular, in his heritage, was love.

Of the later years of his exile not much is known. Several great families—the households of the Scaligeri, of Uguccione della Faggiuola, of Cangrande della Scala—befriended and sheltered him and provided for him. The last years of his life were spent in Ravenna, apparently in peace and relative security. Probably his children and perhaps his wife were able to join him there. He may have lectured there, and he worked at completing the *Commedia*. Shortly after it was finished he went on a diplomatic mission to Venice for Guido da Polenta, and he died on the way home, on September 13 or 14, 1321, four years short of the age of sixty.

He was buried in Ravenna, and despite repeated efforts by the city of Florence to claim them, there his bones remain.

We know as much as we ever will about what he looked like from a description by Boccaccio: a long face, aquiline nose, large jaw, protruding lower lip, large eyes, dark curly hair (and beard), and a melancholy, thoughtful appearance. None of the surviving portraits is entirely trustworthy, though two have become famous and are commonly accepted.

Since adolescence I have felt what I can only describe as reverence for him, a feeling that seems a bit odd in our age. It is there, of course, because of his poetry, and because of some authority of the imagination in the poetry, some wisdom quite distinct from doctrine, though his creed and his reason directed its form. I am as remote from his theological convictions, probably, as he was from the religion of Virgil, but the respect and awed affection he expresses for his guide sound familiar to me.

I have read, more or less at random, and over a long period, in the vast literature of Dante studies—not much, to be sure, in view of how much of it there is. I am particularly grateful for works by Erich Auerbach, Irma Brandeis, Charles S. Singleton, Allan Gilbert, Thomas G. Bergin, Helmut Hatzfeld, Charles Spironi, Francis Fergusson, Robert Briffault, and Philippe Guiberteau. The notes to the individual cantos in the translation are above all indebted to Charles S. Singleton's lifelong dedication to Dante studies and to the notes in his own edition of the poem. But there has been no consistent method in my reading of studies about Dante. I have come upon what seemed to me individual illuminations of his work partly by chance, over a period of time, forgetting as I went, naturally. The one unfaltering presence has been a love of the poem, which has been there from the first inchmeal reading. I am as conscious as ever of the impossibility of putting the original into any words but its own. But I hope this version manages to convey something true and essential of what is there in the words of the poem that Dante wrote.

Inferno
CANTO XXVI

Florence rejoice, oh you that are so great
that over sea and over land you beat
your wings and hell is swollen with your name.

I found among the thieves five citizens   4
of yours and the shame of that stays with me
and your honor is not enlarged thereby.

But if we dream the truth as we near morning   7
you will now be feeling before long
what Prato among others prays down on you.

If it were now it would be none too soon.
Since it is sure to happen, let it come,
for it will weigh upon me worse with time.

We left that place and up by the stone stair
of rock ledges that we came down before
my guide climbed again and drew me after

and following the solitary way
among the rocks and juttings of the cliff
the foot could not move unless the hand was helping.

Then I felt sorrow and I sorrow now
when I turn back my mind to what I saw
and more than usually I restrain my genius

lest it run where Virtue does not guide it,
so that if favoring star or better thing
has given me the good I may accept it.

As many fireflies as the peasant resting
on the hill during that season when
he who gives light to the world hides his face least

at the hour when the fly is yielding to the gnat
sees down the length of the valley perhaps
even there where he harvests the grapes and plows,

with as many flames as that the eighth chasm
was shining, so it appeared to me when
I stood where I could look all the way down.

And even as he whom the bears avenged
beheld Elijah's chariot departing
that time the horses rose straight up to Heaven

so that he could not turn his eyes upon
anything except the flame alone
like a little cloud in its ascending

even so each one moves in the gullet
of the gorge, for in none of them the theft
appears and every flame palms a sinner.

I had climbed up onto the bridge to look
and if I had not held onto a rock
I would have fallen in with none to push me.

And the guide, seeing me so rapt,
said, "Inside those fires are the spirits.
Each one wraps himself in what burns him."

"My master," I said to him, "hearing you
has made me sure, but I had already
guessed it was so and was moved to ask you

who is in that fire that comes divided

10

13

16

19

22

25

28

31

34

37

40

43

46

49

52

at the top as though it rose from the pyre
where Eteocles was put beside his brother?"

He answered me, "Inside that one Ulysses   55
and Diomed suffer and so together
they endure vengeance as they went in anger

and in their flame they groan for the hiding   58
in the horse, which made the doorway for
the noble seed of the Romans to come through.

Inside there they lament the art that causes   61
Deidamia even in death to mourn for Achilles
and there they are punished for Palladium."

"If those who are inside the sparks can speak,"   64
I said, "I beseech you fervently,
and beseech again, beseech you a thousand times

not to refuse to let me wait   67
until the horned flame comes here where we are.
See how the longing is bending me toward it."

And he to me, "What you pray is worthy   70
of much praise, and therefore I accept it,
but you must put a curb on your own tongue.

Leave the speaking to me, for I understand   73
what you desire, and it could be that they,
since they were Greek, might scorn what you would say."

After the flame had arrived somewhere that   76
seemed to my guide to be the time and place
this is what I heard him say to it,

"Oh you that are two within a single fire,   79
if I deserved much of you while I lived,
if I deserved of you much or a little

when in the world I wrote the high verses,   82
do not move on, but one of you say where
when he had lost himself he went to die."

The larger horn of the ancient flame   85
began to shudder, murmuring, the way
a flame does when the wind harries it.

Then the tip, moving back and forth as though   88
it were the tongue that was speaking, flung
a voice out of itself saying, "When

I left Circe who for a year and more   91
had held me back, close to Gaeta there,
before Aeneas gave the place its name,

not affection for my son nor reverence   94
for my old father nor that rightful love

that should have brought joy to Penelope
could subdue the ardor I had in me   97
to become experienced in the world
and in human iniquities and worth,
but I set forth on the open sea   100
with a single ship and that small company
that by then had not deserted me.
One shore and the other I saw as far as Spain,   103
far as Morocco, the isle of Sardinia
and the other islands that sea washes round.
I and my companions were old and near   106
the end when we came to the narrows
where Hercules set up his warning markers
for men, to tell them they should sail no farther.   109
On the right hand I left Seville behind,
on the other I had already left Ceuta.
'Oh brothers,' I said, 'who through a hundred   112
thousand perils have arrived at the west,
do not deny to the little waking
time that remains to your senses knowing   115
for yourselves the world on the far side
of the sun, that has no people in it.
Consider what you rose from: you were not   118
made to live like animals but
for the pursuit of virtue and knowledge.'
With this short speech I so whetted my   121
companions for the journey that I
would hardly have been able to hold them back,
and turning the stern toward the morning we   124
made wings of our oars for the insane flight,
bearing over the whole time toward the left.
Already the night could see all of the stars   127
of the other pole, and ours was so low
it never rose above the ocean floor.
Five times the light under the moon had been   130
lighted and as many times put out
since we had entered on the deep passage
when a mountain appeared dark in the distance   133
and it seemed to me that it was higher
than any I had ever seen before.
At the sight we rejoiced, but that turned quickly   136
to grief, for out of the new land a whirlwind
rose that struck the bow of our vessel.

Three times it spun her round with all the waters.   *139*
On the fourth it lifted the stern up
and drove down the prow, as pleased another,
    until the sea was closed over us."   *142*

CANTO XXVII

    Now the flame burned straight upward and was still,
saying no more, and now from us it
went with the consent of the gentle poet
    when there arrived another from behind it   *4*
that made us turn our eyes to the top of it
toward a confused noise that came out of it.
    As the Sicilian bull that bellowed first   *7*
with the moaning (as was no more than just)
of the one who had tuned it with his file
    bellowed on with the voice of the victim   *10*
so that though it was only a brass thing
it seemed to be transfixed with suffering,
    thus, having from the first no way, no little   *13*
hole out of the fire, the miserable
words were converted into its language,
    but after they had taken their journey   *16*
up through the point, giving it those vibrations
that the tongue had given them on their way,
    we heard it say, "Oh you toward whom I turn   *19*
my voice and who just now were speaking in
Lombard, saying 'Go now, no more I ask you,'
    though perhaps I have come a little late,   *22*
do not be impatient but wait and speak with me.
See, I am not impatient and I burn.
    If you have fallen only now into   *25*
this blind world out of that sweet Italian
land from which all of my guilt I bring,
    say, have the Romagnoli peace or war,   *28*
for I was from the mountains between Urbino there
and the summit from which the Tiber flows."
    I was still bent down and listening   *31*
when my guide touched my side, saying
"You speak, for this is an Italian."
    And I who had my answer ready   *34*
lost no time then but began this way:
"Oh soul that are hidden under there,

your Romagna is not and never was without   37
war in the hearts of its tyrants, though
none was to be seen now as I left it.

Ravenna is as it has been all these years,   40
the eagle of Polenta brooding on it
so that he covers Cervia with his wings.

The city that was put to the long test   43
and then made of the French a bleeding hill
finds itself again under the green claws.

Verrucchio's old mastiff and the young one   46
who had Montagna in his evil keeping
are still gnawing at the same places.

The cities of Lamone and Santerno   49
are led by the young lion of the white lair
who changes sides from winter to summer,

and that city whose flank the Savio washes,   52
just as it lies between plain and mountain
so it lives between tyranny and freedom.

Now I pray you to tell us who you are.   55
Be no harder than one has been toward you,
so may your name advance still through the world."

After the flame had for a moment roared   58
in its own way, the sharp point of it moved
back and forth, and then gave breath like this:

"If I believed that I was answering   61
one who would ever go back to the world
this flame would stand still and shake no further,

but since no one ever returned alive   64
out of this deep if what I hear is true,
without dread of disgrace I answer you.

After a life of arms I turned Franciscan,   67
thinking, girt with that rope, to make amends,
and my belief would have been fulfilled, I am certain,

but for the Great Vicar—evil take him!—   70
who set me back into my early sins.
I want you to hear from me how and why.

While I was the shape of bone and flesh   73
my mother gave me, the things I did
were not those of the lion but the fox.

Intricate strategies and covert means,   76
I knew them all, and used them with such art
that to the end of the earth the sound went out.

When I saw that I myself had reached 79
that part of my age at which everyone
should lower sails and gather the ropes in,

what had pleased me before became my grief, 82
and repenting and confessing I turned friar
—oh misery—and it would have been enough.

The prince of the new Pharisees, finding 85
himself at war close to the Lateran
and not against the Jews or Saracens,

for every enemy of his was Christian, 88
not one of whom had been to conquer Acre
nor been a merchant in the Sultan's land,

regarded neither in himself the highest 91
office, his holy orders, nor in me
that cord that used to make its wearers thin,

but as Constantine sought Silvester on 94
Mount Soracte to cure his leprosy,
so this one sought me out to be the doctor

who would cure him of his proud fever, 97
asking me for advice, and I said nothing
because his words sounded drunk to me.

And then he said to me, 'Put from your heart any 100
fear. Here and now I absolve you. Teach me
how to throw Penestrino to the ground.

Heaven, as you know, I am able 103
to close and open. For this are there two keys
which my predecessor valued little.'

I was moved by the weighty arguments 106
until I thought silence would be the worst course
and I said, 'Father, since you wash me

of this sin into which now I must fall, 109
be long in promises, short in keeping them,
and you will triumph on the high seat.'

Later, when I was dead, Saint Francis came 112
for me, but one of the black cherubim
said, 'Do not take him. Do not do me wrong.

He is bound to come down among my helots, 115
for ever since he gave the fraudulent
counsel I have had him by the hair

for none can be absolved without repenting 118
nor can repent and want at the same time,
the contradiction not permitting it.'

Oh my suffering! How startled I was when 121
he seized me saying, 'Maybe you did not
realize that I was a logician.'

He bore me off to Minos and that one curled 124
his tail eight times around his hardened back
and then biting it in his great rage

said, 'This sinner is for the stealing fire,' 127
so that here where you see me I am lost
in this garment, bitter and wandering."

When he had ended what he had to say 130
with that, the flame, sorrowing, went its way,
writhing and flinging high its pointed horn.

We continued, I and my guide, along 133
the cliff to the next arch which crosses over
the chasm where the penalty is paid

by those whose burden comes from sowing discord. 136

Notes

INFERNO, CANTO XXVI

(The notes appended here and at the back of the book rely on the work of Dante scholars—I am certainly nothing of the kind, myself—and primarily on the commentaries of John D. Sinclair, Philip H. Wicksteed, and above all Charles S. Singleton.)

9 Perhaps in part to evoke the elusive style of prophetic utterances, the allusion here is full of possible interpretations but points clearly to no single, unequivocal object. The probable references seem to be these:

Prato is a Tuscan town between Florence and Pistoia. Smaller than Florence, it remained, in general, on good terms with the larger state, though the allusion here may suggest an ancient jealousy, or a long-restrained resentment at Florentine arrogance. But it seems more likely that the primary reference is to Cardinal Niccolò da Prato, who had tried to pacify the bitter factions in Florence, had failed, and in June of 1304 had left Florence in disgust, excommunicating its inhabitants. The misfortunes to which Dante's "prophecy" refers were attributed to the cardinal's imprecations.

They include a catastrophe at the new Ponte alla Carraia over the Arno, where many spectators had gathered, as Benvenuto wrote, after "the people of the St. Florian quarter had it publicly proclaimed that whoever wanted to have news of the other world should come to the Ponte alla Carraia at the beginning of May. They set up floats on boats and barges and arranged a sort of representation of Hell, with fires and other pains and torments . . . everyone went to see it. . . . Because of that, the Ponte alla Carraia, which was then made of wood . . . crashed into the Arno with all the people on it . . ." and a great many were killed. A while later a fire in the city destroyed over seventeen hundred buildings, including towers and palazzi.

I cannot resolve what seems to me a confusion in the chronology. The cardinal left in June, and if the Ponte alla Carraia collapsed in May of the same year, as Charles Singleton, citing Villari's *Cronica*, tells us, then the curse must have come after the event.

A consideration of the chronology suggests another reason for Dante's putting the dire happenings in the form of a veiled prophecy. If the disasters mentioned above are among those referred to, they took place several years after 1300, the "Ideal Date of Vision" of the *Commedia*.

34   2 Kings 2:23–24 And Eliseus went up from thence to Bethel. And as he was going up by the way, little boys came out of the city and mocked him, saying: Go up, thou bald head. Go up, thou bald head.

And looking back, he saw them, and cursed them in the name of the Lord, and there came forth two bears out of the forest, and tore of them two and forty boys.

35   2 Kings 2:11–12 And as they went on, walking and talking together, behold a fiery chariot, and fiery horses parted them both asunder, and Elias went up by a whirlwind into heaven.

54   Eteocles and Polynices were twin sons of Oedipus and Jocasta. They forced Oedipus to abdicate and leave Thebes, and he prayed that enmity should divide them forever. They agreed to rule Thebes alternately, each one for a year at a time. But Eteocles, at the end of his reign, refused to relinquish the kingdom, and the civil war that led to the Seven Against Thebes broke out. The brothers killed each other in single combat. Their bodies were placed on one pyre, but as the flame rose it split apart.

56   The person of Ulysses, in whatever setting, surely needs no general iden-tification. But it is worth noting that Diomedes, king of Argos and one of the heroes who was with Ulysses in the war against Troy, was his accom-plice in luring Achilles into that war, and in the tactic that led to the cap-ture of the Palladium, the image of Pallas Athena that protected Troy. And Dante appears to have assumed that Diomedes was also a party to Ulysses' famous stratagem of the wooden horse, which led to the sack of Troy. But it should be remembered, in regard both to this and to Dante's account of Ulysses' final voyage, that Dante did not know the *Odyssey*, but only later references to Ulysses. On the other hand, we know and can suppose that Dante knew that two Genoese brothers named Vivaldi, in 1291, sailed through the Straits of Gibraltar, westward, looking for India, and never returned—and the "Americas" were spared thus for another two centuries.

62   Deidamia: Achilles' wife.

91   Circe: Sorceress who transformed men into swine.

92   Gaeta: Seaport in southern Italy, named for Aeneas' nurse.

103–109   An itinerary more imaginary than literal. Spain and Morocco of course are far to the west of Sardinia. At the Straits of Gibraltar, the Pillars of Hercules, according to the tradition, were once a single mountain until they were torn apart by that sun hero. During the later Middle Ages they were taken to represent the western limits of human enterprise, beyond which no one could presume to travel and live to tell of it.

INFERNO, CANTO XXVII

7–12 Phalaris, a tyrant of Agrigentum in Sicily, had his victims locked into a brazen image of a bull, which was then roasted, and the shrieks of the victim, it is said, were like the bellowing of a bull. Perillus, the inventor of the device, was supposedly its first victim.

19–20 This unnamed voice reduced to asking for news of home is Guido da Montefeltro, once known as "the Fox," a brilliant and often successful military leader of the Ghibelline faction, from Romagna. He was excommunicated for returning from exile, to which he had been sentenced by the Vatican. Eventually he left secular life altogether and in 1296 joined the Franciscan order. But according to a tradition, in 1298 Pope Boniface VIII persuaded him to tell how the citadel of Palestrina could be taken, and Guido's advice on that occasion is the basis for Dante's finding him here among the authors of covert operations and fraudulent counsel.

40–51 The references throughout are to municipalities and ruling families of Romagna.

52 On the river Savio, between Forlí and Rimini, at the foothills of the Appenines, the municipality of Cesena.

Guido's advice, according to Riccobaldo, chonicler of Ferrara, was to "promise much and fulfill little"—a practice so generally assumed among those engaged in politics that it seems there must have been something more remarkable and specific which has remained a secret.

88 The war between Pope Boniface VIII and the Colonna family, who contested the succession that had led to the Pope's position and maintained that it was based upon fraud. "Lateran" here refers to Rome itself.

89 Acre: from the French Saint-Jean d'Acre, and Old Testament Accho; a seaport now part of Israel, northwest of Jerusalem. The crusaders took it in 1104, and it was their principal port for eighty-three years, until Saladin recaptured it. In 1191 Richard Coeur de Lion and Philip Augustus of France led the campaign that took the port again, and it remained in Christian hands for a century after that. In 1294 it was taken back by a sultan, thus ending the western kingdom of Jerusalem.

94 In the legend recounted by Jacobus de Varagine, archbishop of Genoa 1292–98, Constantine, as a punishment for persecuting Christians, contracted leprosy. The pagan clergy prescribed a bath in infants' blood. Three thousand babies were brought in, but the shrieks of lamentation touched Constantine and he said he would rather die than butcher these innocents. That night Saints Peter and Paul appeared to him and told him to consult a certain Sylvester, who was living in a cave on Mount Soracte. Sylvester, in due course, baptized Constantine, who was cured on the spot. Constantine went back and converted his mother, and between them they brought about the Christianization of Rome.

102   Penestrino, now Palestrina. The citadel of the Colonna family, some twenty miles southeast of Rome. In 1298, when the Colonnas surrendered to Pope Boniface VIII, who had promised them complete amnesty, the Pope completely destroyed the city.

124   Minos, guardian at the entrance to the second circle of Hell, who hears the offenses of those who come before him and assigns them to their eternal places in the abyss.

PURGATORIO

CANTO I

Per correr miglior acque alza le vele
omai la navicella del mio ingegno,
che lascia dietro a sé mar sì crudele;

e canterò di quel secondo regno   4
·dove l'umano spirito si purga
e di salire al ciel diventa degno.

Ma qui la morta poesì resurga,   7
o sante Muse, poi che vostro sono;
e qui Calïopè alquanto surga,

seguitando il mio canto con quel suono   10
di cui le Piche misere sentiro
lo colpo tal, che disperar perdono.

Dolce color d'orïental zaffiro,   13
che s'accoglieva nel sereno aspetto
del mezzo, puro infino al primo giro,

a li occhi miei ricominciò diletto,   16
tosto ch'io usci' fuor de l'aura morta
che m'avea contristati li occhi e 'l petto.

Lo bel pianeto che d'amar conforta   19
faceva tutto rider l'orïente,
velando i Pesci ch'erano in sua scorta.

I' mi volsi a man destra, e puosi mente   22
a l'altro polo, e vidi quattro stelle
non viste mai fuor ch'a la prima gente.

Goder pareva 'l ciel di lor fiammelle: 25
oh settentrïonal vedovo sito,
poi che privato se' di mirar quelle!

Com' io da loro sguardo fui partito,   28
un poco me volgendo a l'altro polo,
là onde 'l Carro già era sparito,

To course on better waters the little
boat of my wit, that leaves behind her
so cruel a sea, now raises her sails,

and I will sing of that second kingdom   4
in which the human spirit is made clean
and becomes worthy to ascend to Heaven.

But here let poetry rise again from the dead,   7
oh holy Muses, for yours I am,
and here let Calliope rise up for a time

lending my song company with that tone   10
which rang in the ears of the miserable
magpies so that they despaired of pardon.

The tender color of Oriental sapphire   13
that was gathering in the serene countenance
of the clear sky all the way to the horizon

brought to my eyes the start of joy once more   16
when I had come forth out of the dead air
that had filled my eyes and my breast with suffering.

The beautiful planet that to love inclines us   19
brought to a smile the whole of the East,
veiling the Fishes that escorted her.

I turned to my right and fixed my vision   22
on the other pole and saw four stars that no one
had seen before, except the first people.

The sky seemed to rejoice in their points of fire—   25
oh widowed northern country, you that are
deprived of having any sight of them!

As I looked away from gazing at them,   28
turning a little toward the other pole
from which already the Wain had gone,

vidi presso di me un veglio solo, 31
degno di tanta reverenza in vista,
che più non dee a padre alcun figliuolo.

Lunga la barba e di pel bianco mista 34
portava, a' suoi capelli simigliante,
de' quai cadeva al petto doppia lista.

Li raggi de le quattro luci sante 37
fregiavan sì la sua faccia di lume,
ch'i' 'l vedea come 'l sol fosse davante.

"Chi siete voi che contro al cieco fiume 40
fuggita avete la pregione etterna?"
diss' el, movendo quelle oneste piume.

"Chi v'ha guidati, o che vi fu lucerna, 43
uscendo fuor de la profonda notte
che sempre nera fa la valle inferna?

Son le leggi d'abisso così rotte? 46
o è mutato in ciel novo consiglio,
che, dannati, venite a le mie grotte?"

Lo duca mio allor mi diè di piglio, 49
e con parole e con mani e con cenni
reverenti mi fé le gambe e 'l ciglio.

Poscia rispuose lui: "Da me non venni: 52
donna scese del ciel, per li cui prieghi
de la mia compagnia costui sovvenni.

Ma da ch'è tuo voler che più si spieghi 55
di nostra condizion com' ell' è vera,
esser non puote il mio che a te si nieghi.

Questi non vide mai l'ultima sera; 58
ma per la sua follia le fu sì presso,
che molto poco tempo a volger era.

Sì com' io dissi, fui mandato ad esso 61
per lui campare; e non li era altra via
che questa per la quale i' mi son messo.

I saw near me an old man all alone,   31
his face deserving of such reverence
no father is owed more by any son.

A long beard with white strands mingled in it   34
he wore, and his hair resembled it,
falling in two locks down onto his breast.

The rays of the four sacred lights adorned   37
his face so with their shining that I saw him
as though the sun were in front of him.

"Who are you, who against the blind stream   40
have made your escape from the eternal prison?"
he said, with those venerable plumes shaking.

"Who was it that guided you? Who was your light   43
bringing you forth out of the profound night
that keeps the infernal valley black forever?

Are the laws of the abyss broken like this   46
or has a new rule been pronounced in Heaven,
that you that are damned come here to my caverns?"

At that my leader laid hold upon me   49
and with words and with hands and with signs
he made my knees and my brow show reverence.

Then he answered, "I have not come of myself.   52
A lady came down from heaven through whose prayers
I have helped this one with my company.

But since it is your will that our condition   55
in its truth should further be unfolded to you,
it cannot be mine to deny that to you.

This one has not yet seen the final evening   58
but through his folly he had come so near it
that very little time was left for changing.

As I have told you, I was sent to him   61
to save him, and there was no other way
than this one, on which I began my journey.

Mostrata ho lui tutta la gente ria;   64
e ora intendo mostrar quelli spirti
che purgan sé sotto la tua balìa.

Com' io l'ho tratto, saria lungo a dirti;   67
de l'alto scende virtù che m'aiuta
conducerlo a vederti e a udirti.

Or ti piaccia gradir la sua venuta: 70
libertà va cercando, ch'è sì cara,
come sa chi per lei vita rifiuta.

Tu 'l sai, ché non ti fu per lei amara   73
in Utica la morte, ove lasciasti
la vesta ch'al gran dì sarà sì chiara.

Non son li editti etterni per noi guasti,   76
ché questi vive e Minòs me non lega;
ma son del cerchio ove son li occhi casti

di Marzia tua, che 'n vista ancor ti priega,   79
o santo petto, che per tua la tegni:
per lo suo amore adunque a noi ti piega.

Lasciane andar per li tuoi sette regni;   82
grazie riporterò di te a lei,
se d'esser mentovato là giù degni."

"Marzïa piacque tanto a li occhi miei   85
mentre ch'i' fu' di là," diss' elli allora,
"che quante grazie volse da me, fei.

Or che di là dal mal fiume dimora,   88
più muover non mi può, per quella legge
che fatta fu quando me n'usci' fora.

Ma se donna del ciel ti move e regge,   91
come tu di', non c'è mestier lusinghe:
bastisi ben che per lei mi richegge.

Va dunque, e fa che tu costui ricinghe   94
d'un giunco schietto e che li lavi 'l viso,
sì ch'ogne sucidume quindi stinghe;

I have shown him the whole populace of evil   64
and now intend to show him the spirits
who purify themselves under your rule.

The route I brought him would be long to tell you;   67
a virtue comes down from above which helps me
to lead him to behold you and to hear you.

Now may it please you to approve his coming;   70
his goal is liberty, and one who has
forfeited life for that knows how dear it is.

You know, for whom death tasted not bitter   73
in Utica where you laid aside the clothing
that on the great day will give off such shining.

Nor are the eternal edicts broken for us: 76
he is alive, and Minos does not bind me.
I come from the circle where the chaste eyes

of your Marcia in their gazing pray to you,   79
oh holy breast, to hold her as your own.
May her love, then, incline you toward us.

Allow us to journey through your seven kingdoms.   82
I will report this kindness of yours to her
if you deign to be spoken of down there."

"Marcia was such pleasure to my eyes   85
while I was on the far side," then he said,
"that any kindness she asked of me I did.

Now that she abides beyond the evil river   88
she can move me no longer, by that law
that was made when I came from over there.

But if a lady from heaven, as you say,   91
moves and directs you, you need not persuade me.
It is enough to ask me for her sake only.

Go then, and see that you gird this one   94
with a smooth rush, and that you wash his face
so that all the dirt on it is gone,

ché non si converria, l'occhio sorpriso   97
d'alcuna nebbia, andar dinanzi al primo
ministro, ch'è di quei di paradiso.

Questa isoletta intorno ad imo ad imo,   100
là giù colà dove la batte l'onda,
porta di giunchi sovra 'l molle limo:

null' altra pianta che facesse fronda   103
o indurasse, vi puote aver vita,
però ch'a le percosse non seconda.

Poscia non sia di qua vostra reddita;   106
lo sol vi mosterrà, che surge omai,
prendere il monte a più lieve salita."

Così sparì; e io sù mi levai   109
sanza parlare, e tutto mi ritrassi
al duca mio, e li occhi a lui drizzai.

El cominciò: "Figliuol, segui i miei passi: 112
volgianci in dietro, ché di qua dichina
questa pianura a' suoi termini bassi."

L'alba vinceva l'ora mattutina   115
che fuggia innanzi, sì che di lontano
conobbi il tremolar de la marina.

Noi andavam per lo solingo piano   118
com' om che torna a la perduta strada,
che 'nfino ad essa li pare ire in vano.

Quando noi fummo là 've la rugiada   121
pugna col sole, per essere in parte
dove, ad orezza, poco si dirada,

ambo le mani in su l'erbetta sparte   124
soavemente 'l mio maestro pose:
ond' io, che fui accorto di sua arte,

porsi ver' lui le guance lagrimose;   127
ivi mi fece tutto discoverto
quel color che l'inferno mi nascose.

for it would not be right to go with eyes
obscured by any cloud before the first
of the ministers who are from Paradise.

97

This little island, in the lowest places
around it, down there where the wave beats
upon it, bears on the soft mud rushes.

100

No other plant that might make leaves or stiffen
would be able to stay alive there
because it would not bend under the pounding.

103

When you have been there do not come back this way.
The sun that just now is rising will show you
where to approach the mountain more easily."

106

At that he vanished, and I rose to my feet
without saying a word, and I came
close to my leader and kept my eyes on him.

109

He began, "Follow me as I go.
Let us turn back, for the plain from here descends
all the way to the bottom, where it ends."

112

The dawn was overcoming the pallor of daybreak
which fled before it, so that I could see
off in the distance the trembling of the sea.

115

We went on across the solitary plain
like someone who has found the lost road again,
who until then seems to have traveled in vain.

118

When we had come to a place where the dew
fends off the sun, there where it dries
hardly at all because of the sea breeze,

121

my master spread out both his hands and laid them
gently upon the grass, and I who
understood what he intended to do

124

leaned toward him my cheeks with their tear stains
and he made visible once again
all that color of mine which Hell had hidden.

127

Venimmo poi in sul lito diserto,   130
che mai non vide navicar sue acque
omo, che di tornar sia poscia esperto.

Quivi mi cinse sì com' altrui piacque: 133
oh maraviglia! ché qual elli scelse
l'umile pianta, cotal si rinacque

subitamente là onde l'avelse.   136

Then we came along to the desert shore   *130*
that had never seen anyone sail upon
its waters who had known a return after.

There he bound me as pleased another.   *133*
Oh wonder! The moment that he pulled up
the humble plant it was reborn there

where it had been, just as it was before.   *136*

CANTO II

Già era 'l sole a l'orizzonte giunto
lo cui meridïan cerchio coverchia
Ierusalèm col suo più alto punto;

e la notte, che opposita a lui cerchia,   4
uscia di Gange fuor con le Bilance,
che le caggion di man quando soverchia;

sì che le bianche e le vermiglie guance,   7
là dov' i' era, de la bella Aurora
per troppa etate divenivan rance.

Noi eravam lunghesso mare ancora,   10
come gente che pensa a suo cammino,
che va col cuore e col corpo dimora.

Ed ecco, qual, sorpreso dal mattino,   13
per li grossi vapor Marte rosseggia
giù nel ponente sovra 'l suol marino,

cotal m'apparve, s'io ancor lo veggia,   16
un lume per lo mar venir sì ratto,
che 'l muover suo nessun volar pareggia.

Dal qual com' io un poco ebbi ritratto   19
l'occhio per domandar lo duca mio,
rividil più lucente e maggior fatto.

Poi d'ogne lato ad esso m'appario   22
un non sapeva che bianco, e di sotto
a poco a poco un altro a lui uscìo.

Lo mio maestro ancor non facea motto,   25
mentre che i primi bianchi apparver ali;
allor che ben conobbe il galeotto,

gridò: "Fa, fa che le ginocchia cali.   28
Ecco l'angel di Dio: piega le mani;
omai vedrai di sì fatti officiali.

By then the sun had come to the horizon
the circle of whose meridian
at its high point covers Jerusalem

and Night, circling on the opposite side,   4
was emerging from the Ganges with the Scales
that fall out of her hands when she prevails,

so that the white and vermilion cheeks   7
of lovely Dawn, in the place where I was,
were growing old and turning orange.

We were still beside the edge of the sea   10
like people who are thinking about their journey
who in their hearts go and their bodies stay

and there, as when Mars in the flush of dawn   13
reddens low in the west through the heavy
vapors, over the floor of the ocean,

may I see it again as it appeared to me: 16
across the sea a light was coming so swiftly
that no flight could compare with its motion.

When I had taken my eyes away from it   19
only for a moment to question my leader,
I saw it again grown brighter and larger.

Then there appeared to me on each side of it   22
something that I could not make out, something white,
and another was emerging little by little below it.

All that time until the first white things appeared   25
to be wings my master uttered not a word,
then when he was sure who the pilot was

he shouted, "Down, down on your knees! There is   28
the angel of God. Put your hands together.
From now on you will see such emissaries.

Vedi che sdegna li argomenti umani,   31
sì che remo non vuol, né altro velo
che l'ali sue, tra liti sì lontani.

Vedi come l'ha dritte verso 'l cielo,   34
trattando l'aere con l'etterne penne,
che non si mutan come mortal pelo."

Poi, come più e più verso noi venne   37
l'uccel divino, più chiaro appariva:
per che l'occhio da presso nol sostenne,

ma chinail giuso; e quei sen venne a riva   40
con un vasello snelletto e leggero,
tanto che l'acqua nulla ne 'nghiottiva.

Da poppa stava il celestial nocchiero,   43
tal che parea beato per iscripto;
e più di cento spirti entro sediero.

"In exitu Isräel de Aegypto,"   46
cantavan tutti insieme ad una voce
con quanto di quel salmo è poscia scripto.

Poi fece il segno lor di santa croce;   49
ond' ei si gittar tutti in su la piaggia:
ed el sen gì, come venne, veloce.

La turba che rimase lì, selvaggia   52
parea del loco, rimirando intorno
come colui che nove cose assaggia.

Da tutte parti saettava il giorno   55
lo sol, ch'avea con le saette conte
di mezzo 'l ciel cacciato Capricorno,

quando la nova gente alzò la fronte   58
ver' noi, dicendo a noi: "Se voi sapete,
mostratene la via di gire al monte."

E Virgilio rispuose: "Voi credete   61
forse che siamo esperti d'esto loco;
ma noi siam peregrin come voi siete.

See how he scorns any human contrivance,   31
wanting no oar nor any sail between
shores so remote, except for his own wings.

See how he has pointed them toward the sky,   34
plying the air with the eternal pinions
which unlike mortal plumage never change."

Then as the divine bird came closer and closer   37
to us he appeared brighter, so that my eyes
could not bear the sight when he was near us,

but I looked down, and he came to the land   40
with so fleet and so light a vessel
that it seemed to draw no water at all.

At its stern was the celestial helmsman,   43
blessedness like a writing upon him,
and seated in it were more than a hundred spirits.

When out of Egypt Israel came forth,   46
all sang together with their voices as one,
and the rest of that psalm as it is written,

then he made the sign of the holy cross   49
over them and they all flung themselves on the shore
and as he had come he was gone, with the same swiftness.

The crowd that was left there did not seem to know   52
anything of the place, looking around them
like those who are trying things for the first time.

On all sides the sun was firing arrows   55
of day, and its sharp arrows had driven
Capricorn out of mid-heaven

when the new people lifted their faces   58
toward us, saying to us, "If you know
the way up the mountain, show it to us."

And Virgil answered, "Possibly you believe   61
that this is a place with which we are familiar,
but we are pilgrims even as you are.

Dianzi venimmo, innanzi a voi un poco,   64
per altra via, che fu sì aspra e forte,
che lo salire omai ne parrà gioco."

L'anime, che si fuor di me accorte,   67
per lo spirare, ch'i' era ancor vivo,
maravigliando diventaro smorte.

E come a messagger che porta ulivo   70
tragge la gente per udir novelle,
e di calcar nessun si mostra schivo,

così al viso mio s'affisar quelle   73
anime fortunate tutte quante,
quasi oblïando d'ire a farsi belle.

Io vidi una di lor trarresi avante   76
per abbracciarmi, con sì grande affetto,
che mosse me a far lo somigliante.

Ohi ombre vane, fuor che ne l'aspetto!   79
tre volte dietro a lei le mani avvinsi,
e tante mi tornai con esse al petto.

Di maraviglia, credo, mi dipinsi;   82
per che l'ombra sorrise e si ritrasse,
e io, seguendo lei, oltre mi pinsi.

Soavemente disse ch'io posasse;   85
allor conobbi chi era, e pregai
che, per parlarmi, un poco s'arrestasse.

Rispuosemi: "Così com' io t'amai   88
nel mortal corpo, così t'amo sciolta:
però m'arresto; ma tu perché vai?"

"Casella mio, per tornar altra volta   91
là dov' io son, fo io questo vïaggio,"
diss' io; "ma a te com' è tanta ora tolta?"

Ed elli a me: "Nessun m'è fatto oltraggio,   94
se quei che leva quando e cui li piace,
più volte m'ha negato esto passaggio;

We came here just now, a little before you did,   64
by another way that was so rough and hard
that the climb must seem like play now, after it."

The souls who had perceived that I was breathing   67
and understood that I was alive still
marveled so that they became deathly pale.

And as people crowd to a messenger   70
bearing an olive branch, so they can hear
the news and no one is afraid of trampling,

in the same way every one of those   73
fortunate souls kept staring at my face,
forgetting, it seemed, to go and see to their own beauty.

I saw one rush ahead of the rest of them   76
to embrace me with so much affection
that he moved me to do the same.

Oh shadows that, except to the eye, are vain!   79
Three times my hands came together behind him
and as often returned to my breast again.

My wonder, I think, must have been painted on me,   82
because the shadow smiled and drew away
and I pushed forward, following after him.

Gently he told me to remain still. Then I   85
knew who he was and I begged him to stay
for a little so he could talk with me.

He answered me, "Even as I loved you   88
in my mortal body, I do now that I am free,
and so I stay. But why are you on this way?"

"My Casella, so that I may return   91
here where I am," I said, "I am making this journey.
But how has so much time been taken from you?"

And he to me, "No wrong was done to me   94
if he who takes up when and whom he pleases
denied this passage many times to me,

ché di giusto voler lo suo si face: 97
veramente da tre mesi elli ha tolto
chi ha voluto intrar, con tutta pace.

Ond' io, ch'era ora a la marina vòlto   100
dove l'acqua di Tevero s'insala,
benignamente fu' da lui ricolto.

A quella foce ha elli or dritta l'ala,   103
però che sempre quivi si ricoglie
qual verso Acheronte non si cala."

E io: "Se nuova legge non ti toglie   106
memoria o uso a l'amoroso canto
che mi solea quetar tutte mie voglie,

di ciò ti piaccia consolare alquanto   109
l'anima mia, che, con la sua persona
venendo qui, è affannata tanto!"

"Amor che ne la mente mi ragiona,"   112
cominciò elli allor sì dolcemente,
che la dolcezza ancor dentro mi suona.

Lo mio maestro e io e quella gente   115
ch'eran con lui parevan sì contenti,
come a nessun toccasse altro la mente.

Noi eravam tutti fissi e attenti   118
a le sue note; ed ecco il veglio onesto
gridando: "Che è ciò, spiriti lenti?

qual negligenza, quale stare è questo?   121
Correte al monte a spogliarvi lo scoglio
ch'esser non lascia a voi Dio manifesto."

Come quando, cogliendo biado o loglio,   124
li colombi adunati a la pastura,
queti, sanza mostrar l'usato orgoglio,

se cosa appare ond' elli abbian paura,   127
subitamente lasciano star l'esca,
perch' assaliti son da maggior cura;

for out of a just will his own is made   97
and in truth for three months now he has taken
with all peace whoever has wished to come.

So I, who had turned at that time to the shore   100
where the water grows salty in the Tiber,
was gathered up by him in his kindness.

Now he has set wing for the mouth of that river   103
since that is where the souls are forever
gathering who do not sink to Acheron."

And I, "If a new law does not take from you   106
the memory or the mode of singing
of love that used to quiet all my longings,

may it please you for a while to comfort   109
with it my soul which, on the journey
here with its body, has become so weary."

Love that speaks in my mind persuading me,   112
he began then, so sweetly that even now
the sweetness goes on sounding in me.

My master and I and the people who   115
were with him seemed as content as though
there was nothing else touching their minds.

All of us were caught up listening   118
to his notes, and here is the venerable
old man shouting, "What is this, lingering spirits?

What is this negligence, this standing still?   121
On your way to the mountain, running, and peel
away the dead skin that keeps you from seeing God."

As doves when they are picking up wheat or weed seeds   124
all together, quietly feeding
without their usual puffed-up displaying,

if something should appear that frightens them   127
suddenly abandon what had tempted them,
seized as they are by what matters more to them,

così vid' io quella masnada fresca   130
lasciar lo canto, e fuggir ver' la costa,
com' om che va, né sa dove rïesca;

né la nostra partita fu men tosta.   133

so I saw that fresh troop abandon 130
the singing and wheel away toward the slope
like one who goes without knowing the direction

nor were we less prompt in our leaving. 133

CANTO III

Avvegna che la subitana fuga
dispergesse color per la campagna,
rivolti al monte ove ragion ne fruga,

i' mi ristrinsi a la fida compagna: 4
e come sare' io sanza lui corso?
chi m'avria tratto su per la montagna?

El mi parea da sé stesso rimorso: 7
o dignitosa coscïenza e netta,
come t'è picciol fallo amaro morso!

Quando li piedi suoi lasciar la fretta,   10
che l'onestade ad ogn' atto dismaga,
la mente mia, che prima era ristretta,

lo 'ntento rallargò, sì come vaga,   13
e diedi 'l viso mio incontr' al poggio
che 'nverso 'l ciel più alto si dislaga.

Lo sol, che dietro fiammeggiava roggio,   16
rotto m'era dinanzi a la figura,
ch'avëa in me de' suoi raggi l'appoggio.

Io mi volsi dallato con paura   19
d'essere abbandonato, quand' io vidi
solo dinanzi a me la terra oscura;

e 'l mio conforto: "Perché pur diffidi?"   22
a dir mi cominciò tutto rivolto;
"non credi tu me teco e ch'io ti guidi?

Vespero è già colà dov' è sepolto   25
lo corpo dentro al quale io facea ombra;
Napoli l'ha, e da Brandizio è tolto.

Ora, se innanzi a me nulla s'aombra,   28
non ti maravigliar più che d'i cieli
che l'uno a l'altro raggio non ingombra.

Even as the sudden flight cast them across
the open land I turned toward the mountain
where the sense of things makes its way into us,

and came closer to my faithful companion,   4
and how would I have made my way without him?
Who would have taken me up the mountain?

He appeared to me to be reproaching himself.   7
Oh noble and unstained conscience, how
bitter is the bite of a slight fault to you!

When his feet had given up the haste   10
that mars the dignity of any action,
my mind, which I had kept in check at first,

widened its scope so that it searched at will   13
and I directed my vision to the hill
that climbs highest from the water against the sky.

The sun, which was flaming red behind me,   16
was broken in front of me in the form
that its rays made when they rested upon me.

I turned to the side, because I was frightened   19
that I had been abandoned, when I saw
that only in front of me the earth was darkened.

And my comfort, turning around all the way,   22
began, "Why are you still mistrustful? Do you
not believe I am with you and guide you?

It is already evening where the body   25
is buried in which I made a shadow.
Naples has it. It was taken from Brindisi.

Now if no shadow is cast before me   28
you should be no more astonished than you are
that the heavens do not keep the light from each other.

A sofferir tormenti, caldi e geli   31
simili corpi la Virtù dispone
che, come fa, non vuol ch'a noi si sveli.

Matto è chi spera che nostra ragione   34
possa trascorrer la infinita via
che tiene una sustanza in tre persone.

State contenti, umana gente, al *quia;*   37
ché, se potuto aveste veder tutto,
mestier non era parturir Maria;

e disïar vedeste sanza frutto   40
tai che sarebbe lor disio quetato,
ch'etternalmente è dato lor per lutto:

io dico d'Aristotile e di Plato   43
e di molt' altri;" e qui chinò la fronte,
e più non disse, e rimase turbato.

Noi divenimmo intanto a piè del monte;   46
quivi trovammo la roccia sì erta,
che 'ndarno vi sarien le gambe pronte.

Tra Lerice e Turbìa la più diserta,   49
la più rotta ruina è una scala,
verso di quella, agevole e aperta.

"Or chi sa da qual man la costa cala,"   52
disse 'l maestro mio fermando 'l passo,
"sì che possa salir chi va sanz'ala?"

E mentre ch'e' tenendo 'l viso basso   55
essaminava del cammin la mente,
e io mirava suso intorno al sasso,

da man sinistra m'apparì una gente   58
d'anime, che movieno i piè ver' noi,
e non pareva, sì venïan lente.

"Leva," diss' io, "maestro, li occhi tuoi: 61
ecco di qua chi ne darà consiglio,
se tu da te medesmo aver nol puoi."

That Power that will not allow its ways 31
to be revealed to us gives us bodies like this
to suffer torments and to burn and freeze.

Only a fool could hope that our reason 34
would be able to trace the infinite way
that one substance takes in three persons.

Oh humans, be content with the fact itself, 37
for if you had been able to see the whole
Mary would not have had to bear her child.

And you have seen their fruitless longing, whose 40
longing would have been fulfilled, that was
given them for their everlasting mourning.

I speak of Aristotle and of Plato 43
and of many others," and there he bowed his forehead
and said no more, and he remained troubled.

With that we came to the foot of the mountain 46
where we found the rock face was so steep
that nimbleness of legs would have been in vain.

Between Lerice and Turbia, the most naked place, 49
where the scree is broken smallest, is a spacious
and gradual staircase compared to this.

"Now who knows on which hand the slope may rise," 52
my master said as he came to a stop,
"so that someone who has no wings can go up."

And as he was considering the way 55
in his mind, with his face turned toward the ground,
and I was looking along the rock above me,

a company of souls appeared to me 58
from the left, moving their feet toward us
and seeming not to, they were coming so slowly.

"Master," I said, "look up. There are those 61
over there who will give us direction
if you cannot find the way alone."

Guardò allora, e con libero piglio 64
rispuose: "Andiamo in là, ch'ei vegnon piano;
e tu ferma la spene, dolce figlio."

Ancora era quel popol di lontano, 67
i' dico dopo i nostri mille passi,
quanto un buon gittator trarria con mano,

quando si strinser tutti ai duri massi 70
de l'alta ripa, e stetter fermi e stretti
com' a guardar chi va, dubbiando stassi.

"O ben finiti, o già spiriti eletti," 73
Virgilio incominciò, "per quella pace
ch'i' credo che per voi tutti s'aspetti,

ditene dove la montagna giace, 76
sì che possibil sia l'andare in suso;
ché perder tempo a chi più sa più spiace."

Come le pecorelle escon del chiuso 79
a una, a due, a tre, e l'altre stanno
timidette atterrando l'occhio e 'l muso;

e ciò che fa la prima, e l'altre fanno, 82
addossandosi a lei, s'ella s'arresta,
semplici e quete, e lo 'mperché non sanno;

sì vid' io muovere a venir la testa 85
di quella mandra fortunata allotta,
pudica in faccia e ne l'andare onesta.

Come color dinanzi vider rotta 88
la luce in terra dal mio destro canto,
sì che l'ombra era da me a la grotta,

restaro, e trasser sé in dietro alquanto, 91
e tutti li altri che venieno appresso,
non sappiendo 'l perché, fenno altrettanto.

"Sanza vostra domanda io vi confesso 94
che questo è corpo uman che voi vedete;
per che 'l lume del sole in terra è fesso.

Then he looked up and his countenance was clear, 64
and he answered, "Let us go there, since they are
coming so slowly. And be of good hope, dear son."

Those people were still as far away— 67
when we had gone a thousand of our steps, I mean—
as the throw from a good hand will carry

when they all crowded against the hard rocks 70
of the tall cliff and stood still, huddled and quiet
as people stop and watch when in doubt.

"Oh you who ended well," Virgil began, 73
"oh spirits already chosen, by that peace
which I believe awaits you every one,

tell us in what place the mountain slopes 76
so that it would be possible to climb,
for who knows most grieves most at the loss of time."

As the sheep make their way out of the fold, 79
one, then two, then three, and the rest stay behind
timid, with eyes and noses to the ground

and whatever the first one does the others do, 82
piling up on top of it if it stops,
simple and quiet and without knowing why,

so I saw the van of that fortunate flock 85
make a movement toward us, modesty
in their features, and stepping with dignity.

As soon as those in front saw that the light 88
was broken on the ground there to my right
so that my shadow reached to the rock face

they stopped and went back a step or two 91
and all the others who were coming behind them,
without knowing why, acted like that too.

"I will tell you what you have not asked me: 94
this is a human body that you see
which has parted the sunlight on the ground.

Non vi maravigliate, ma credete   97
che non sanza virtù che da ciel vegna
cerchi di soverchiar questa parete."

Così 'l maestro; e quella gente degna   100
"Tornate," disse, "intrate innanzi dunque,"
coi dossi de le man faccendo insegna.

E un di loro incominciò: "Chiunque   103
tu se', così andando, volgi-'l viso:
pon mente se di là mi vedesti unque."

Io mi volsi ver' lui e guardail fiso: 106
biondo era e bello e di gentile aspetto,
ma l'un de' cigli un colpo avea diviso.

Quand' io mi fui umilmente disdetto   109
d'averlo visto mai, el disse: "Or vedi";
e mostrommi una piaga a sommo 'l petto.

Poi sorridendo disse: "Io son Manfredi,   112
nepote di Costanza imperadrice;
ond' io ti priego che, quando tu riedi,

vadi a mia bella figlia, genitrice   115
de l'onor di Cicilia e d'Aragona,
e dichi 'l vero a lei, s'altro si dice.

Poscia ch'io ebbi rotta la persona   118
di due punte mortali, io mi rendei,
piangendo, a quei che volontier perdona.

Orribil furon li peccati miei;   121
ma la bontà infinita ha sì gran braccia,
che prende ciò che si rivolge a lei.

Se 'l pastor di Cosenza, che a la caccia   124
di me fu messo per Clemente allora,
avesse in Dio ben letta questa faccia,

l'ossa del corpo mio sarieno ancora   127
in co del ponte presso a Benevento,
sotto la guardia de la grave mora.

Do not wonder at it, but be certain   97
that not without power that comes from Heaven
he is trying to find the way over this rampart."

So my master. And that deserving band   100
said, "Turn back then, and go ahead of us,"
waving us that way with the back of the hand.

And one of them began, "Whoever   103
you are, turn your face as you are going.
Think whether you ever saw me over there."

I turned toward him and looked at him closely: 106
he was fair-haired, beautiful, a noble expression,
but a blow had split one of his eyebrows open.

When I had denied humbly that I had   109
ever seen him before, "Now look," he said,
and showed me a wound at the top of his breast.

Then, smiling, he said, "I am Manfred, grandson   112
of the Empress Costanza. I beg you
therefore, when you have returned again,

to go to my beautiful daughter who is mother   115
of the pride of Sicily and Aragon,
and whatever else they are saying, tell the truth to her.

After my body had been cloven by   118
two mortal blows, in tears I surrendered
myself to her who pardons willingly.

Horrible were the sins I had committed,   121
but so wide are the arms of infinite
goodness that it takes in all who turn to it.

If the pastor of Cosenza whom Clement then   124
sent out with the order to hunt me down
had read that page of God's as he should have done,

the bones of my body would still be lying   127
at the bridgehead next to Benevento
under the keeping of the heavy cairn.

Or le bagna la pioggia e move il vento   *130*
di fuor dal regno, quasi lungo 'l Verde,
dov' e' le trasmutò a lume spento.

Per lor maladizion sì non si perde,   *133*
che non possa tornar, l'etterno amore,
mentre che la speranza ha fior del verde.

Vero è che quale in contumacia more   *136*
di Santa Chiesa, ancor ch'al fin si penta,
star li convien da questa ripa in fore,

per ognun tempo ch'elli è stato, trenta,   *139*
in sua presunzïon, se tal decreto
più corto per buon prieghi non diventa.

Vedi oggimai se tu mi puoi far lieto,   *142*
revelando a la mia buona Costanza
come m'hai visto, e anco esto divieto;

ché qui per quei di là molto s'avanza."   *145*

Now the rain washes them and the wind moves them   *130*
outside the kingdom, almost to the Verde,
where, with torches extinguished, he had them taken.

No one is so lost through their malediction   *133*
that eternal love cannot return
as long as hope keeps the least bit of green.

It is true that whoever dies outlawed   *136*
by the Holy Church, even if at the end
he repents, must wait out on this bankside

thirty times as long as he continued   *139*
in his presumption, unless there are good
prayers prevailing to make the sentence shorter.

See now whether you can make me happy,   *142*
revealing to my good Costanza how you
have seen me, and then this ban upon me,

for much is accomplished here by those back there."   *145*

CANTO IV

Quando per dilettanze o ver per doglie,
che alcuna virtù nostra comprenda,
l'anima bene ad essa si raccoglie,

par ch'a nulla potenza più intenda;   4
e questo è contra quello error che crede
ch'un'anima sovr' altra in noi s'accenda.

E però, quando s'ode cosa o vede   7
che tegna forte a sé l'anima volta,
vassene 'l tempo e l'uom non se n'avvede;

ch'altra potenza è quella che l'ascolta,   10
e altra è quella c'ha l'anima intera:
questa è quasi legata e quella è sciolta.

Di ciò ebb' io esperïenza vera,   13
udendo quello spirto e ammirando;
ché ben cinquanta gradi salito era

lo sole, e io non m'era accorto, quando   16
venimmo ove quell' anime ad una
gridaro a noi: "Qui è vostro dimando."

Maggiore aperta molte volte impruna   19
con una forcatella di sue spine
l'uom de la villa quando l'uva imbruna,

che non era la calla onde salìne   22
lo duca mio, e io appresso, soli,
come da noi la schiera si partìne.

Vassi in Sanleo e discendesi in Noli,   25
montasi su in Bismantova e 'n Cacume
con esso i piè; ma qui convien ch'om voli;

dico con l'ale snelle e con le piume   28
del gran disio, di retro a quel condotto
che speranza mi dava e facea lume.

Whenever one of our faculties becomes
so conscious of some pleasure or some pain
that the soul turns toward it all its attention,

it seems to heed none of its other powers,   4
and this contradicts the error of believing
that one soul is kindled in us above another.

And so it is that when one hears or sees   7
something that keeps the soul bent tightly to it,
time will go by before one notices,

because the listening faculty   10
differs from that which holds the entire soul:
the latter somewhat captive, the former free.

I had a true experience of this   13
as I listened to that spirit, marveling,
for the sun had risen full fifty degrees

and I had not been aware of it, when   16
we came to where those souls called out as one
to us, "Here is what you were asking for."

Often the peasant closes a wider breach   19
in the hedge with a forkful of his sloe-thorns
at the season when the grapes begin to darken

than the passage through which my leader climbed   22
and I behind him, only the two of us
after that company had departed from us.

One can walk to San Leo and go down into Noli,   25
one can climb Bismantova to the very top
with the feet alone, but here one has to fly—

with the racing wings, I mean, and the plumage   28
of great desire, following that guidance
which gave me hope and made a light for me.

Noi salavam per entro 'l sasso rotto,   31
e d'ogne lato ne stringea lo stremo,
e piedi e man volea il suol di sotto.

Poi che noi fummo in su l'orlo suppremo   34
de l'alta ripa, a la scoperta piaggia,
"Maestro mio," diss' io, "che via faremo?"

Ed elli a me: "Nessun tuo passo caggia;   37
pur su al monte dietro a me acquista,
fin che n'appaia alcuna scorta saggia."

Lo sommo er' alto che vincea la vista,   40
e la costa superba più assai
che da mezzo quadrante a centro lista.

Io era lasso, quando cominciai: 43
"O dolce padre, volgiti, e rimira
com' io rimango sol, se non restai."

"Figliuol mio," disse, "infin quivi ti tira,"   46
additandomi un balzo poco in sùe
che da quel lato il poggio tutto gira.

Sì mi spronaron le parole sue,   49
ch'i' mi sforzai carpando appresso lui,
tanto che 'l cinghio sotto i piè mi fue.

A seder ci ponemmo ivi ambedui   52
vòlti a levante ond' eravam saliti,
che suole a riguardar giovare altrui.

Li occhi prima drizzai ai bassi liti;   55
poscia li alzai al sole, e ammirava
che da sinistra n'eravam feriti.

Ben s'avvide il poeta ch'ïo stava   58
stupido tutto al carro de la luce,
ove tra noi e Aquilone intrava.

Ond' elli a me: "Se Castore e Poluce   61
fossero in compagnia di quello specchio
che sù e giù del suo lume conduce,

We climbed up inside where the rock was split   31
and the surface pressed upon us on all sides
and we needed hands, for the ground, as well as feet.

When we had come out at the upper margin   34
of the high bank, onto the open hillside,
I said, "My master, which way do we turn?"

And he to me, "Do not take one step downward.   37
Make your way on up the mountain behind me
until some wise escort appears to us."

The summit was higher than the eye could reach   40
and the slope of the mountain was much steeper
than the line from the mid-quadrant to the center.

I was exhausted when I began to say,   43
"Oh sweet father, turn your head and see:
I will be here alone unless you wait for me."

"My son," he said, "haul yourself up that far,"   46
pointing to a ledge, a little higher,
that ran around that whole side of the hill.

His words had such power to spur me on   49
that I made myself crawl up after him
until I had the terrace under my feet.

There both of us sat down, with our faces   52
turned to the east, where we had come from,
for often, facing that way, the heart rises.

First I looked down to the shores below us   55
and then up toward the sun, and I marveled
to see it was on our left that it struck us.

It was clear to the poet that my confusion   58
was complete when I saw the chariot of the light
passing between us and Aquilon;

therefore he said to me, "If Castor   61
and Pollux were in the company of that mirror
that conducts its light upward and downward,

tu vedresti il Zodïaco rubecchio 64
ancora a l'Orse più stretto rotare,
se non uscisse fuor del cammin vecchio.

Come ciò sia, se 'l vuoi poter pensare, 67
dentro raccolto, imagina Sïòn
con questo monte in su la terra stare

sì, ch'amendue hanno un solo orizzòn 70
e diversi emisperi; onde la strada
che mal non seppe carreggiar Fetòn,

vedrai come a costui convien che vada 73
da l'un, quando a colui da l'altro fianco,
se lo 'ntelletto tuo ben chiaro bada."

"Certo, maestro mio," diss' io, "unquanco 76
non vid' io chiaro sì com' io discerno
là dove mio ingegno parea manco,

che 'l mezzo cerchio del moto superno, 79
che si chiama Equatore in alcun' arte,
e che sempre riman tra 'l sole e 'l verno,

per la ragion che di', quinci si parte 82
verso settentrïon, quanto li Ebrei
vedevan lui verso la calda parte.

Ma se a te piace, volontier saprei 85
quanto avemo ad andar; ché 'l poggio sale
più che salir non posson li occhi miei."

Ed elli a me: "Questa montagna è tale, 88
che sempre al cominciar di sotto è grave;
e quant' om più va sù, e men fa male.

Però, quand' ella ti parrà soave 91
tanto, che sù andar ti fia leggero
com' a seconda giù andar per nave,

allor sarai al fin d'esto sentiero; 94
quivi di riposar l'affanno aspetta.
Più non rispondo, e questo so per vero."

you would see the glowing Zodiac   64
revolving even closer to the Bears
unless it were to leave its ancient track.

If you wish to know how that is possible,   67
concentrate, and imagine Zion
so placed on earth that it and this mountain

in opposite hemispheres have between them   70
a single horizon. Then you will see
how that road which Phaëton, to his misfortune,

could not keep to, must pass this mountain   73
on the one side and the other on the other side,
if you grasp it clearly with your reason."

"Truly, my master, at no time," I said,   76
"have I seen so clearly as I do now,
there where my understanding seemed limited,

that the mid-circle of the heavenly motion   79
which is called the Equator in one discipline,
lying always between the sun and winter,

is as far north from us, for the reason   82
you gave me, as the Hebrews saw it
when they were looking toward the torrid zone.

But if you please, I would be glad to know   85
how far we have to go, for the hill rises
up beyond where my eyes can follow."

And he to me, "It is the way of this mountain   88
always to seem hard at the beginning
and become easier as one goes on climbing.

Therefore when it has become so easy   91
for you that going up is as light
as drifting downstream in a boat would be,

you will have come to the end of this path.   94
There you can hope to rest your weariness.
I say no more, and I know this is the truth."

E com' elli ebbe sua parola detta,   97
una voce di presso sonò: "Forse
che di sedere in pria avrai distretta!"

Al suon di lei ciascun di noi si torse,   100
e vedemmo a mancina un gran petrone,
del qual né io né ei prima s'accorse.

Là ci traemmo; e ivi eran persone   103
che si stavano a l'ombra dietro al sasso
come l'uom per negghienza a star si pone.

E un di lor, che mi sembiava lasso,   106
sedeva e abbracciava le ginocchia,
tenendo 'l viso giù tra esse basso.

"O dolce segnor mio," diss' io, "adocchia   109
colui che mostra sé più negligente
che se pigrizia fosse sua serocchia."

Allor si volse a noi e puose mente,   112
movendo 'l viso pur su per la coscia,
e disse: "Or va tu sù, che se' valente!"

Conobbi allor chi era, e quella angoscia   115
che m'avacciava un poco ancor la lena,
non m'impedì l'andare a lui; e poscia

ch'a lui fu' giunto, alzò la testa a pena,   118
dicendo: "Hai ben veduto come 'l sole
da l'omero sinistro il carro mena?"

Li atti suoi pigri e le corte parole   121
mosser le labbra mie un poco a riso;
poi cominciai: "Belacqua, a me non dole

di te omai; ma dimmi: perché assiso   124
quiritto se'? attendi tu iscorta,
o pur lo modo usato t'ha' ripriso?"

Ed elli: "O frate, andar in sù che porta?   127
ché non mi lascerebbe ire a' martìri
l'angel di Dio che siede in su la porta.

And his words had hardly been spoken   97
when a voice sounded from beside us, "Maybe
before you get there you will have to sit down."

At that sound we both turned and saw there   100
on our left a massive boulder
which neither he nor I had noticed before.

We went over to it and there were people   103
resting in the shade behind the rock, looking
like those who settle down to do nothing.

And one of them, who seemed to be tired,   106
sat with his arms around his knees and held
his face between them, looking downward.

"Oh my sweet lord," I said, "let your eye linger   109
on that one who appears to be lazier
than if he had sloth for his little sister."

At that he turned to us and looked us over,   112
moving his face up slightly on his leg,
and said, "Well, go on up, you rugged pair."

Then I knew who he was, and the exhaustion   115
from which I still had not caught my breath
did not detain me from going to him, and when

I came to him he raised his head scarcely   118
at all, saying, "Have you noticed how the sun
is driving his chariot past your left shoulder?"

The languor of his moving and his brief   121
words brought a little smile to my lips
and I began, "Belacqua, now I grieve

for you no longer. But tell me, why are you   124
sitting there? Are you waiting for an escort
or have you simply returned to what you are used to?"

And he, "Oh brother, what would be the point   127
of my going up? For God's angel sits in the doorway
and would not let me pass through to the torments.

Prima convien che tanto il ciel m'aggiri   130
di fuor da essa, quanto fece in vita,
per ch'io 'ndugiai al fine i buon sospiri,

se orazïone in prima non m'aita   133
che surga sù di cuor che in grazia viva;
l'altra che val, che 'n ciel non è udita?"

E già il poeta innanzi mi saliva,   136
e dicea: "Vienne omai; vedi ch'è tocco
meridïan dal sole, e a la riva

cuopre la notte già col piè Morrocco."   139

I will have to wait outside while the heavens   130
revolve around me for as long as I lived
since I put off the good sighs to the end,

unless prayer rising from a heart that lives   133
in grace comes to my help before then.
What use are the others, that are not heard in heaven?"

And already the poet had begun   136
to climb ahead of me, and he said, "Come now.
See: the meridian is touched by the sun,

and on the shore night has set foot on Morocco."   139

CANTO V

Io era già da quell' ombre partito,
e seguitava l'orme del mio duca,
quando di retro a me, drizzando 'l dito,

una gridò: "Ve' che non par che luca   4
lo raggio da sinistra a quel di sotto,
e come vivo par che si conduca!"

Li occhi rivolsi al suon di questo motto,   7
e vidile guardar per maraviglia
pur me, pur me, e 'l lume ch'era rotto.

"Perché l'animo tuo tanto s'impiglia,"   10
disse 'l maestro, "che l'andare allenti?
che ti fa ciò che quivi si pispiglia?

Vien dietro a me, e lascia dir le genti: 13
sta come torre ferma, che non crolla
già mai la cima per soffiar di venti;

ché sempre l'omo in cui pensier rampolla   16
sovra pensier, da sé dilunga il segno,
perché la foga l'un de l'altro insolla."

Che potea io ridir, se non "Io vegno"?   19
Dissilo, alquanto del color consperso
che fa l'uom di perdon talvolta degno.

E 'ntanto per la costa di traverso   22
venivan genti innanzi a noi un poco,
cantando 'Miserere' a verso a verso.

Quando s'accorser ch'i' non dava loco   25
per lo mio corpo al trapassar d'i raggi,
mutar lor canto in un "oh!" lungo e roco;

e due di loro, in forma di messaggi,   28
corsero incontr' a noi e dimandarne:
"Di vostra condizion fatene saggi."

I had already left those shades and was
following the footsteps of my leader
when from behind me, pointing the finger,

someone called out, "Look how the ray seems not   4
to shine on the left of that one down there,
and he seems to act as though he were alive!"

At the sound of those words I turned my eyes   7
and saw them staring in amazement
at me, at me, and the light that was broken.

"How is it that your spirit is so ensnared,"   10
the master said, "that you slacken your pace?
What is it to you what they whisper there?

Follow behind me and let the people talk.   13
Stand like a firm tower that never trembles
at the top though the wind blows upon it:

for always that man in whom thought wells up   16
over thought puts his goal farther from him
as the one weakens the force of the other."

What could I answer except "I come"?   19
I said it, flushed a little with that color
that makes a man worthy, sometimes, of pardon.

And as I did, there were people coming   22
along the hillside, a little way before us,
singing the *Miserere* line by line.

When it had struck them that I gave no place   25
for the rays of light to pass through my body,
their song changed into a long, hoarse "Oh."

And two of them in the role of messengers   28
ran to meet us and put their question:
"Let us know something of your condition."

E 'l mio maestro: "Voi potete andarne 31
e ritrarre a color che vi mandaro
che 'l corpo di costui è vera carne.

Se per veder la sua ombra restaro, 34
com' io avviso, assai è lor risposto:
fàccianli onore, ed esser può lor caro."

Vapori accesi non vid' io sì tosto 37
di prima notte mai fender sereno,
né, sol calando, nuvole d'agosto,

che color non tornasser suso in meno; 40
e, giunti là, con li altri a noi dier volta,
come schiera che scorre sanza freno.

"Questa gente che preme a noi è molta, 43
e vegnonti a pregar," disse 'l poeta:
"però pur va, e in andando ascolta."

"O anima che vai per esser lieta 46
con quelle membra con le quai nascesti,"
venian gridando, "un poco il passo queta.

Guarda s'alcun di noi unqua vedesti, 49
sì che di lui di là novella porti:
deh, perché vai? deh, perché non t'arresti?

Noi fummo tutti già per forza morti, 52
e peccatori infino a l'ultima ora;
quivi lume del ciel ne fece accorti,

sì che, pentendo e perdonando, fora 55
di vita uscimmo a Dio pacificati,
che del disio di sé veder n'accora."

E io: "Perché ne' vostri visi guati, 58
non riconosco alcun; ma s'a voi piace
cosa ch'io possa, spiriti ben nati,

voi dite, e io farò per quella pace 61
che, dietro a' piedi di sì fatta guida,
di mondo in mondo cercar me si face."

And my master: "You can return again 31
and make it plain to those who have sent you
that it is made of flesh, the body of this one.

If what they stopped at was the sight of his shadow, 34
as I suppose, there they all have their answer;
let them honor him and it may be dear to them."

I never saw lit vapors so quickly 37
just at nightfall split the calm of the sky
nor clouds in August as the sun was setting;

these took less time to return above 40
and when they arrived they wheeled back toward us
with the others like unreined cavalry.

"There are many people crowding upon us 43
and they come to ask something of you," the poet said,
"but keep straight on and listen as you go."

"Oh soul who go your way to become happy 46
in those same limbs that you were born into,"
they called as they came, "Slow your steps a little.

See whether you ever set eyes on any of us, 49
so that you can take news of him back there.
Oh why are you going? Oh why will you not stay?

All of us met our deaths by violence 52
and we were sinners until the last hour
when light from heaven brought understanding to us,

so that we came out of life repenting 55
and forgiving and at peace with God
who makes our hearts suffer longing to see Him."

And I, "However I study your faces 58
I cannot recognize one, but if something
I can do would please you, spirits born fortunate,

tell me and I will do it, by that peace 61
which in the footsteps of such a guide
draws me from world to world in search of it."

E uno incominciò: "Ciascun si fida   64
del beneficio tuo sanza giurarlo,
pur che 'l voler nonpossa non ricida.

Ond' io, che solo innanzi a li altri parlo,   67
ti priego, se mai vedi quel paese
che siede tra Romagna e quel di Carlo,

che tu mi sie di tuoi prieghi cortese   70
in Fano, sì che ben per me s'adori
pur ch'i' possa purgar le gravi offese.

Quindi fu' io; ma li profondi fóri   73
ond' uscì 'l sangue in sul quale io sedea,
fatti mi fuoro in grembo a li Antenori,

là dov' io più sicuro esser credea: 76
quel da Esti il fé far, che m'avea in ira
assai più là che dritto non volea.

Ma s'io fosse fuggito inver' la Mira,   79
quando fu' sovragiunto ad Orïaco,
ancor sarei di là dove si spira.

Corsi al palude, e le cannucce e 'l braco   82
m'impigliar sì ch'i' caddi; e lì vid' io
de le mie vene farsi in terra laco."

Poi disse un altro: "Deh, se quel disio   85
si compia che ti tragge a l'alto monte,
con buona pïetate aiuta il mio!

Io fui di Montefeltro, io son Bonconte;   88
Giovanna o altri non ha di me cura;
per ch'io vo tra costor con bassa fronte."

E io a lui: "Qual forza o qual ventura   91
ti travïò sì fuor di Campaldino,
che non si seppe mai tua sepultura?"

"Oh!" rispuos' elli, "a piè del Casentino   94
traversa un'acqua c'ha nome l'Archiano,
che sovra l'Ermo nasce in Apennino.

And one began, "Each of us has faith   64
in your good will without your swearing to it,
though you may not be able to do all you would.

So I who speak alone before the others   67
beseech you, if ever you see that land again
which lies between Romagna and Charles's kingdom,

as a courtesy to me beg them in   70
Fano to say such orisons for me
that I may be purged of my heavy sins.

I came from there, but those deep wounds that blood   73
poured from, which a moment before had been me
were dealt me in the lap of the Antenori

where I had thought to be safer than anywhere.   76
He of Este had it done, who was more angry
with me than he had any reason to be.

But if only I had turned toward La Mira fleeing   79
from Oriaco when I was overtaken
I would still be there where they are breathing.

I ran to the marsh and the reeds and slime   82
caught me so that I fell and there I saw
a lake grow on the ground out of my veins."

Then another said, "Oh, so may that desire be   85
satisfied that brings you to the high mountain,
out of compassion lend your help to mine.

I was of Montefeltro; I am Buonconte.   88
Giovanna cares nothing about me, nor does anyone,
which is why I go among these with my face down."

And I to him, "What force or fortune   91
took you so far away from Campaldino
that no one ever knew where you were buried?"

"Oh," he answered, "at the foot of the Casentino   94
a stream that is called the Archiano crosses
from above the Hermitage, in the Apennines.

Là 've 'l vocabol suo diventa vano,   97
arriva' io forato ne la gola,
fuggendo a piede e sanguinando il piano.

Quivi perdei la vista e la parola;   100
nel nome di Maria fini', e quivi
caddi, e rimase la mia carne sola.

Io dirò vero, e tu 'l ridì tra ' vivi: 103
l'angel di Dio mi prese, e quel d'inferno
gridava: 'O tu del ciel, perché mi privi?

Tu te ne porti di costui l'etterno   106
per una lagrimetta che 'l mi toglie;
ma io farò de l'altro altro governo!'

Ben sai come ne l'aere si raccoglie   109
quell' umido vapor che in acqua riede,
tosto che sale dove 'l freddo il coglie.

Giunse quel mal voler che pur mal chiede   112
con lo 'ntelletto, e mosse il fummo e 'l vento
per la virtù che sua natura diede.

Indi la valle, come 'l dì fu spento,   115
da Pratomagno al gran giogo coperse
di nebbia; e 'l ciel di sopra fece intento,

sì che 'l pregno aere in acqua si converse;   118
la pioggia cadde, e a' fossati venne
di lei ciò che la terra non sofferse;

e come ai rivi grandi si convenne,   121
ver' lo fiume real tanto veloce
si ruinò, che nulla la ritenne.

Lo corpo mio gelato in su la foce   124
trovò l'Archian rubesto; e quel sospinse
ne l'Arno, e sciolse al mio petto la croce

ch'i' fe' di me quando 'l dolor mi vinse;   127
voltòmmi per le ripe e per lo fondo,
poi di sua preda mi coperse e cinse."

There where its name grows empty of it 97
I came with the cut across my throat
fleeing on foot and bloodying the plain.

There I lost the sight of my eyes, and my speech, 100
ending with the name of Mary, and there
I fell and only my flesh was left of me.

I will tell the truth, and you repeat it to the living: 103
the angel of God took me and the one from Hell
shouted, 'Oh you from heaven, why do you rob me?

You carry off with you the eternal part 106
of this one for one little tear that rips him from me,
but I will handle the other another way.'

You know well enough how in the air 109
that damp vapor gathers that turns to water
the moment it comes where the cold seizes it.

He joined that evil will that wants ill only 112
with intellect, and stirred the mists and the wind
using the power that his nature gave him.

Then from the valley of Pratomagno to 115
the great peaks, as the day was ending, he covered
with cloud and made the sky brood overhead

so that the pregnant air changed into water; 118
the rain fell and came to the gullies
after the ground could not take any more

and it flowed together in great streams, 121
tearing its way with such speed toward the royal
river that nothing could stand against it.

Close to its mouth the raging Archiano 124
found my frozen body and into the Arno
heaved it and undid on my breast the cross

I had made of my arms when the pain overcame me; 127
against its banks and down its bed it rolled me
and then it covered and bound me in its spoils."

"Deh, quando tu sarai tornato al mondo   130
e riposato de la lunga via,"
seguitò 'l terzo spirito al secondo,

"ricorditi di me, che son la Pia;   133
Siena mi fé, disfecemi Maremma:
salsi colui che 'nnanellata pria

disposando m'avea con la sua gemma."   136

"Oh when you are back in the world again 130
and are rested after the long journey,"
the third spirit followed upon the second,

"pray you, remember me who am La Pia. 133
Siena made me, Maremma unmade me;
he knows it who, with his ring taking me,

first had me for his wife with his gem." 136

CANTO VI

Quando si parte il gioco de la zara,
colui che perde si riman dolente,
repetendo le volte, e tristo impara;

con l'altro se ne va tutta la gente;   4
qual va dinanzi, e qual di dietro il prende,
e qual dallato li si reca a mente;

el non s'arresta, e questo e quello intende;   7
a cui porge la man, più non fa pressa;
e così da la calca si difende.

Tal era io in quella turba spessa,   10
volgendo a loro, e qua e là, la faccia,
e promettendo mi sciogliea da essa.

Quiv' era l'Aretin che da le braccia   13
fiere di Ghin di Tacco ebbe la morte,
e l'altro ch'annegò correndo in caccia.

Quivi pregava con le mani sporte   16
Federigo Novello, e quel da Pisa
che fé parer lo buon Marzucco forte.

Vidi conte Orso e l'anima divisa   19
dal corpo suo per astio e per inveggia,
com' e' dicea, non per colpa commisa;

Pier da la Broccia dico; e qui proveggia,   22
mentr' è di qua, la donna di Brabante,
sì che però non sia di peggior greggia.

Come libero fui da tutte quante   25
quell' ombre che pregar pur ch'altri prieghi,
sì che s'avacci lor divenir sante,

io cominciai: "El par che tu mi nieghi,   28
o luce mia, espresso in alcun testo
che decreto del cielo orazion pieghi;

When the game of dice breaks up, the one
who loses is left with his sorrow,
repeating the throws, and his sad lesson;

all the rest go off with the other,   4
one in front, one behind, hanging on,
one at his side trying to get his attention.

He does not stop, he listens to this one and that one,   7
and the one to whom he holds out his hand nags him
no longer, and in that way he escapes them.

So it was with me in that dense swarm,   10
turning my face from one to another of them,
promising until I was free of them.

There was the Aretine whose death came to him   13
from the brutal hands of Ghino di Tacco, and
the other who was drowned in the hunt as he ran.

There was Federigo Novello, begging,   16
holding his hands out, and from Pisa the one who
revealed the strength of the good Marzucco.

I saw Count Orso, and the soul cut away   19
from its body by malice and envy,
and for nothing he had done, as he told me,

I refer to Pierre de la Brosse, and while she is   22
here, let the lady of Brabant take it
to heart, lest she end in a worse flock, for this.

When I was free of the last of those   25
who prayed only for the prayers of others
to bring them sooner to their blessedness

I began, "It seems to me that in one   28
passage, oh my light, you expressly deny
that prayer can deflect the decree of Heaven,

e questa gente prega pur di questo: 31
sarebbe dunque loro speme vana,
o non m'è 'l detto tuo ben manifesto?"

Ed elli a me: "La mia scrittura è piana; 34
e la speranza di costor non falla,
se ben si guarda con la mente sana;

ché cima di giudicio non s'avvalla 37
perché foco d'amor compia in un punto
ciò che de' sodisfar chi qui s'astalla;

e là dov' io fermai cotesto punto, 40
non s'ammendava, per pregar, difetto,
perché 'l priego da Dio era disgiunto.

Veramente a così alto sospetto 43
non ti fermar, se quella nol ti dice
che lume fia tra 'l vero e lo 'ntelletto.

Non so se 'ntendi: io dico di Beatrice; 46
tu la vedrai di sopra, in su la vetta
di questo monte, ridere e felice."

E io: "Segnore, andiamo a maggior fretta, 49
ché già non m'affatico come dianzi,
e vedi omai che 'l poggio l'ombra getta."

"Noi anderem con questo giorno innanzi," 52
rispuose, "quanto più potremo omai;
ma 'l fatto è d'altra forma che non stanzi.

Prima che sie là sù, tornar vedrai 55
colui che già si cuopre de la costa,
sì che ' suoi raggi tu romper non fai.

Ma vedi là un'anima che, posta 58
sola soletta, inverso noi riguarda:
quella ne 'nsegnerà la via più tosta."

Venimmo a lei: o anima lombarda, 61
come ti stavi altera e disdegnosa
e nel mover de li occhi onesta e tarda!

and these people are praying for that alone.   31
Is their hope then finally in vain,
or have I not truly understood what you mean?"

And he to me, "What I wrote is plain,   34
and the hope of these is not mistaken
if you consider it with a clear mind.

For it does not reduce the height of justice   37
if the fire of love fulfills in one moment
what each one owes who lives in this place,

and in the passage where I said the same,   40
prayer did not redeem the fault, because
it was never to God that the prayer came.

Nevertheless, in so lofty a question   43
do not make up your mind until she says to
who will be light between truth and your reason.

I do not know whether you grasp my meaning.   46
I am speaking of Beatrice, whom you will see
at the top of this mountain, happy and smiling."

And I, "My lord, let us walk faster, for   49
I do not feel tired as I did before,
and see how the hill now casts its shadow."

"We will go on by the light of this day,"   52
he answered, "as much farther as we may,
but the fact is not what you take it to be.

Before you are there you will see him reappear   55
who is already hidden by the slope
so that you break off his beams no longer.

But see, there is a soul sitting alone,   58
off by himself, who is looking toward us.
He will point out the quickest way for us."

We approached him. O Lombard soul, with what   61
haughtiness and what disdain you stood
and with what slow dignity your eyes turned!

Ella non ci dicëa alcuna cosa,   64
ma lasciavane gir, solo sguardando
a guisa di leon quando si posa.

Pur Virgilio si trasse a lei, pregando   67
che ne mostrasse la miglior salita;
e quella non rispuose al suo dimando,

ma di nostro paese e de la vita   70
ci 'nchiese; e 'l dolce duca incominciava
"Mantüa . . . ," e l'ombra, tutta in sé romita,

surse ver' lui del loco ove pria stava,   73
dicendo: "O Mantoano, io son Sordello
de la tua terra!"; e l'un l'altro abbracciava.

Ahi serva Italia, di dolore ostello,   76
nave sanza nocchiere in gran tempesta,
non donna di provincie, ma bordello!

Quell' anima gentil fu così presta,   79
sol per lo dolce suon de la sua terra,
di fare al cittadin suo quivi festa;

e ora in te non stanno sanza guerra   82
li vivi tuoi, e l'un l'altro si rode
di quei ch'un muro e una fossa serra.

Cerca, misera, intorno da le prode   85
le tue marine, e poi ti guarda in seno,
s'alcuna parte in te di pace gode.

Che val perché ti racconciasse il freno   88
Iustinïano, se la sella è vòta?
Sanz' esso fora la vergogna meno.

Ahi gente che dovresti esser devota,   91
e lasciar seder Cesare in la sella,
se bene intendi ciò che Dio ti nota,

guarda come esta fiera è fatta fella   94
per non esser corretta da li sproni,
poi che ponesti mano a la predella.

Not a thing did he have to say to us,   64
but was letting us pass, only watching us
as a lion watches from where it lies.

But Virgil went closer to him and asked him   67
to show us the best way up from there,
and that one never answered his question

but asked to know our country and our station,   70
and the gentle leader began, "Mantuan—"
and that shade, all into himself withdrawn,

sprang toward him, from the place where he had been,   73
saying, "Oh Mantuan, I am Sordello,
from your own country," and they embraced each other.

Oh slavish Italy, hostel of wretchedness,   76
ship with no pilot in the great tempest,
no mistress of provinces but a whorehouse,

that noble soul, at the sweet name alone   79
of his own city, was so eager
to make welcome a citizen from there,

while those now living in you are forever   82
at war, and those whom one wall and one
moat enclose are gnawing on each other.

Unhappy spirit, search along the seashore   85
around you, then look into your own breast;
see whether you enjoy peace anywhere.

Justinian repaired the reins for you;   88
what good is that if the saddle is empty?
it would not be so shameful were it not so.

Oh you who are supposed to show devotion   91
ought to let Caesar sit in the saddle,
if you had comprehended God's instruction.

See how this beast has grown ungovernable   94
for want of any spur to discipline her
since you have laid your hand upon the bridle.

O Alberto tedesco ch'abbandoni 97
costei ch'è fatta indomita e selvaggia,
e dovresti inforcar li suoi arcioni,

giusto giudicio da le stelle caggia 100
sovra 'l tuo sangue, e sia novo e aperto,
tal che 'l tuo successor temenza n'aggia!

Ch'avete tu e 'l tuo padre sofferto, 103
per cupidigia di costà distretti,
che 'l giardin de lo 'mperio sia diserto.

Vieni a veder Montecchi e Cappelletti, 106
Monaldi e Filippeschi, uom sanza cura:
color già tristi, e questi con sospetti!

Vien, crudel, vieni, e vedi la pressura 109
d'i tuoi gentili, e cura lor magagne;
e vedrai Santafior com' è oscura!

Vieni a veder la tua Roma che piagne 112
vedova e sola, e dì e notte chiama:
"Cesare mio, perché non m'accompagne?"

Vieni a veder la gente quanto s'ama! 115
e se nulla di noi pietà ti move,
a vergognar ti vien de la tua fama.

E se licito m'è, o sommo Giove 118
che fosti in terra per noi crucifisso,
son li giusti occhi tuoi rivolti altrove?

O è preparazion che ne l'abisso 121
del tuo consiglio fai per alcun bene
in tutto de l'accorger nostro scisso?

Ché le città d'Italia tutte peine 124
son di tiranni, e un Marcel diventa
ogne villan che parteggiando viene.

Fiorenza mia, ben puoi esser contenta 127
di questa digression che non ti tocca,
mercé del popol tuo che si argomenta.

Oh German Albert who abandon her   97
when she has become wild and unbreakable,
you who should be set firmly in the saddle,

    may a just judgment rain down from the stars   100
upon your blood, and be so strange and clear
that your successor may be struck with fear,

    for you and your father were distracted   103
by your greed, far away there, and you let
the garden of the empire run to waste.

    Come look at the Montecchis and Cappellettis,   106
Monaldis and Filippeschis, those grieving
already and these in dread, and you not caring.

    Come, come, you with no heart, behold the anguish   109
of your nobly born, look to their injuries
and you will see how safe Santafiore is.

    Come look upon your Rome as she is weeping,   112
widowed and alone, calling, "My Caesar,"
day and night, "why are you not with me here?"

    Come and see how your people love each other,   115
and though nothing may move you to pity us,
come if only out of shame, for your honor.

    And if I have a right to ask, oh highest   118
Jove who on earth were crucified for us,
are your just eyes turned to some other place,

    or in the abyss of your wisdom   121
is this the preparation of some good
cut off utterly from our perception?

    For all the cities of Italy are full   124
of tyrants, and each peasant who becomes
a partisan turns into a Marcellus.

    Let your content remain complete, my Florence,   127
through this digression, which does not concern you,
thanks to the good sense of your citizens.

Molti han giustizia in cuore, e tardi scocca   130
per non venir sanza consiglio a l'arco;
ma il popol tuo l'ha in sommo de la bocca.

Molti rifiutan lo comune incarco;   133
ma il popol tuo solicito risponde
sanza chiamare, e grida: "I' mi sobbarco!"

Or ti fa lieta, ché tu hai ben onde: 136
tu ricca, tu con pace e tu con senno!
S'io dico 'l ver, l'effetto nol nasconde.

Atene e Lacedemona, che fenno   139
l'antiche leggi e furon sì civili,
fecero al viver bene un picciol cenno

verso di te, che fai tanto sottili   142
provedimenti, ch'a mezzo novembre
non giugne quel che tu d'ottobre fili.

Quante volte, del tempo che rimembre,   145
legge, moneta, officio e costume
hai tu mutato, e rinovate membre!

E se ben ti ricordi e vedi lume,   148
verdrai te somigliante a quella inferma
che non può trovar posa in su le piume,

ma con dar volta suo dolore scherma.   151

Many have justice in their hearts but are slow   *130*
to find reason to bring the arrow to the bow,
but your people keep it on the tip of the tongue.

Many refuse to bear the common burden,   *133*
but your people answer before anyone
asks them, they call eagerly, "Let me take it on."

Rejoice then, you that have such reason to,   *136*
you that are rich, and are at peace, and wise.
Facts will not hide my words if they are true.

Athens and Lacedaemon, which composed   *139*
the ancient laws and were so civilized,
in the matter of righteous living, compared to you

were next to nothing, whose provisions are   *142*
so subtle that the thread spun in October
runs out before the middle of November.

How often, in the time you can remember,   *145*
have you changed laws, money, offices,
customs, and remodeled every member,

and if you look clearly at what you were   *148*
you will see yourself as that sick woman never
still on her bed of down, turning over

and over to find some way not to suffer.   *151*

CANTO VII

Poscia che l'accoglienze oneste e liete
furo iterate tre e quattro volte,
Sordel si trasse, e disse: "Voi, chi siete?"

"Anzi che a questo monte fosser volte   4
l'anime degne di salire a Dio,
fur l'ossa mie per Ottavian sepolte.

Io son Virgilio; e per null' altro rio   7
lo ciel perdei che per non aver fé."
Così rispuose allora il duca mio.

Qual è colui che cosa innanzi sé   10
sùbita vede ond' e' si maraviglia,
che crede e non, dicendo "Ella è . . . non è . . . ,"

tal parve quelli; e poi chinò le ciglia,   13
e umilmente ritornò ver' lui,
e abbracciòl là 've 'l minor s'appiglia.

"O gloria d'i Latin," disse, "per cui   16
mostrò ciò che potea la lingua nostra,
o pregio etterno del loco ond' io fui,

qual merito o qual grazia mi ti mostra?   19
S'io son d'udir le tue parole degno,
dimmi se vien d'inferno, e di qual chiostra."

"Per tutt' i cerchi del dolente regno,"   22
rispuose lui, "son io di qua venuto;
virtù del ciel mi mosse, e con lei vegno.

Non per far, ma per non fare ho perduto   25
a veder l'alto Sol che tu disiri
e che fu tardi per me conosciuto.

Luogo è là giù non tristo di martìri,   28
ma di tenebre solo, ove i lamenti
non suonan come guai, ma son sospiri.

After the unaffected joyful greetings
had been said over again three and four times
Sordello drew back and said, "Who are you both?"

"Before the first souls worthy of making   4
the ascent to God had turned to this mountain
my bones were buried by Octavian.

I am Virgil, and lost heaven only   7
for one fault: that the faith was not in me."
That was his answer, then, who was leading me.

As one who sees before him suddenly   10
something at which he marvels so that he
believes, not believing, saying, "It is . . . it is not . . ."

the other seemed, and then with lowered brow   13
and humbly he drew close to him again
and embraced him as one does of lower station.

"Oh glory of the Latins," he said, "through whom   16
our tongue revealed what it had power to say,
oh eternal honor of the place I came from,

what merit shows you to me, or what favor?   19
If I am worthy to hear your words, tell me
whether you come from Hell, and from which cloister."

"Through all the circles of the suffering kingdom," 22
he answered him, "I have come here. Power from
Heaven moved me and by its strength I came.

Not by doing but by not doing I   25
have lost the sight of the high sun you long for
which when it was too late was known to me.

There is a place down there sad not with torments   28
but only with darkness, where the laments
are not the moans of anguish but are sighs.

Quivi sto io coi pargoli innocenti   31
dai denti morsi de la morte avante
che fosser da l'umana colpa essenti;

quivi sto io con quei che le tre sante   34
virtù non si vestiro, e sanza vizio
conobber l'altre e seguir tutte quante.

Ma se tu sai e puoi, alcuno indizio   37
dà noi per che venir possiam più tosto
là dove purgatorio ha dritto inizio."

Rispuose: "Loco certo non c'è posto;   40
licito m'è andar suso e intorno;
per quanto ir posso, a guida mi t'accosto.

Ma vedi già come dichina il giorno,   43
e andar sù di notte non si puote;
però è buon pensar di bel soggiorno.

Anime sono a destra qua remote;   46
se mi consenti, io ti merrò ad esse,
e non sanza diletto ti fier note."

"Com' è ciò?" fu risposto. "Chi volesse   49
salir di notte, fora elli impedito
d'altrui, o non sarria ché non potesse?"

E 'l buon Sordello in terra fregò 'l dito,   52
dicendo: "Vedi? sola questa riga
non varcheresti dopo 'l sol partito:

non però ch'altra cosa desse briga,   55
che la notturna tenebra, ad ir suso;
quella col nonpoder la voglia intriga.

Ben si poria con lei tornare in giuso   58
e passeggiar la costa intorno errando,
mentre che l'orizzonte il dì tien chiuso."

Allora il mio segnor, quasi ammirando,   61
"Menane," disse, "dunque là 've dici
ch'aver si può diletto dimorando."

There I stay with the infant innocents 31
whom the fangs of death fastened upon
before they were exempted from human sin.

There I stay with those who did not put on 34
the three holy virtues, and without sin
knew the others and kept to every one.

But tell us, if you know and can, of any 37
way that we may take to come more quickly
to the true beginning of Purgatory."

He answered, "To no place are we assigned. 40
I am allowed to go up and around.
I will go with you and guide you while I can.

But see, already the day is going down 43
and no one can go up at all at night.
We should be thinking of a good place to rest in.

There are souls off on the right, over here. 46
If you allow me, I will lead you to them
and they will be known to you, not without great pleasure."

"How is that," was the reply, "if someone 49
wanted to go up at night would anyone
prevent him, or would he not be able to?"

And the good Sordello ran his finger along 52
the ground, saying, "Look, not even this line
could you step across after the sun has gone,

not because anything else would be in the way 55
of going up, but only the night's darkness
that enmeshes the will and leaves it helpless.

It would be easy, though, to go back down 58
around the hill in the dark, wandering on
while the horizon has the day shut in."

Then my lord, seeming to wonder at it, 61
said, "Lead us, then, to that place where you say
it will be pleasant for us, while we are there."

Poco allungati c'eravam di lici,   64
quand' io m'accorsi che 'l monte era scemo,
a guisa che i vallon li sceman quici.

"Colà," disse quell' ombra, "n'anderemo 67
dove la costa face di sé grembo;
e là il novo giorno attenderemo."

Tra erto e piano era un sentiero schembo, 70
che ne condusse in fianco de la lacca,
là dove più ch'a mezzo muore il lembo.

Oro e argento fine, cocco e biacca,   73
indaco, legno lucido e sereno,
fresco smeraldo in l'ora che si fiacca,

da l'erba e da li fior, dentr' a quel seno 76
posti, ciascun saria di color vinto,
come dal suo maggiore è vinto il meno.

Non avea pur natura ivi dipinto,   79
ma di soavità di mille odori
vi facea uno incognito e indistinto.

"Salve, Regina" in sul verde e 'n su' fiori 82
quindi seder cantando anime vidi,
che per la valle non parean di fuori.

"Prima che 'l poco sole omai s'annidi," 85
cominciò 'l Mantoan che ci avea vòlti,
"tra color non vogliate ch'io vi guidi.

Di questo balzo meglio li atti e ' volti 88
conoscerete voi di tutti quanti,
che ne la lama giù tra essi accolti.

Colui che più siede alto e fa sembianti 91
d'aver negletto ciò che far dovea,
e che non move bocca a li altrui canti,

Rodolfo imperador fu, che potea   94
sanar le piaghe c'hanno Italia morta,
sì che tardi per altri si ricrea.

We had gone only a little way from there   64
when I could see a hollow in the mountain
such as the valleys make in the mountains here.

"Over there," that shade said, "we will make our way,   67
to where the hillside forms a lap of itself,
and that is where we will wait for the new day."

Part steep, part level, there was a winding way   70
that led us in to the side of the valley
where the edge above it half dies away.

Gold and fine silver, cochineal, white lead,   73
or the wood indigo with its lucid sheen,
fresh emerald at the moment it breaks open,

each would have been overcome in color   76
by the grass and flowers in that valley
as the less is overcome by the greater.

Nature there had not kept to painting alone   79
but from the fragrance of a thousand scents
made one that was none of them and unknown.

There on the green and the flowers, singing   82
"Salve Regina," I saw souls sitting
whom I could not see from outside the valley.

"Before the small sun to its nest has gone,"   85
the Mantuan who had led us there began,
"do not ask me to guide you among them.

You will be better able to see the faces   88
from this bank and the gestures of each of them
than if you were received down on the level with them.

He that sits highest and looks like someone   91
who has neglected what he should have done
and does not move his mouth when the others sing

was the Emperor Rudolf who could have healed   94
the wounds of Italy that have killed her
so that another tries, too late, to raise her.

L'altro che ne la vista lui conforta,   97
resse la terra dove l'acqua nasce
che Molta in Albia, e Albia in mar ne porta:

Ottacchero ebbe nome, e ne le fasce   100
fu meglio assai che Vincislao suo figlio
barbuto, cui lussuria e ozio pasce.

E quel nasetto che stretto a consiglio   103
par con colui c'ha sì benigno aspetto,
morì fuggendo e disfiorando il giglio:

guardate là come si batte il petto!   106
L'altro vedete c'ha fatto a la guancia
de la sua palma, sospirando, letto.

Padre e suocero son del mal di Francia: 109
sanno la vita sua viziata e lorda,
e quindi viene il duol che sì li lancia.

Quel che par sì membruto e che s'accorda,   112
cantando, con colui dal maschio naso,
d'ogne valor portò cinta la corda;

e se re dopo lui fosse rimaso   115
lo giovanetto che retro a lui siede,
ben andava il valor di vaso in vaso,

che non si puote dir de l'altre rede;   118
Iacomo e Federigo hanno i reami;
del retaggio miglior nessun possiede.

Rade volte risurge per li rami   121
l'umana probitate; e questo vole
quei che la dà, perché da lui si chiami.

Anche al nasuto vanno mie parole   124
non men ch'a l'altro, Pier, che con lui canta,
onde Puglia e Proenza già si dole.

Tant' è del seme suo minor la pianta,   127
quanto, più che Beatrice e Margherita,
Costanza di marito ancor si vanta.

The other who seems to be comforting him   97
ruled the land that the waters come from
that Moldau bears to Elbe and Elbe to the sea.

Ottokar was his name, and of more worth in his   100
swaddling clothes than bearded Wenceslas,
his son, with his diet of lewdness and idleness.

The one with the small nose, in close counsel   103
with that one whose countenance shows him to be
so kind, died in flight, deflowering the lily.

Look at the way he beats his breast! See   106
how the other has made for his
cheek a bed with his palm, and sighs.

They are father and father-in-law of the plague   109
of France, know his foul, vicious life, and from
that comes the suffering which so pierces them.

That one who looks so strong and sings in time   112
with the one who has the manly nose
wore the cord of every virtue about him,

and if the young man sitting there behind him   115
had been the king who succeeded him
his strength would have flowed from vessel to vessel,

which cannot be said of the other heirs   118
now James and Frederick have the kingdoms
and neither heritage exceeds the other's.

Rarely does human integrity climb into   121
the branches, which is the will of the one who
gave it, so they must ask it of him again.

My words concern him with the nose no less   124
than that other, Peter, who is singing with him.
Puglia and Provence suffer because of him.

So much less the plant is than the seed   127
Constance still boasts of her own husband more
than Beatrice and Margaret do of theirs.

Vedete il re de la semplice vita   130
seder là solo, Arrigo d'Inghilterra:
questi ha ne' rami suoi migliore uscita.

Quel che più basso tra costor s'atterra,   133
guardando in suso, è Guiglielmo marchese,
per cui e Alessandria e la sua guerra

fa pianger Monferrato e Canavese."   136

See, there is the king of the simple life,   130
Henry of England, sitting alone, who has
a finer issue in his branches.

The one who sits on the ground, lowest among them,   133
looking up, is the marquis William
because of whom Alessandria and its war

have Montferrat and Canavese grieving."   136

CANTO VIII

Era già l'ora che volge il disio
ai navicanti e 'ntenerisce il core
lo dì c'han detto ai dolci amici addio;

e che lo novo peregrin d'amore   4
punge, se ode squilla di lontano
che paia il giorno pianger che si more;

quand' io incominciai a render vano   7
l'udire e a mirare una de l'alme
surta, che l'ascoltar chiedea con mano.

Ella giunse e levò ambo le palme,   10
ficcando li occhi verso l'orïente,
come dicesse a Dio: "D'altro non calme."

"*Te lucis ante*" sì devotamente   13
le uscìo di bocca e con sì dolci note,
che fece me a me uscir di mente;

e l'altre poi dolcemente e devote   16
seguitar lei per tutto l'inno intero,
avendo li occhi a le superne rote.

Aguzza qui, lettor, ben li occhi al vero,   19
ché 'l velo è ora ben tanto sottile,
certo che 'l trapassar dentro è leggero.

Io vidi quello essercito gentile   22
tacito poscia riguardare in sùe,
quasi aspettando, palido e umìle;

e vidi uscir de l'alto e scender giùe   25
due angeli con due spade affocate,
tronche e private de le punte sue.

Verdi come fogliette pur mo nate   28
erano in veste, che da verdi penne
percosse traean dietro e ventilate.

Then it was the hour that brings longing again
to melt the hearts of those out on the sea
the day they have said goodbye to their dear friends,

and when love stabs the new pilgrim who hears   4
far off in the distance a bell ringing
as though mourning the day that is dying,

when I found I was no longer hearing his words   7
and was staring at one who had risen,
holding up his hand, wishing to be heard.

He joined his palms and raised them together,   10
fixing his eyes on the east, as though to say
to God, "There is nothing else I care for."

Out of his lips the *Te lucis ante*   13
issued with such devotion and so sweetly
that the notes drew me up out of me,

and then the others joined in after him   16
sweetly and devoutly through the whole hymn
with their eyes fixed upon the wheels of heaven.

Reader, sharpen your own eyes here to see   19
the truth, for now the veil is certainly
so fine that passing through it will be easy.

I saw that noble army then gazing   22
upward in silence, pallid and humble;
it seemed clear that they were waiting for something.

And from high up I saw two angels come   25
who descended with two flaming swords
shortened and with the points broken off them.

Green as small leaves at the moment they are born   28
were the robes they wore, and those were whipped and blown
by their green wings, and trailed out behind them.

L'un poco sovra noi a star si venne,   31
e l'altro scese in l'opposita sponda,
sì che la gente in mezzo si contenne.

Ben discernëa in lor la testa bionda;   34
ma ne la faccia l'occhio si smarria,
come virtù ch'a troppo si confonda.

"Ambo vegnon del grembo di Maria,"   37
disse Sordello, "a guardia de la valle,
per lo serpente che verrà vie via."

Ond' io, che non sapeva per qual calle,   40
mi volsi intorno, e stretto m'accostai,
tutto gelato, a le fidate spalle.

E Sordello anco: "Or avvalliamo omai   43
tra le grandi ombre, e parleremo ad esse;
grazïoso fia lor vedervi assai."

Solo tre passi credo ch'i' scendesse,   46
e fui di sotto, e vidi un che mirava
pur me, come conoscer mi volesse.

Temp' era già che l'aere s'annerava,   49
ma non sì che tra li occhi suoi e ' miei
non dichiarisse ciò che pria serrava.

Ver' me si fece, e io ver' lui mi fei: 52
giudice Nin gentil, quanto mi piacque
quando ti vidi non esser tra ' rei!

Nullo bel salutar tra noi si tacque;   55
poi dimandò: "Quant' è che tu venisti
a piè del monte per le lontane acque?"

"Oh!" diss' io lui, "per entro i luoghi tristi   58
venni stamane, e sono in prima vita,
ancor che l'altra, sì andando, acquisti."

E come fu la mia risposta udita,   61
Sordello ed elli in dietro si raccolse
come gente di sùbito smarrita.

One came to stand still almost overhead
and the other descended onto the far side
so that everyone there was between them.

31

I could see plainly the blond hair of their heads,
but my eyes were dazzled by their faces
as any faculty is confused by excess.

34

"Both have come from the bosom of Mary,"
Sordello said, "to protect the valley
because of the serpent that before long you will see."

37

So that I, not knowing which way it would
come from, turned around, with cold all through me,
and drew close to the shoulders I trusted.

40

And Sordello went on, "Now let us go down
among the great shades and speak with them;
seeing you will be a pleasure to them."

43

I seemed to take only three steps before
I was down there and saw watching me one
who thought I might be someone he had known.

46

The time had come when the air was darkening
but it was not so dark that, between his eyes and mine,
something shut off before could not be seen.

49

He made his way toward me and I toward him.
Noble Judge Nino, what joy I had
when I saw you were not down with the wicked!

52

No grace of greeting went unsaid between us.
Then he asked, "How long ago did you come
to the foot of the mountain, over the far waters?"

55

"Oh," I said to him, "by way of the regions of sorrow
I came this morning, and I am still in my
first life, seeking another with this journey."

58

And Sordello and he, when they had heard
the answer I had made, drew back the way
people do who are suddenly bewildered.

61

L'uno a Virgilio e l'altro a un si volse   64
che sedea lì, gridando: "Sù, Currado!
vieni a veder che Dio per grazia volse."

Poi, vòlto a me: "Per quel singular grado   67
che tu dei a colui che sì nasconde
lo suo primo perché, che non li è guado,

quando sarai di là da le larghe onde,   70
dì a Giovanna mia che per me chiami
là dove a li 'nnocenti si risponde.

Non credo che la sua madre più m'ami,   73
poscia che trasmutò le bianche bende,
le quai convien che, misera!, ancor brami.

Per lei assai di lieve si comprende   76
quanto in femmina foco d'amor dura,
se l'occhio o 'l tatto spesso non l'accende.

Non le farà sì bella sepultura   79
la vipera che Melanesi accampa,
com' avria fatto il gallo di Gallura."

Così dicea, segnato de la stampa,   82
nel suo aspetto, di quel dritto zelo
che misuratamente in core avvampa.

Li occhi miei ghiotti andavan pur al cielo,   85
pur là dove le stelle son più tarde,
sì come rota più presso a lo stelo.

E 'l duca mio: "Figliuol, che là sù guarde?"   88
E io a lui: "A quelle tre facelle
di che 'l polo di qua tutto quanto arde."

Ond' elli a me: "Le quattro chiare stelle   91
che vedevi staman, son di là basse,
e queste son salite ov' eran quelle."

Com' ei parlava, e Sordello a sé il trasse   94
dicendo: "Vedi là 'l nostro avversaro";
e drizzò il dito perché 'n là guardasse.

One turned to Virgil and the other to   64
someone sitting there, calling, "Stand up, Corrado.
Come and see what God in His grace has willed."

Then, turning to me, "By that singular   67
gratitude that you owe Him who so hides
his primal Why that there is no way there,

when you are beyond the wide waters   70
tell my Giovanna to plead for me
there where the innocent receive answers.

I do not think her mother has loved me   73
since she took off the white widow's veil which she
must now be longing for in her misery.

It is easy enough to see in her how long   76
the fire of love lasts in a woman, if sight
and touch are not always keeping it alight.

The viper that leads the Milanese to the field   79
will never raise for her a tomb so fine
as the cock of Gallura would have done."

So he spoke, his face bearing the mark   82
stamped on it of that righteous zeal which glows
on at its proper measure in the heart.

My eyes kept straying greedily to the sky   85
there where the stars, like the part of a wheel
nearest the axle, move most slowly.

And my leader said, "Son, what is it up there   88
you are gazing at?" And I said, "Those three torches
that have set the entire pole here on fire."

And he to me, "The four bright stars   91
you saw this morning went down over there,
and these have risen where those others were."

As he was speaking Sordello drew him closer,   94
saying, "See, there is the adversary,"
pointing a finger for him to look that way.

Da quella parte onde non ha riparo   97
la picciola vallea, era una biscia,
forse qual diede ad Eva il cibo amaro.

Tra l'erba e ' fior venìa la mala striscia,   100
volgendo ad ora ad or la testa, e 'l dosso
leccando come bestia che si liscia.

Io non vidi, e però dicer non posso,   103
come mosser li astor celestïali;
ma vidi bene e l'uno e l'altro mosso.

Sentendo fender l'aere a le verdi ali,   106
fuggì 'l serpente, e li angeli dier volta,
suso a le poste rivolando iguali.

L'ombra che s'era al giudice raccolta   109
quando chiamò, per tutto quello assalto
punto non fu da me guardare sciolta.

"Se la lucerna che ti mena in alto   112
truovi nel tuo arbitrio tanta cera
quant' è mestiere infino al sommo smalto,"

cominciò ella, "se novella vera   115
di Val di Magra o di parte vicina
sai, dillo a me, che già grande là era.

Fui chiamato Currado Malaspina;   118
non son l'antico, ma di lui discesi;
a' miei portai l'amor che qui raffina."

"Oh!" diss' io lui, "per li vostri paesi   121
già mai non fui; ma dove si dimora
per tutta Europa ch'ei non sien palesi?

La fama che la vostra casa onora,   124
grida i segnori e grida la contrada,
sì che ne sa chi non vi fu ancora;

e io vi giuro, s'io di sopra vada,   127
che vostra gente onrata non si sfregia
del pregio de la borsa e de la spada.

On that side where the small valley has 97
no ramparts was a snake. Maybe it was
that kind that gave the bitter food to Eve.

Through the grass and flowers came the streak of evil, 100
turning its head to the side, and again, and again,
licking its back like a preening animal.

I did not see and so I cannot tell 103
of the motion of the celestial
falcons, though I saw them both plainly in motion.

Hearing the green wings split the air, the serpent 106
fled and the angels together wheeled around,
flying back up to their posts again.

The shade who had come to the judge's side 109
when he called, through all that assault had not
for one moment taken his eyes from me.

"So may the lantern that leads you to the height 112
find in your will the wax that it requires
all the way up to the enameled summit,"

he began, "tell me if you have any news 115
that is true of Val di Magra or that country,
for I was important, at one time, in that place.

I was called Corrado Malaspina. Not 118
the elder, but his descendant. I bore
to my own kin the love that is refined here."

"Oh," I said to him, "I have never been 121
through your lands, but is there any place
in all Europe where they are not renowned?

The fame that is the honor of your household 124
praises alike the lords and their domains,
making them known to those who never saw them,

and as I hope to reach the heights, I swear 127
that your honored family still has not squandered
the glory of the purse and of the sword.

Uso e natura sì la privilegia,   130
che, perché il capo reo il mondo torca,
sola va dritta e 'l mal cammin dispregia."

Ed elli: "Or va; che 'l sol non si ricorca   133
sette volte nel letto che 'l Montone
con tutti e quattro i piè cuopre e inforca,

che cotesta cortese oppinïone   136
ti fia chiavata in mezzo de la testa
con maggior chiovi che d'altrui sermone,

se corso di giudicio non s'arresta."   139

Custom and nature have endowed it so   130
that, though the guilty head turns the world awry,
it alone keeps straight and scorns the evil way."

And he, "Go now, for before the sun has come   133
seven times to the bed that the Ram
bestrides with all four feet, standing over it,

you will have this courteous opinion   136
nailed in the center of your head with nails
that will be stronger than the talk of men

if the course of judgment is not halted."   139

CANTO IX

La concubina di Titone antico
già s'imbiancava al balco d'orïente,
fuor de le braccia del suo dolce amico;

di gemme la sua fronte era lucente,   4
poste in figura del freddo animale
che con la coda percuote la gente;

e la notte, de' passi con che sale,   7
fatti avea due nel loco ov' eravamo,
e 'l terzo già chinava in giuso l'ale;

quand' io, che meco avea di quel d'Adamo,   10
vinto dal sonno, in su l'erba inchinai
là 've già tutti e cinque sedavamo.

Ne l'ora che comincia i tristi lai   13
la rondinella presso a la mattina,
forse a memoria de' suo' primi guai,

e che la mente nostra, peregrina   16
più da la carne e men da' pensier presa,
a le sue visïon quasi è divina,

in sogno mi parea veder sospesa   19
un'aguglia nel ciel con penne d'oro,
con l'ali aperte e a calare intesa;

ed esser mi parea là dove fuoro   22
abbandonati i suoi da Ganimede,
quando fu ratto al sommo consistoro.

Fra me pensava: "Forse questa fiede   25
pur qui per uso, e forse d'altro loco
disdegna di portarne suso in piede."

Poi mi parea che, poi rotata un poco,   28
terribil come folgor discendesse,
e me rapisse suso infino al foco.

Leaving the arms of her tender lover
the mistress of old Tithonus already
was appearing, white, on the eastern balcony,

her forehead all alight with jewels set   4
in the outline of that cold animal
that lashes out at people with its tail,

and in the place where we were the night had climbed   7
two of the paces that she takes, by then,
and the wings of the third were folding down

when I, who had something of Adam with me,   10
lay down in the grass where all five of us
had seated ourselves, and sleep overcame me.

Close to dawn, at the hour when the swallow   13
begins her sad songs, out of memory,
as it may be, of her earliest woe,

and when our mind, a pilgrim farther from   16
the flesh, and captive less to thoughts, is in
its vision almost able to divine,

it seemed to me that I saw in a dream   19
an eagle with golden feathers in heaven
with wings spread wide, ready to swoop down,

and I seemed to be there where those with him   22
were abandoned by Ganymede when he
was caught up to the highest consistory.

I thought to myself, "It may be that only here   25
it is used to striking, and from no other
place, perhaps, takes anyone in its talons."

Then it seemed to me that after wheeling for   28
a moment, terrible as lightning it
dropped and snatched me up all the way to the fire.

Ivi parea che ella e io ardesse; 31
e sì lo 'ncendio imaginato cosse,
che convenne che 'l sonno si rompesse.

Non altrimenti Achille si riscosse, 34
li occhi svegliati rivolgendo in giro
e non sappiendo là dove si fosse,

quando la madre da Chirón a Schiro 37
trafuggò lui dormendo in le sue braccia,
là onde poi li Greci il dipartiro;

che mi scoss' io, sì come da la faccia 40
mi fuggì 'l sonno, e diventa' ismorto,
come fa l'uom che, spaventato, agghiaccia.

Dallato m'era solo il mio conforto, 43
e 'l sole er' alto già più che due ore,
e 'l viso m'era a la marina torto.

"Non aver tema," disse il mio segnore; 46
"fatti sicur, chè noi semo a buon punto;
non stringer, ma rallarga ogne vigore.

Tu se' omai al purgatorio giunto: 49
vedi là il balzo che 'l chiude dintorno;
vedi l'entrata là 've par digiunto.

Dianzi, ne l'alba che procede al giorno, 52
quando l'anima tua dentro dormia
sovra li fiori ond' è là giù addorno,

venne una donna, e disse: 'I' son Lucia; 55
lasciatemi pigliar costui che dorme;
sì l'agevolerò per la sua via.'

Sordel rimase e l'altre genti forme; 58
ella ti tolse, e come 'l dì fu chiaro,
sen venne suso; e io per le sue orme.

Qui ti posò, ma pria mi dimostraro 61
li occhi suoi belli quella intrata aperta;
poi ella e 'l sonno ad una se n'andaro."

There it seemed that it burned and I burned with it   31
and such was the heat of that imagined blaze
that my sleep could not but be broken by it.

It was no different, the surprise   34
of Achilles, turning his wakened eyes
around him without knowing where he was

after his mother had smuggled him   37
asleep in her arms from Chiron to Schiro,
the place the Greeks later took him from,

such was my own surprise as sleep was fleeing   40
from my face, and I became no color
as someone does who is frozen with fear.

There was no one beside me, except my comfort,   43
and the sun had climbed two hours already
and I was facing with my eyes toward the sea.

"Do not be afraid," my lord said to me,   46
"Take heart. It is good to be where we are.
Do not hold back, but unleash all your valor.

Now you have arrived at Purgatory.   49
See, there is the cliff that runs all around it.
See the way in there, where the cliff seems to split.

A while ago, in the dawn before morning,   52
while the soul within you was still sleeping
on the flowers that adorn the place down there

a lady came and said, 'I am Lucy.   55
Let me take up this one who is asleep
and in that way ease him on his journey.'

Sordello stayed with the other noble shapes.   58
She took you up, and with the clear daylight
came up from there, and I in her footsteps.

Here she set you down, but before she did that   61
her beautiful eyes showed me that open
entrance. Then she and sleep went away as one."

A guisa d'uom che 'n dubbio si raccerta 64
e che muta in conforto sua paura,
poi che la verità li è discoperta,

mi cambia' io; e come sanza cura 67
vide me 'l duca mio, su per lo balzo
si mosse, e io di rietro inver' l'altura.

Lettor, tu vedi ben com' io innalzo 70
la mia matera, e però con più arte
non ti maravigliar s'io la rincalzo.

Noi ci appressammo, ed eravamo in parte 73
che là dove pareami prima rotto,
pur come un fesso che muro diparte,

vidi una porta, e tre gradi di sotto 76
per gire ad essa, di color diversi,
e un portier ch'ancor non facea motto.

E come l'occhio più e più v'apersi, 79
vidil seder sovra 'l grado sovrano,
tal ne la faccia ch'io non lo soffersi;

e una spada nuda avëa in mano, 82
che reflettëa i raggi sì ver' noi,
ch'io dirizzava spesso il viso in vano.

"Dite costinci: che volete voi?" 85
cominciò elli a dire, "ov' è la scorta?
Guardate che 'l venir sù non vi nòi."

"Donna del ciel, di queste cose accorta," 88
rispuose 'l mio maestro a lui, "pur dianzi
ne disse: 'Andate là: quivi è la porta.'"

"Ed ella i passi vostri in bene avanzi," 91
ricominciò il cortese portinaio:
"Venite dunque a' nostri gradi innanzi."

Là ne venimmo; e lo scaglion primaio 94
bianco marmo era sì pulito e terso,
ch'io mi specchiai in esso qual io paio.

As a man in doubt who is reassured   64
and whose fear, after he has discovered
the truth, changes to confidence again,

so I was changed, and when my leader saw   67
that I was untroubled, he set out
up the slope, and I followed toward the height.

Reader, you can see that I am raising   70
my theme higher. It should not be surprising
to you if I sustain it with greater art.

We came closer and arrived at a place   73
where what seemed no more to me at first than a cleft,
as when a wall is broken by a crevice,

I saw was a gate, and under it, leading   76
up to it, three steps each of a different color,
and a gatekeeper who still had said nothing.

And as I brought my eye to bear upon him   79
I saw that he was sitting on the top step
and his face was such that I could not look at him,

and in his hand he had a naked sword   82
reflecting the rays toward us so that again
and again I turned my eyes toward it in vain.

"Say it from where you are: what have you come for?"   85
he began. "Where is your escort? Take care
or else you will suffer for this climb."

"A lady from heaven who knows these things,"   88
my master answered him, "a moment ago said
to us, 'Go that way. There is the gate.' "

"And may she further your footsteps to the good,"   91
the courteous gatekeeper replied.
"In that case come forward to our stairs."

Then we came on, and the first of the stairs   94
was white marble so smooth and clear
that I was reflected in it as I appear.

Era il secondo tinto più che perso,
d'una petrina ruvida e arsiccia,
crepata per lo lungo e per traverso. 97

Lo terzo, che di sopra s'ammassiccia,
porfido mi parea, sì fiammeggiante
come sangue che fuor di vena spiccia. 100

Sovra questo tenëa ambo le piante
l'angel di Dio sedendo in su la soglia
che mi sembiava pietra di diamante. 103

Per li tre gradi sù di buona voglia
mi trasse il duca mio, dicendo: "Chiedi
umilemente che 'l serrame scioglia." 106

Divoto mi gittai a' santi piedi;
misericordia chiesi e ch'el m'aprisse,
ma tre volte nel petto pria mi diedi. 109

Sette P ne la fronte mi descrisse
col punton de la spada, e "Fa che lavi,
quando se' dentro, queste piaghe" disse. 112

Cenere, o terra che secca si cavi,
d'un color fora col suo vestimento;
e di sotto da quel trasse due chiavi. 115

L'una era d'oro e l'altra era d'argento;
pria con la bianca e poscia con la gialla
fece a la porta sì, ch'i' fu' contento. 118

"Quandunque l'una d'este chiavi falla,
che non si volga dritta per la toppa,"
diss' elli a noi, "non s'apre questa calla. 121

Più cara è l'una; ma l'altra vuol troppa
d'arte e d'ingegno avanti che diserri,
perch' ella è quella che 'l nodo digroppa. 124

Da Pier le tegno; e dissemi ch'i' erri
anzi ad aprir ch'a tenerla serrata,
pur che la gente a' piedi mi s'atterri." 127

The second was of a dark purpled color, 97
of some rough stone that had been through the fire,
cracked from one end and one side to the other.

The third, massed in place on top of them, 100
seemed to me to be porphyry, aflame,
like blood when it gushes out of a vein.

The angel of God had both of his feet 103
on that one, as he sat on the threshold
the stone of which was adamant, I thought.

Up the three steps my leader drew me, 106
willing as I was to follow, and said to me,
"Ask him humbly to draw back the bolt."

Devoutly I threw myself at the holy feet, 109
for mercy's sake asking him—and three times I beat
my breast before I asked him—to open it.

With the point of his sword, on my forehead 112
he drew seven P's, and "When you are inside
be sure to wash these wounds away," he said.

Earth that is dry when it is dug, or ashes, 115
would be one in color with his garment,
and from beneath it he drew forth two keys.

One was of gold and the other of silver. 118
First he put the white one into the door,
then the yellow, so that I was satisfied.

"Whenever one of these keys cannot turn 121
in the lock as it should," he said to us,
"the passage through here will not open.

One of them is more precious, but the other 124
requires great skill and wisdom before
it will open, and that one undoes the knot.

I have them from Peter, who told me rather 127
to err in opening than in locking out
those who come if they cast themselves at my feet."

Poi pinse l'uscio a la porta sacrata,   130
dicendo: "Intrate; ma facciovi accorti
che di fuor torna chi 'n dietro si guata."

E quando fuor ne' cardini distorti   133
li spigoli di quella regge sacra,
che di metallo son sonanti e forti,

non rugghiò sì né si mostrò sì acra   136
Tarpëa, come tolto le fu il buono
Metello, per che poi rimase macra.

Io mi rivolsi attento al primo tuono,   139
e *"Te Deum laudamus"* mi parea
udire in voce mista al dolce suono.

Tale imagine a punto mi rendea   142
ciò ch'io udiva, qual prender si suole
quando a cantar con organi si stea;

ch'or sì or no s'intendon le parole.   145

Then he pushed, in the opening, the sacred door,   130
saying, "Enter. But know that whoever
looks behind him finds himself back outside."

And when the hinges of massive metal   133
that resounded were twisted around
the pivots of that sacred portal

not the Tarpeian roared as loudly nor   136
stood as stubborn when the good Metellus
was taken from it, so that it was left bare.

I turned toward the first note, and listening   139
I thought I heard *Te Deum laudamus*
in voices through that sweet sound mingling.

What I heard came to me as it happens   142
sometimes when an organ is playing
and at the same time they are singing

so that now the words are heard and now are not.   145

CANTO X

Poi fummo dentro al soglio de la porta
che 'l mal amor de l'anime disusa,
perché fa parer dritta la via torta,

sonando la senti' esser richiusa;   4
e s'io avesse li occhi vòlti ad essa,
qual fora stata al fallo degna scusa?

Noi salavam per una pietra fessa,   7
che si moveva e d'una e d'altra parte,
sì come l'onda che fugge e s'appressa.

"Qui si conviene usare un poco d'arte,"   10
cominciò 'l duca mio, "in accostarsi
or quinci, or quindi al lato che si parte."

E questo fece i nostri passi scarsi,   13
tanto che pria lo scemo de la luna
rigiunse al letto suo per ricorcarsi,

che noi fossimo fuor di quella cruna;   16
ma quando fummo liberi e aperti
sù dove il monte in dietro si rauna,

ïo stancato e amendue incerti   19
di nostra via, restammo in su un piano
solingo più che strade per diserti.

Da la sua sponda, ove confina il vano,   22
al piè de l'alta ripa che pur sale,
misurrebbe in tre volte un corpo umano;

e quanto l'occhio mio potea trar d'ale,   25
or dal sinistro e or dal destro fianco,
questa cornice mi parea cotale.

Là sù non eran mossi i piè nostri anco,   28
quand' io conobbi quella ripa intorno
che dritto di salita aveva manco,

When we were in over the sill of the gate
which is neglected by the soul's wrong love
that makes the crooked way seem to be straight,

the loud sound told me it had closed again   4
and if I had turned back to look at it
what excuse could have wiped that error out?

We were climbing through a fissure in the stone   7
that kept turning from one side to the other
as a wave that flows out and runs in again.

"Some skill is needed in this place," my leader   10
began, "to keep one side or the other
close at those points where either turns away."

That so much limited the steps we took   13
that the moon, past the full then, had gone back
into her bed, and to her rest, before

we made our way out of that needle's eye,   16
but once we were in the open, and free,
up where the mountain draws back toward itself,

I was weary and we were both uncertain   19
of our way. We stopped at a level place
more solitary than a track in the wilderness.

From the edge of it, where it borders the void,   22
to the high bank rising from it would be
three times the length of a human body,

and as far as my eye could take wing   25
both to the left and to the right it seemed
to me that this cornice was the same.

Our feet had not yet set out upon it   28
when I saw that the inner bank, which rose up straight
so that no one would have been able to climb it,

esser di marmo candido e addorno 31
d'intagli sì, che non pur Policleto,
ma la natura lì avrebbe scorno.

L'angel che venne in terra col decreto 34
de la molt' anni lagrimata pace,
ch'aperse il ciel del suo lungo divieto,

dinanzi a noi pareva sì verace 37
quivi intagliato in un atto soave,
che non sembiava imagine che tace.

Giurato si saria ch'el dicesse *"Ave!"*; 40
perché iv' era imaginata quella
ch'ad aprir l'alto amor volse la chiave;

e avea in atto impressa esta favella 43
"Ecce ancilla Deï," propriamente
come figura in cera si suggella.

"Non tener pur ad un loco la mente," 46
disse 'l dolce maestro, che m'avea
da quella parte onde 'l cuore ha la gente.

Per ch'i' mi mossi col viso, e vedea 49
di retro da Maria, da quella costa
onde m'era colui che mi movea,

un'altra storia ne la roccia imposta; 52
per ch'io varcai Virgilio, e fe'mi presso,
acciò che fosse a li occhi miei disposta.

Era intagliato lì nel marmo stesso 55
lo carro e ' buoi, traendo l'arca santa,
per che si teme officio non commesso.

Dinanzi parea gente; e tutta quanta, 58
partita in sette cori, a' due mie' sensi
faceva dir l'un "No," l'altro "Sì, canta."

Similemente al fummo de li 'ncensi 61
che v'era imaginato, li occhi e 'l naso
e al sì e al no discordi fensi.

was of white marble, and with such sculpture   31
embellished as would have put to shame there
not only Polycletus but even nature.

The angel who came to earth announcing   34
the peace that for many years had been
wept for, opening the long ban of Heaven,

appeared there before us so truthfully   37
carved with such an expression of gentleness
that the image did not seem to be speechless.

One would have sworn that he said *"Ave,"*   40
for there was her image who had opened
the highest love with a turn of the key,

and there was graven in her expression   43
the phrase "Behold the handmaiden
of God," as clearly as a figure stamped in wax.

"Do not let your mind stay in one single place,"   46
said the kind master. I was to that
side of him where, in people, the heart lies.

So I turned my face, and beyond Mary   49
I saw, over to that side
where he was who was leading me,

another story set into the stone,   52
so that I passed Virgil and went close
until I had it in front of my eyes.

There were the cart and oxen, in the same   55
marble carved, drawing the holy ark
that makes men fear tasks not assigned to them.

Before them people appeared, all divided   58
into seven choirs. Two senses I had.
One said, "No," the other, "Yes, they are singing."

The smoke of the incense, in its image there,   61
in the same way left my nose and my eyes
arguing yes and no with each other.

Lì precedeva al benedetto vaso,
trescando alzato, l'umile salmista,
e più e men che re era in quel caso.   64

Di contra, effigïata ad una vista
d'un gran palazzo, Micòl ammirava
sì come donna dispettosa e trista.   67

I' mossi i piè del loco dov' io stava,
per avvisar da presso un'altra istoria,
che di dietro a Micòl mi biancheggiava.   70

Quiv' era storïata l'alta gloria
del roman principato, il cui valore
mosse Gregorio a la sua gran vittoria;   73

i' dico di Traiano imperadore;
e una vedovella li era al freno,
di lagrime atteggiata e di dolore.   76

Intorno a lui parea calcato e pieno
di cavalieri, e l'aguglie ne l'oro
sovr'essi in vista al vento si movieno.   79

La miserella intra tutti costoro
pareva dir: "Segnor, fammi vendetta
di mio figliuol ch'è morto, ond' io m'accoro";   82

ed elli a lei rispondere: "Or aspetta
tanto ch'i' torni"; e quella: "Segnor mio,"
come persona in cui dolor s'affretta,   85

"se tu non torni?"; ed ei: "Chi fia dov' io,
la ti farà"; ed ella: "L'altrui bene
a te che fia, se 'l tuo metti in oblio?";   88

ond' elli: "Or ti conforta; ch'ei convene
ch'i' solva il mio dovere anzi ch'i' mova:
giustizia vuole e pietà mi ritene."   91

Colui che mai non vide cosa nova
produsse esto visibile parlare,
novello a noi perché qui non si trova.   94

There in front of the blessèd vessel went   64
the humble psalmist with his robe caught up, dancing,
and at that moment he was less and more than a king.

Across from him, a sculpture in a window   67
of a great palace, Michael was looking on
like a malicious and sullen woman.

I moved my feet from where I had been standing,   70
past Michael, to be able to look closely
at the whitening of another story.

There it portrayed the exalted glory   73
of that prince of Rome whose virtue moved
Gregory to his great victory.

I am speaking of the Emperor Trajan,   76
and at his bridle there was a poor widow
with an expression of tears and sorrow.

Around him appeared a crowd and trampling   79
of knights, and in the gold above him
the eagles could be seen, in the wind, moving.

In the midst of all of them the poor woman   82
seemed to be saying, "Lord, avenge my son
who is dead, and it tears at my heart."

And he answering her, "Wait now until   85
I return." And she, "My lord," as a person will
whom suffering has made impatient,

"if you do not return?" And he, "Whoever   88
is in my place will do it for you." And she, "What good will
another's good do you, if you forget your own?"

Then he, "Now take comfort. I must satisfy   91
the duty that is mine before I go.
Justice requires it and pity retains me."

He who has never seen anything new   94
made this visible speech that appears new
to us because it is not to be found here.

Mentr' io mi dilettava di guardare   97
l'imagini di tante umilitadi,
e per lo fabbro loro a veder care,

"Ecco di qua, ma fanno i passi radi,"   100
mormorava il poeta, "molte genti:
questi ne 'nvïeranno a li alti gradi."

Li occhi miei, ch'a mirare eran contenti   103
per veder novitadi ond' e' son vaghi,
volgendosi ver' lui non furon lenti.

Non vo' però, lettor, che tu ti smaghi   106
di buon proponimento per udire
come Dio vuol che 'l debito si paghi.

Non attender la forma del martìre: 109
pensa la succession; pensa ch'al peggio
oltre la gran sentenza non può ire.

Io cominciai: "Maestro, quel ch'io veggio   112
muovere a noi, non mi sembian persone,
e non so che, sì nel veder vaneggio."

Ed elli a me: "La grave condizione   115
di lor tormento a terra li rannicchia,
sì che ' miei occhi pria n'ebber tencione.

Ma guarda fiso là, e disviticchia   118
col viso quel che vien sotto a quei sassi:
già scorger puoi come ciascun si picchia."

O superbi cristian, miseri lassi,   121
che, de la vista de la mente infermi,
fidanza avete ne' retrosi passi,

non v'accorgete voi che noi siam vermi   124
nati a formar l'angelica farfalla,
che vola a la giustizia sanza schermi?

Di che l'animo vostro in alto galla,   127
poi siete quasi antomata in difetto,
sì come vermo in cui formazion falla?

While I was gazing with delight upon   97
the images of such great humilities,
dearer to my sight for their artisan,

"Look over here," the poet murmured. "Many   100
people, but they are coming with slow steps. They
will tell us the way to the high stairs."

My eyes, which were looking intently,   103
eager for any new thing they could see,
were not slow in turning toward him.

Reader, I would not have you fall away   106
from your good resolution to hear the way
God wills that what is owed is to be paid.

Do not linger on the form of the torment.   109
Think of what follows it. At the worst, think
it cannot go beyond the great judgment.

I began, "Master, those I see coming toward us   112
do not look like people, and I cannot tell
what they are, so bewildered my sight is."

And he to me, "The grave condition   115
of their torment doubles them to the ground
so that my eyes at first argued about them.

But look there closely, and with looking   118
untangle what, under those stones, is coming.
You can see already how they beat their breasts."

Oh proud Christians, wretched and weary,   121
who, in the sickness of the way you see
in your minds, put your faith in walking backward,

is it not plain to you that we are worms   124
born to form the angelic butterfly
and fly up to judgment, without defenses?

Why is your mind floating at such a height   127
when you are, as it were, imperfect insects
like the worm that has not assumed its form yet?

Come per sostentar solaio o tetto,   130
per mensola talvolta una figura
si vede giugner le ginocchia al petto,

  la qual fa del non ver vera rancura   133
nascere 'n chi la vede; così fatti
vid' io color, quando puosi ben cura.

  Vero è che più e meno eran contratti   136
secondo ch'avien più e meno a dosso;
e qual più pazïenza avea ne li atti,

  piangendo parea dicer: "Più non posso."   139

As a figure sometimes is seen with its 130
knees drawn clear up to its chest, supporting,
the way a corbel does, a roof or ceiling,

and though it is unreal begets a real 133
discomfort in the beholder, such I
saw was their shape when I looked carefully.

It is true they were shrunken less or more, 136
as what was on their backs was lighter or heavier,
and the one with most patience in his face

seemed to be saying through tears, "I can do no more." 139

CANTO XI

"O Padre nostro, che ne' cieli stai,
non circunscritto, ma per più amore
ch'ai primi effetti di là sù tu hai,

laudato sia 'l tuo nome e 'l tuo valore   4
da ogne creatura, com' è degno
di render grazie al tuo dolce vapore.

Vegna ver' noi la pace del tuo regno,   7
ché noi ad essa non potem da noi,
s'ella non vien, con tutto nostro ingegno.

Come del suo voler li angeli tuoi   10
fan sacrificio a te, cantando *osanna*,
così facciano li uomini de' suoi.

Dà oggi a noi la cotidiana manna,   13
sanza la qual per questo aspro diserto
a retro va chi più di gir s'affanna.

E come noi lo mal ch'avem sofferto   16
perdoniamo a ciascuno, e tu perdona
benigno, e non guardar lo nostro merto.

Nostra virtù che di legger s'adona,   19
non spermentar con l'antico avversaro,
ma libera da lui che sì la sprona.

Quest' ultima preghiera, segnor caro,   22
già non si fa per noi, ché non bisogna,
ma per color che dietro a noi restaro."

Così a sé e noi buona ramogna   25
quell' ombre orando, andavan sotto 'l pondo,
simile a quel che talvolta si sogna,

disparmente angosciate tutte a tondo   28
e lasse su per la prima cornice,
purgando la caligine del mondo.

"Our Father, who are in heaven, encircled by
nothing except the greater love you have
for the first works that you made there on high,

praised be your name and your power by   4
every creature, with those thanks that are due
for the sweet emanation that flows from you.

May the peace of your kingdom come to us   7
who are not able to reach it by ourselves,
try as we may, unless it comes to us.

As your angels make sacrifice to you   10
of their wills, singing hosannas, even so
may humans offer their own wills to you.

Give us today the manna of every day,   13
for without it, in this harsh desert we
go backward, straining forward as we may.

And as we pardon each one for the harm   16
that we have suffered, in loving kindness
overlook what we deserve, and pardon us.

Do not oppose to the old adversary   19
our virtue which gives way so easily
but deliver us from his goading of it.

This last request we make not for ourselves,   22
dear Lord, because we do not need it.
It is for those who remain behind us."

Thus praying for godspeed for themselves   25
and us, those souls went on under their burden
like that which one bears sometimes in a dream,

their torment differing, all of them wearily   28
making the circuit of the first terrace,
purging the mists of the world away.

Se di là sempre ben per noi si dice,   31
di qua che dire e far per lor si puote
da quei c'hanno al voler buona radice?

Ben si de' loro atar lavar le note   34
che portar quinci, sì che, mondi e lievi,
possano uscire a le stellate ruote.

"Deh, se giustizia e pietà vi disgrievi   37
tosto, sì che possiate muover l'ala,
che secondo il disio vostro vi lievi,

mostrate da qual mano inver' la scala   40
si va più corto; e se c'è più d'un varco,
quel ne 'nsegnate che men erto cala;

ché questi che vien meco, per lo 'ncarco   43
de la carne d'Adamo onde si veste,
al montar sù, contra sua voglia, è parco."

Le lor parole, che rendero a queste   46
che dette avea colui cu' io seguiva,
non fur da cui venisser manifeste;

ma fu detto: "A man destra per la riva   49
con noi venite, e troverete il passo
possibile a salir persona viva.

E s'io non fossi impedito dal sasso   52
che la cervice mia superba doma,
onde portar convienmi il viso basso,

cotesti, ch'ancor vive e non si noma,   55
guardere' io, per veder s'i' 'l conosco,
e per farlo pietoso a questa soma.

Io fui latino e nato d'un gran Tosco: 58
Guiglielmo Aldobrandesco fu mio padre;
non so se 'l nome suo già mai fu vosco.

L'antico sangue e l'opere leggiadre   61
d'i miei maggior mi fer sì arrogante,
che, non pensando a la comune madre,

If they are always praying for us there, 31
what can be said and done for them from here
by those whose will is rooted in the good?

We should help them to wash away the stains 34
they took there, so they can be light and pure
to go out to the wheeling of the stars.

"Oh, so may justice and mercy free you 37
soon of your burden and let you move the wing
which, according to your longing, lifts you,

show us on which hand is the shorter way 40
to the stair, and if there is more than one,
tell us which passage is less steep,

for, as the one who comes with me is clothed in 43
the burden of Adam, against his own
will, when it comes to climbing, he goes slowly."

It was not clear whose words of theirs 46
came in answer after these had been
spoken by the one I was following,

but they said, "To the right. Come with us 49
along the bank and you will find the pass
where a living person would be able to climb,

and if I were not hindered by the stone 52
that overpowers my neck for its pride
so that I have to go with my face down

I would look at this one who is still alive 55
and is not named, and see whether I
know him, and have his pity for this weight I carry.

I was Italian and born of a great Tuscan. 58
Guiglielmo Aldobrandesco was my father's name.
I wonder whether you ever heard of him.

The ancient blood and my ancestors' 61
gallant deeds made me so arrogant
that without thinking of our common mother

ogn' uomo ebbi in despetto tanto avante, 64
ch'io ne mori'; come, i Sanesi sanno,
e sallo in Campagnatico ogne fante.

Io sono Omberto; e non pur a me danno 67
superbia fa, ché tutti miei consorti
ha ella tratti seco nel malanno.

E qui convien ch'io questo peso porti 70
per lei, tanto che a Dio si sodisfaccia,
poi ch'io nol fe' tra ' vivi, qui tra ' morti."

Ascoltando chinai in giù la faccia; 73
e un di lor, non questi che parlava,
si torse sotto il peso che li 'mpaccia,

e videmi e conobbemi e chiamava, 76
tenendo li occhi con fatica fisi
a me che tutto chin con loro andava.

"Oh!" diss' io lui, "non se' tu Oderisi, 79
l'onor d'Agobbio e l'onor di quell' arte
ch'alluminar chiamata è in Parisi?"

"Frate," diss' elli, "più ridon le carte 82
che pennelleggia Franco Bolognese;
l'onore è tutto or suo, e mio in parte.

Ben non sare' io stato sì cortese 85
mentre ch'io vissi, per lo gran disio
de l'eccellenza ove mio core intese.

Di tal superbia qui si paga il fio; 88
e ancor non sarei qui, se non fosse
che, possendo peccar, mi volsi a Dio.

Oh vana gloria de l'umane posse! 91
com' poco verde in su la cima dura,
se non è giunta da l'etati grosse!

Credette Cimabue ne la pittura 94
tener lo campo, e ora ha Giotto il grido,
sì che la fama di colui è scura.

I took my scorn of every man so far   64
it was the death of me, as in Siena they know
and every child in Campagnatico.

I am Omberto, and pride has brought injury   67
not only to me but my whole family,
dragging them with it into calamity.

And here I must bear this because of that   70
until God is satisfied. What I would not
do among the living I do here among the dead."

I had put my face down where I could listen,   73
and one of them, not the one who had spoken,
twisted under the weight that held him down

and saw me and knew me and called as he   76
went on struggling to keep his eyes on me
while I went along bent over with them.

"Oh," I said to him, "are you not Oderisi,   79
the honor of Gubbio, the honor of that art which in
Paris they call illumination?"

"Brother," he said, "the pages smile more   82
from the brushstrokes of Franco of Bologna.
Now the honor is all his, apart from my share.

I would not, indeed, have been so courteous   85
while I was living, because of the great
desire to excel, on which my heart was set.

This is where the fine for such pride is paid,   88
and I would not be here yet, were it not
that while I could still sin I turned to God.

Oh the vain glory in human powers!   91
How briefly, at the top, the green endures,
or else an age of ignorance follows it!

In painting Cimabue thought the field   94
was his alone. Now the cry is Giotto,
so the fame of the other is in shadow,

Così ha tolto l'uno a l'altro Guido   97
la gloria de la lingua; e forse è nato
chi l'uno e l'altro caccerà del nido.

Non è il mondan romore altro ch'un fiato   100
di vento, ch'or vien quinci e or vien quindi,
e muta nome perché muta lato.

Che voce avrai tu più, se vecchia scindi   103
da te la carne, che se fossi morto
anzi che tu lasciassi il "pappo" e 'l "dindi,"

pria che passin mill' anni? ch'è più corto   106
spazio a l'etterno, ch'un muover di ciglia
al cerchio che più tardi in cielo è torto.

Colui che del cammin sì poco piglia   109
dinanzi a me, Toscana sonò tutta;
e ora a pena in Siena sen pispiglia,

ond' era sire quando fu distrutta   112
la rabbia fiorentina, che superba
fu a quel tempo sì com' ora è putta.

La vostra nominanza è color d'erba,   115
che viene e va, e quei la discolora
per cui ella esce de la terra acerba."

E io a lui: "Tuo vero dir m'incora   118
bona umiltà, e gran tumor m'appiani;
ma chi è quei di cui tu parlavi ora?"

"Quelli è," rispuose, "Provenzan Salvani;   121
ed è qui perché fu presuntüoso
a recar Siena tutta a le sue mani.

Ito è così e va, sanza riposo,   124
poi che morì; cotal moneta rende
a sodisfar chi è di là troppo oso."

E io: "Se quello spirito ch'attende,   127
pria che si penta, l'orlo de la vita,
là giù dimora e qua sù non ascende,

and so the glory of our tongue was taken   97
from one Guido by another, and one
is born now, perhaps, who will push both from the nest.

The noise the world makes is only a breath   100
of wind from time to time blowing back and forth,
the name changing according to where it comes from.

Do you think you will have more fame if you strip away   103
the flesh in age than if you die as a baby
still babbling baby words for bread and money

after a thousand years have passed, which is shorter   106
compared to eternity than the blink of an eye
is to that circle of Heaven that turns most slowly?

That one inching so slowly ahead of me,   109
once all Tuscany rang with the sound of him,
and now in Siena there is hardly a whisper of him,

and he was a lord there when they destroyed   112
the haughty rabble of Florence that was as proud
at the time as now it is prostitute.

Your renown is the color of the grass   115
that comes and goes, and that which fades it is
what brings it green out of the ground at first."

And I to him, "The truth you say humbles   118
my heart as it should, and shrinks a great swelling in me,
but the one you were just talking about, who is he?"

"That one," he answered, "is Provenzan Salvani,   121
who is here because in his presumption he
wanted to have all Siena in his hands.

The way he is going is the way he has gone   124
ever since he died. That is the coin
in which he makes good his rashness over there."

And I, "If a spirit waits until the edge   127
of life before repenting, and remains there
down below and does not come up here

se buona orazïon lui non aita,   130
prima che passi tempo quanto visse,
come fu la venuta lui largita?"

"Quando vivea più glorïoso," disse,   133
"liberamente nel Campo di Siena,
ogne vergogna diposta, s'affisse;

e lì, per trar l'amico suo di pena,   136
ch'e' sostenea ne la prigion di Carlo,
si condusse a tremar per ogne vena.

Più non dirò, e scuro so che parlo;   139
ma poco tempo andrà, che ' tuoi vicini
faranno sì che tu potrai chiosarlo.

Quest' opera li tolse quei confini."   142

until as much time passes as he lived 130
unless he is assisted by good prayer,
how was he given leave to come here?"

"When he was living in his glory," he said, 133
"one time, putting aside all shame, he stood,
by his own will, in the marketplace of Siena,

where, to ransom a friend from the pains 136
he was suffering in Charles' prison, he
brought himself to tremble in all his veins.

I will say no more, and I speak, as I know, 139
darkly, but something your neighbors will do
before long will allow you to expound this.

What he did there released him from those confines." 142

CANTO XII

Di pari, come buoi che vanno a giogo,
m'andava io con quell' anima carca,
fin che 'l sofferse il dolce pedagogo.

Ma quando disse: "Lascia lui e varca;   4
ché qui è buono con l'ali e coi remi,
quantunque può, ciascun pinger sua barca";

dritto sì come andar vuolsi rife'mi   7
con la persona, avvegna che i pensieri
mi rimanessero e chinati e scemi.

Io m'era mosso, e seguia volontieri   10
del mio maestro i passi, e amendue
già mostravam com' eravam leggeri;

ed el mi disse: "Volgi li occhi in giùe: 13
buon ti sarà, per tranquillar la via,
veder lo letto de le piante tue."

Come, perché di lor memoria sia,   16
sovra i sepolti le tombe terragne
portan segnato quel ch'elli eran pria,

onde lì molte volte si ripiagne   19
per la puntura de la rimembranza,
che solo a' pïi dà de le calcagne;

sì vid' io lì, ma di miglior sembianza   22
secondo l'artificio, figurato
quanto per via di fuor del monte avanza.

Vedea colui che fu nobil creato   25
più ch'altra creatura, giù dal cielo
folgoreggiando scender, da l'un lato.

Vedëa Brïareo fitto dal telo   28
celestïal giacer, da l'altra parte,
grave a la terra per lo mortal gelo.

Side by side, as oxen yoked together,
I went on with that laden soul as long
as I was allowed to by my gentle teacher,

but when he said, "Leave them now and pass on,   4
for here it is best for each one, with sail and oar,
to move his bark forward as well as he can,"

I straightened up my body again to the way   7
a man should walk, but my thoughts were bent down
and went on still brought low, as they had been.

I had moved ahead and followed willingly   10
my master's footsteps, and we both together
showed at that moment how light we were,

and he said to me, "Turn your eyes and look down.   13
It will be good for you and will ease the way
to see the bed your soles are walking on."

Even as, in their memory, over   16
those buried there, the tombs in the church floor
bear figures to show what they were before,

so that tears time and again are shed there   19
in response to the jab of memory,
whose spur is felt by the faithful only,

so I saw, but with better likeness   22
as the skill was greater, sculptures carved in
that whole pathway jutting out from the mountain.

I saw that one who was created more   25
noble than any creature, on the one
side falling as lightning from heaven.

I saw Briareus lying pierced with   28
the arrow from Heaven, on the other side,
heavy on the ground, in the cold of death.

Vedea Timbreo, vedea Pallade e Marte,   31
armati ancora, intorno al padre loro,
mirar le membra d'i Giganti sparte.

Vedea Nembròt a piè del gran lavoro   34
quasi smarrito, e riguardar le genti
che 'n Sennaàr con lui superbi fuoro.

O Nïobè, con che occhi dolenti   37
vedea io te segnata in su la strada,
tra sette e sette tuoi figliuoli spenti!

O Saùl, come in su la proprìa spada   40
quivi parevi morto in Gelboè,
che poi non sentì pioggia né rugiada!

O folle Aragne, sì vedea io te   43
già mezza ragna, trista in su li stracci
de l'opera che mal per te si fé.

O Roboàm, già non par che minacci   46
quivi 'l tuo segno; ma pien di spavento
nel porta un carro, sanza ch'altri il cacci.

Mostrava ancor lo duro pavimento   49
come Almeon a sua madre fé caro
parer lo sventurato addornamento.

Mostrava come i figli si gittaro   52
sovra Sennacherìb dentro dal tempio,
e come, morto lui, quivi il lasciaro.

Mostrava la ruina e 'l crudo scempio   55
che fé Tamiri, quando disse a Ciro:
"Sangue sitisti, e io di sangue t'empio."

Mostrava come in rotta si fuggiro   58
li Assiri, poi che fu morto Oloferne,
e anche le reliquie del martiro.

Vedeva Troia in cenere e in caverne;   61
o Ilïón, come te basso e vile
mostrava il segno che lì si discerne!

I saw Thymbraeus, I saw Pallas and Mars   *31*
around their father, still with their weapons,
staring at the giants' scattered limbs.

I saw Nimrod at the foot of the great   *34*
work, looking bewildered, and the staring
peoples of Shinar who had shared his pride.

Oh Niobe, with what sorrow in your eyes   *37*
I saw you graven in the road between
the seven and seven of your dead children!

Oh Saul, how you appeared there, dead upon   *40*
your own sword, in Gilboa which never
after that felt rain or dew again.

O foolish Arachne, as I saw you, already   *43*
half turned to spider, in misery
on the shreds of the work you made for your undoing.

O Rehoboam, the figure of you there   *46*
seems not to threaten now, but a chariot
bears it off, full of terror, with none chasing it.

It showed besides, the hard paving stone,   *49*
the way Alcmaeon revealed to his mother
how much the ill-fated jewelry had cost her.

It showed how his sons flung themselves upon   *52*
Sennacherib inside the temple, and when
he was dead how they had left him there.

It showed the ruin and the raw bloodshed   *55*
Tomyris wrought when she said to Cyrus,
"You thirsted for blood and I fill you with blood."

It showed how the routed Assyrians   *58*
after the death of Holofernes fled
and of that slaughter also the remains.

I saw Troy turned to ashes and to caverns.   *61*
Oh Ilion, how low and base you were
in the picture that was seen of you there!

Qual di pennel fu maestro o di stile   64
che ritraesse l'ombre e ' tratti ch'ivi
mirar farieno uno ingegno sottile?

Morti li morti e i vivi parean vivi: 67
non vide mei di me chi vide il vero,
quant' io calcai, fin che chinato givi.

Or superbite, e via col viso altero,   70
figliuoli d'Eva, e non chinate il volto
sì che veggiate il vostro mal sentero!

Più era già per noi del monte vòlto   73
e del cammin del sole assai più speso
che non stimava l'animo non sciolto,

quando colui che sempre innanzi atteso   76
andava, cominciò: "Drizza la testa;
non è più tempo di gir sì sospeso.

Vedi colà un angel che s'appresta   79
per venir verso noi; vedi che torna
dal servigio del dì l'ancella sesta.

Di reverenza il viso e li atti addorna,   82
sì che i diletti lo 'nvïarci in suso;
pensa che questo dì mai non raggiorna!"

Io era ben del suo ammonir uso   85
pur di non perder tempo, sì che 'n quella
materia non potea parlarmi chiuso.

A noi venìa la creatura bella,   88
biancovestito e ne la faccia quale
par tremolando mattutina stella.

Le braccia aperse, e indi aperse l'ale;   91
disse: "Venite: qui son presso i gradi,
e agevolemente omai si sale.

A questo invito vegnon molto radi: 94
o gente umana, per volar sù nata,
perché a poco vento così cadi?"

Who had the mastery of brush or pencil
so to portray the shades and features there
that they would fill any mind that saw them with wonder?

64

The dead looked dead and the living seemed alive.
He who saw the truth of it could see it
no better than I, bent down and walking on it.

67

Now be proud, and proceed with haughty look,
children of Eve, and never turn the face
down to see the evil path you take.

70

We had already gone farther around
the mountain, and the sun's course had raced on
more than my mind, held as it was, imagined,

73

when he who always as he went was looking
ahead began, "Lift up your head. There is
no more time for us to suspend in this.

76

See, there is an angel preparing
to come toward us, and from the service of
the day the sixth handmaiden is returning.

79

Let reverence grace your bearing and regard
so it may be his pleasure to send us upward.
Think that this day will never dawn again."

82

I had become used to his prompting me
never to lose time, so upon that
subject his words could not seem closed to me.

85

Toward us came the beautiful creature
clothed in white, and his face appearing
like the morning star in its shimmering.

88

He opened his arms and then he opened
his wings and said, "Come. The steps are here at hand,
and from here on the way up is easy.

91

Rarely does anyone reach this welcome.
Oh race of humans, born to fly upward,
why do you fall, as you do, at the slightest wind?"

94

Menocci ove la roccia era tagliata;   97
quivi mi batté l'ali per la fronte;
poi mi promise sicura l'andata.

Come a man destra, per salire al monte   100
dove siede la chiesa che soggioga
la ben guidata sopra Rubaconte,

si rompe del montar l'ardita foga   103
per le scalee che si fero ad etade
ch'era sicuro il quaderno e la doga;

così s'allenta la ripa che cade   106
quivi ben ratta da l'altro girone;
ma quinci e quindi l'alta pietra rade.

Noi volgendo ivi le nostre persone,   109
"Beati pauperes spiritu!" voci
cantaron sì, che nol diria sermone.

Ahi quanto son diverse quelle foci   112
da l'infernali! ché quivi per canti
s'entra, e là giù per lamenti feroci.

Già montavam su per li scaglion santi,   115
ed esser mi parea troppo più lieve
che per lo pian non mi parea davanti.

Ond' io: "Maestro, dì, qual cosa greve   118
levata s'è da me, che nulla quasi
per me fatica, andando, si riceve?"

Rispuose: "Quando i P che son rimasi   121
ancor nel volto tuo presso che stinti,
saranno, com' è l'un, del tutto rasi,

fier li tuoi piè dal buon voler sì vinti,   124
che non pur non fatica sentiranno,
ma fia diletto loro esser sù pinti."

Allor fec' io come color che vanno   127
con cosa in capo non da lor saputa,
se non che ' cenni altrui sospecciar fanno;

He led us to where the rock had been split.   97
There on my forehead, with his wings, he struck me.
Then he promised me safety on the journey.

As on the right hand, to go up the hill   100
on which the church stands above Rubaconte,
dominating the well-guided city,

the climb up the jutting hill is broken   103
by the stairs that were built there in an age when
the records and the measures were kept safe,

so the bank falling away steeply from   106
the other circle is made easier
but the high rock presses from one side and the other.

As we were turning there, voices were   109
singing, *"Blessed are the poor in spirit,"*
so that there are no words to tell of it.

Oh how different are these openings   112
from those in Hell. Here one enters to singing
and there below to fierce lamentations.

Now we were climbing up the sacred stairs   115
and seemed much lighter than I had been where
I was walking on level ground, before,

so that I said, "Master, tell me, what heavy   118
thing has been lifted from me, letting me
walk and feel almost no effort in it?"

He answered, "When the P's that are still there,   121
much faded, on your forehead, are altogether
wiped away, as one of them has been,

your feet will be overcome so utterly   124
with goodwill that not only will they not be
weary, but urging them on will make them happy."

Then I did as they do who have something   127
on their heads and do not know what it is
but the looks of others set them wondering,

per che la mano ad accertar s'aiuta, 130
e cerca e truova e quello officio adempie
che non si può fornir per la veduta;

e con le dita de la destra scempie 133
trovai pur sei le lettere che 'ncise
quel da le chiavi a me sovra le tempie:

a che guardando, il mio duca sorrise. 136

so the hand tries to make out what it is   130
and gropes and finds, and fulfills the office
that seeing is unable to perform,

and with the spread fingers of my right hand   133
I found only six of the letters imprinted,
by the one with the keys, across my forehead,

and as he watched me do it my leader smiled.   136

CANTO XIII

Noi eravamo al sommo de la scala,
dove secondamente si risega
lo monte che salendo altrui dismala.

Ivi così una cornice lega   4
dintorno il poggio, come la primaia;
se non che l'arco suo più tosto piega.

Ombra non li è né segno che si paia: 7
parsi la ripa e parsi la via schietta
col livido color de la petraia.

"Se qui per dimandar gente s'aspetta,"   10
ragionava il poeta, "io temo forse
che troppo avrà d'indugio nostra eletta."

Poi fisamente al sole li occhi porse;   13
fece del destro lato a muover centro,
e la sinistra parte di sé torse.

"O dolce lume a cui fidanza i' entro   16
per lo novo cammin, tu ne conduci,"
dicea, "come condur si vuol quinc' entro.

Tu scaldi il mondo, tu sovr' esso luci;   19
s'altra ragione in contrario non ponta,
esser dien sempre li tuoi raggi duci."

Quanto di qua per un migliaio si conta,   22
tanto di là eravam noi già iti,
con poco tempo, per la voglia pronta;

e verso noi volar furon sentiti,   25
non però visti, spiriti parlando
a la mensa d'amor cortesi inviti.

La prima voce che passò volando   28
"Vinum non habent" altamente disse,
e dietro a noi l'andò reïterando.

We had come to the top of the stairway
where the mountain which takes from those who climb
their evils is cut back a second time.

In the same way there a ledge is wound   4
around the hillside like the first one
but the arc bends sooner in this one.

There is no figure nor image to be seen.   7
In front of us the bank and the bare road
in the same livid color as the stone.

"If we were to wait here to ask someone,"   10
the poet said, "I am afraid it might be
too long before we came to a decision."

Then he set his eyes steadily on the sun,   13
made his right side the center of his motion
and brought his left side in a turn around it.

"Oh sweet light in which I trust to enter   16
upon the new road, guide us," he said,
"with the guidance that we have need of here.

You warm the world and send light down upon us.   19
Unless some other reason holds against it,
yours are the rays that must always lead us."

As far as what we take to be a mile here   22
we had traveled in a little while there
already, as our will urged us on,

and toward us were heard flying, although they   25
were not seen, spirits speaking, courteously
inviting us to the table of love.

The first voice, as it flew past us, loudly   28
cried, *"They have no wine,"* and then went on
behind us calling that again and again,

E prima che del tutto non si udisse 31
per allungarsi, un'altra "I' sono Oreste"
passò gridando, e anco non s'affisse.

"Oh!" diss' io, "padre, che voci son queste?" 34
E com' io domandai, ecco la terza
dicendo: "Amate da cui male aveste."

E 'l buon maestro: "Questo cinghio sferza 37
la colpa de la invidia, e però sono
tratte d'amor le corde de la ferza.

Lo fren vuol esser del contrario suono; 40
credo che l'udirai, per mio avviso,
prima che giunghi al passo del perdono.

Ma ficca li occhi per l'aere ben fiso, 43
e vedrai gente innanzi a noi sedersi,
e ciascun è lungo la grotta assiso."

Allora più che prima li occhi apersi; 46
guarda'mi innanzi, e vidi ombre con manti
al color de la pietra non diversi.

E poi che fummo un poco più avanti, 49
udia gridar: "Maria, òra per noi":
gridar "Michele" e "Pietro" e "Tutti santi."

Non credo che per terra vada ancoi 52
omo sì duro, che non fosse punto
per compassion di quel ch'i' vidi poi;

ché, quando fui sì presso di lor giunto, 55
che li atti loro a me venivan certi,
per li occhi fui di grave dolor munto.

Di vil ciliccio mi parean coperti, 58
e l'un sofferia l'altro con la spalla,
e tutti da la ripa eran sofferti.

Così li ciechi a cui la roba falla, 61
stanno a' perdoni a chieder lor bisogna,
e l'uno il capo sopra l'altro avvalla,

and before it was so far that we could not
hear it at all another passed us, shouting,
"I am Orestes," it too without staying.

31

"Oh," said I, "Father, what voices are these?"
And as I asked, the third one came
saying, "Love them from whom you suffered harm."

34

And the good master, "This circle scourges
the sin of envy, and so for the lash
the source from which the cords are taken is love.

37

The curb must be of the opposing sound.
You will hear it, if I am not mistaken,
before you come to the pass of pardon.

40

But go on looking steadily through the air
and you will see people ahead of us
every one sitting along the rock face."

43

Then I opened my eyes more than they were before
to look ahead, and saw shades, the color
of whose cloaks was no different from the stone.

46

And when we had come a little farther I
heard a cry of "Mary, pray for us,"
and cries to "Michael" and "Peter" and "all saints."

49

I do not think there is today a man
on earth so hard that he would not have been
pierced by pity for what I saw then,

52

for when I had come up closer to them
where I could see plainly what they were doing,
out of my eyes a heavy grief was wrung.

55

They appeared to me to be covered with
coarse haircloth, holding each other up
with their shoulders, and the bank holding them all up,

58

the way the blind who lack everything
beg, where pardons are given, for what they need,
with one resting the head upon another,

61

perché 'n altrui pietà tosto si pogna,   64
non pur per lo sonar de le parole,
ma per la vista che non meno agogna.

E come a li orbi non approda il sole,   67
così a l'ombre quivi, ond' io parlo ora,
luce del ciel di sé largir non vole;

ché a tutti un fil di ferro i cigli fóra   70
e cusce sì, come a sparvier selvaggio
si fa però che queto non dimora.

A me pareva, andando, fare oltraggio,   73
veggendo altrui, non essendo veduto:
per ch'io mi volsi al mio consiglio saggio.

Ben sapev' ei che volea dir lo muto;   76
e però non attese mia dimanda,
ma disse: "Parla, e sie breve e arguto."

Virgilio mi venìa da quella banda   79
de la cornice onde cader si puote,
perché da nulla sponda s'inghirlanda;

da l'altra parte m'eran le divote   82
ombre, che per l'orribile costura
premevan sì, che bagnavan le gote.

Volsimi a loro e: "O gente sicura,"   85
incominciai, "di veder l'alto lume
che 'l disio vostro solo ha in sua cura,

se tosto grazia resolva le schiume   88
di vostra coscïenza sì che chiaro
per essa scenda de la mente il fiume,

ditemi, ché mi fia grazioso e caro,   91
s'anima è qui tra voi che sia latina;
e forse lei sarà buon s'i' l'apparo."

"O frate mio, ciascuna è cittadina   94
d'una vera città; ma tu vuo' dire
che vivesse in Italia peregrina."

so that pity may wake more readily   64
in others, not from the words only,
but at the sight, pleading as sorely for them.

And as the sun never comes to the blind,   67
so to the shades there, in the place that now I
tell of, the light of Heaven withholds its bounty,

for all of them have an iron wire run through   70
their eyelids, stitching them up, as they do
when the unbroken hawk will not hold still.

It seemed to me that I was doing them   73
an outrage as I went on seeing them
unseen, and I turned to my wise counselor.

Well he knew what the dumb wanted to say,   76
and so, not waiting for my question,
he said, "Speak, and be brief and to the point."

Virgil was coming with me along that   79
side of the ledge where one could have fallen
since there was no parapet around it,

on the other side of me were the devout   82
shades, through the horrible stitches squeezing out
so much that their cheeks were being bathed in it.

I turned to them and began, "Oh you   85
people who are sure of seeing the light
above, which is all that your desire looks to,

so may grace soon from your conscience rinse away   88
the scum, letting the stream of memory
run clear as it makes its way down through there,

tell me, and your grace will be dear to me,   91
whether there is among the souls here any
Italian; it might be well for him if I knew it."

"Oh my brother, each is a citizen   94
of one true city. You mean is there any
who as a pilgrim lived in Italy."

Questo mi parve per risposta udire   97
più innanzi alquanto che là dov' io stava,
ond' io mi feci ancor più là sentire.

Tra l'altre vidi un'ombra ch'aspettava   100
in vista; e se volesse alcun dir "Come?"
lo mento a guisa d'orbo in sù levava.

"Spirto," diss' io, "che per salir ti dome,   103
se tu se' quelli che mi rispondesti,
fammiti conto o per luogo o per nome."

"Io fui sanese," rispuose, "e con questi   106
altri rimendo qui la vita ria,
lagrimando a colui che sé ne presti.

Savia non fui, avvegna che Sapìa   109
fossi chiamata, e fui de li altrui danni
più lieta assai che di ventura mia.

E perché tu non creda ch'io t'inganni,   112
odi s'i' fui, com' io ti dico, folle,
già discendendo l'arco d'i miei anni.

Eran li cittadin miei presso a Colle   115
in campo giunti co' loro avversari,
e io pregava Iddio di quel ch'e' volle.

Rotti fuor quivi e vòlti ne li amari   118
passi di fuga; e veggendo la caccia,
letizia presi a tutte altre dispari,

tanto ch'io volsi in sù l'ardita faccia,   121
gridando a Dio: 'Omai più non ti temo!'
come fé 'l merlo per poca bonaccia.

Pace volli con Dio in su lo stremo   124
de la mia vita; e ancor non sarebbe
lo mio dover per penitenza scemo,

se ciò non fosse, ch'a memoria m'ebbe   127
Pier Pettinaio in sue sante orazioni,
a cui di me per caritate increbbe.

This I thought I heard by way of answer   97
coming from somewhat farther ahead of me,
so I made sure they heard me coming there.

Among the others I saw a shade who   100
seemed to expect something. If one were to ask, "How?"
the chin was raised up the way the blind do.

"Spirit," I said, "who tame yourself to rise,   103
if you are the one who has answered me,
make yourself known by place or name to me."

"I was from Siena," came the answer, "and with these   106
others here I mend my sinful life,
weeping to Him to grant Himself to us.

Wise I was not, though Sapia was the name   109
I bore, and I rejoiced in others' harm
far more than in good fortune of my own.

And so you will not think that I deceive you,   112
hear whether I was mad, as I will tell you.
I was already descending the arc of my years;

the people of my town had joined in battle   115
near Colle with their enemies, and I
prayed to God for what then was His will.

They were routed there and whirled into the bitter   118
footsteps of flight, and when I saw the chase
I was happy beyond any measure,

so that I turned up my impudent face,   121
shouting to God, 'Now I fear you no longer,'
like the blackbird with a little good weather.

At the end of my life I wished for peace   124
with God, and would not have been able yet
to reduce, with penitence, my debt

had it not been that Peter the comb maker   127
took pity on me out of charity
and in his holy prayers remembered me.

Ma tu chi se', che nostre condizioni   130
vai dimandando, e porti li occhi sciolti,
sì com' io credo, e spirando ragioni?"

"Li occhi," diss' io, "mi fieno ancor qui tolti,   133
ma picciol tempo, ché poca è l'offesa
fatta per esser con invidia vòlti.

Troppa è più la paura ond' è sospesa   136
l'anima mia del tormento di sotto,
che già lo 'ncarco di là giù mi pesa."

Ed ella a me: "Chi t'ha dunque condotto   139
qua sù tra noi, se giù ritornar credi?"
E io: "Costui ch'è meco e non fa motto.

E vivo sono; e però mi richiedi,   142
spirito eletto, se tu vuo' ch'i' mova
di là per te ancor li mortai piedi."

"Oh, questa è a udir sì cosa nuova,"   145
rispuose, "che gran segno è che Dio t'ami;
però col priego tuo talor mi giova.

E cheggioti, per quel che tu più brami,   148
se mai calchi la terra di Toscana,
che a' miei propinqui tu ben mi rinfami.

Tu li vedrai tra quella gente vana   151
che spera in Talamone, e perderagli
più di speranza ch'a trovar la Diana;

ma più vi perderanno li ammiragli."   154

But who are you, who go asking of our   130
condition, and have, I believe, your
eyes free, and are breathing as you speak?"

"My eyes," I said, "will yet be taken from me   133
here, but not for long, for they have not
offended, much, with glances of envy.

Much greater is the dread in which my soul   136
is kept hanging of the torment there below;
the load down there weighs on me even now."

And she to me, "Who has led you up among   139
us here then, if you think to go down again?"
And I, "He who is with me saying nothing.

And I am alive, and so, spirit elect,   142
if you would have me move my mortal feet
later, back there, for your sake, ask it of me."

"Oh what a strange thing," she said, "to my ears   145
this is, and what a great sign that God loves you.
Since that is so, help me, sometimes, with your prayers.

And I beg you, if ever again you tread   148
the land of Tuscany, by all you long for most,
restore my name among my kindred.

You will see them among that vain people   151
whose hope is in Talamone and who will lose more
hope there than in finding the Diana,

though there the admirals will lose still more."   154

"Chi è costui che 'l nostro monte cerchia
prima che morte li abbia dato il volo,
e apre li occhi a sua voglia e coverchia?"

"Non so chi sia, ma so ch'e' non è solo;   4
domandal tu che più li t'avvicini,
e dolcemente, sì che parli, acco'lo."

Così due spirti, l'uno a l'altro chini,   7
ragionavan di me ivi a man dritta;
poi fer li visi, per dirmi, supini;

e disse l'uno: "O anima che fitta   10
nel corpo ancora inver' lo ciel ten vai,
per carità ne consola e ne ditta

onde vieni e chi se;' ché tu ne fai   13
tanto maravigliar de la tua grazia,
quanto vuol cosa che non fu più mai."

E io: "Per mezza Toscana si spazia   16
un fiumicel che nasce in Falterona,
e cento miglia di corso nol sazia.

Di sovr' esso rech' io questa persona: 19
dirvi ch'i' sia, saria parlare indarno,
ché 'l nome mio ancor molto non suona."

"Se ben lo 'ntendimento tuo accarno   22
con lo 'ntelletto," allora mi rispuose
quei che diceva pria, "tu parli d'Arno."

E l'altro disse lui: "Perché nascose   25
questi il vocabol di quella riviera,
pur com' om fa de l'orribili cose?"

E l'ombra che di ciò domandata era,   28
si sdebitò così: "Non so; ma degno
ben è che 'l nome di tal valle pèra;

"Who is this who travels around our mountain
before death has given flight to him
and opens his eyes at will and closes them?"

"I do not know who he is, but I can tell   4
that he is not alone. You are nearer.
Greet him kindly so that he will answer."

So two spirits leaning upon each other   7
at my right hand were talking about me.
Then they tipped back their faces to speak to me

and one of them said, "Oh soul who, lodged within   10
your body still, are journeying toward Heaven,
console us, out of charity, and tell us

where you came from and who you are, for you   13
make us wonder at this grace granted to you
as at something that never was before."

And I, "Midway through Tuscany a stream   16
runs from its birth in Falterona and
in a hundred miles still has not reached its end.

From above its current I bring this body.   19
It would be in vain if I told you who I am,
for there is not much sound yet to my name."

"If I am able to grasp with my mind   22
what you mean," that one answered me who
had spoken first, "you are talking about the Arno."

And the other one said to him, "Why did he   25
hide the name of that river as somebody
would have done with a horrible thing?"

And the shade thus questioned unburdened himself   28
this way: "I do not know, but I think it would be
good for the name of such a valley to die,

ché dal principio suo, ov' è sì pregno 31
l'alpestro monte ond' è tronco Peloro,
che 'n pochi luoghi passa oltra quel segno,

infin là 've si rende per ristoro 34
di quel che 'l ciel de la marina asciuga,
ond' hanno i fiumi ciò che va con loro,

vertù così per nimica si fuga 37
da tutti come biscia, o per sventura
del luogo, o per mal uso che li fruga:

ond' hanno sì mutata lor natura 40
li abitator de la misera valle,
che par che Circe li avesse in pastura.

Tra brutti porci, più degni di galle 43
che d'altro cibo fatto in uman uso,
dirizza prima il suo povero calle.

Botoli trova poi, venendo giuso, 46
ringhiosi più che non chiede lor possa,
e da lor disdegnosa torce il muso.

Vassi caggendo; e quant' ella più 'ngrossa, 49
tanto più trova di can farsi lupi
la maladetta e sventurata fossa.

Discesa poi per più pelaghi cupi, 52
trova le volpi sì piene di froda,
che non temono ingegno che le occùpi.

Né lascerò di dir perch' altri m'oda; 55
e buon sarà costui, s'ancor s'ammenta
di ciò che vero spirto mi disnoda.

Io veggio tuo nepote che diventa 58
cacciator di quei lupi in su la riva
del fiero fiume, e tutti li sgomenta.

Vende la carne loro essendo viva; 61
poscia li ancide come antica belva;
molti di vita e sé di pregio priva.

for from its source in the range of jagged peaks   31
Pelorus broke from, where so swollen are
its waters that few surpass them anywhere,

to where it gives itself up to restore   34
what the sky draws back out of the ocean
with which the rivers' courses become their own

virtue is fled from as an enemy   37
or a snake, by everyone either from some
bad luck in the place, or bad habit that spurs them,

so that the inhabitants of that wretched   40
valley have been so altered in their nature
it seems as though Circe had them at pasture.

Among filthy hogs better suited to acorns   43
than any food prepared for human use
it directs from the start its ill-fed course.

As it descends it finds small noisy dogs   46
with more bark than they can live up to
and in scorn it turns its muzzle away from them.

It falls farther and the more it fattens   49
the more the accursed, ill-fated ditch finds
that the dogs have been turning into wolves.

Then running down through a series of hollow   52
gorges it finds foxes that are so
full of tricks they know no trap can catch them.

Nor will I stop speaking about it for   55
fear someone might hear me. Good for them
to heed what the spirit of truth unties to me.

I see your grandson becoming a hunter   58
of those wolves along the savage stream
and putting panic into all of them.

He offers their flesh for sale while they are alive,   61
then slaughters them like old cattle, depriving
many of life, and himself of honor.

Sanguinoso esce de la trista selva;   64
lasciala tal, che di qui a mille anni
ne lo stato primaio non si rinselva."

Com' a l'annunzio di dogliosi danni   67
si turba il viso di colui ch'ascolta,
da qual che parte il periglio l'assanni,

    così vid' io l'altr' anima, che volta   70
stava a udir, turbarsi e farsi trista,
poi ch'ebbe la parola a sé raccolta.

Lo dir de l'una e de l'altra la vista   73
mi fer voglioso di saper lor nomi,
e dimanda ne fei con prieghi mista;

    per che lo spirto che di pria parlòmi   76
ricominciò: "Tu vuo' ch'io mi deduca
nel fare a te ciò che tu far non vuo'mi.

Ma da che Dio in te vuol che traluca   79
tanto sua grazia, non ti sarò scarso;
però sappi ch'io fui Guido del Duca.

Fu il sangue mio d'invidia sì rïarso,   82
che se veduto avesse uom farsi lieto,
visto m'avresti di livore sparso.

Di mia semente cotal paglia mieto;   85
o gente umana, perché poni 'l core
là 'v' è mestier di consorte divieto?

Questi è Rinier; questi è 'l pregio e l'onore   88
de la casa da Calboli, ove nullo
fatto s'è reda poi del suo valore.

E non pur lo suo sangue è fatto brullo,   91
tra 'l Po e 'l monte e la marina e 'l Reno,
del ben richesto al vero e al trastullo;

    ché dentro a questi termini è ripieno   94
di venenosi sterpi, sì che tardi
per coltivare omai verrebber meno.

He emerges bloody from the dismal wood,   64
leaving it so that a thousand years from now
it will not again have the forest it once had."

As the announcement of terrible evils   67
fills a listener's face with trouble,
wherever the danger may be coming from,

so I saw the other soul that had turned   70
to listen become troubled and sad
as it took in what was said to it.

The speech of the one and the other's expression   73
made me want to know what their names were,
and with careful entreaty I questioned them,

at which the spirit who had first spoken to me   76
began again, "You would have me agree
to do for you what you would not do for me.

But since God wills to have His grace so shine   79
in you, I will not withhold from you mine,
so you may know I am Guido del Duca.

So heated up with envy was my blood   82
that seeing someone become happy
would make me turn to the color of lead.

Of my sowing this is the straw I reap.   85
Oh humankind, why set your hearts where you
have to drive any partner away from you?

This is Rinier. This is the honor and glory   88
of the house of Calboli, where nobody
after him has been a worthy heir.

And his is not the only blood gone worthless   91
between Po and mountain, from the Reno to the sea,
whether for serious matters or for play,

for within these bounds by now there are so many   94
poisonous growths it would take a long time
to clear them out again with cultivation.

Ov' è 'l buon Lizio e Arrigo Mainardi?   97
Pier Traversaro e Guido di Carpigna?
Oh Romagnuoli tornati in bastardi!

Quando in Bologna un Fabbro si ralligna?   100
quando in Faenza un Bernardin di Fosco,
verga gentil di picciola gramigna?

Non ti maravigliar s'io piango, Tosco,   103
quando rimembro, con Guido da Prata,
Ugolin d'Azzo che vivette nosco,

Federigo Tignoso e sua brigata,   106
la casa Traversara e li Anastagi
(e l'una gente e l'altra è diretata),

le donne e ' cavalier, li affanni e li agi   109
che ne 'nvogliava amore e cortesia
là dove i cuor son fatti sì malvagi.

O Bretinoro, ché non fuggi via,   112
poi che gita se n'è la tua famiglia
e molta gente per non esser ria?

Ben fa Bagnacaval, che non rifiglia;   115
e mal fa Castrocaro, e peggio Conio,
che di figliar tai conti più s'impiglia.

Ben faranno i Pagan, da che 'l demonio   118
lor sen girà; ma non però che puro
già mai rimagna d'essi testimonio.

O Ugolin de' Fantolin, sicuro   121
è 'l nome tuo, da che più non s'aspetta
chi far lo possa, tralignando, scuro.

Ma va via, Tosco, omai; ch'or mi diletta   124
troppo di pianger più che di parlare,
sì m'ha nostra ragion la mente stretta."

Noi sapavam che quell' anime care   127
ci sentivano andar; però, tacendo,
facëan noi del cammin confidare.

Where is good Lizio, and Arrigo Mainardi,   97
Pier Traversaro and Guido di Carpigna?
You have all become bastards, you of Romagna.

When will a Fabbro take root again in Bologna,   100
or a Bernardin di Fosco in Faenza,
the noble shoot of a lowly weed?

If I weep, Tuscan, do not be surprised   103
when I remember Guido da Prata,
Ugolin d'Azzo who once lived among us,

Federico Tignoso and his men,   106
the house of Traversara and the Anastagi
with no heir now to either family,

the knights and ladies, the labors and the games   109
that love and courtesy once brought us to
there where hearts are so full of evil now.

Oh Bretinoro, why do you not flee   112
in the footsteps of the rest of your family
and many others, rather than be corrupted?

Bagnacavallo does well to have no more children,   115
and Castrocaro ill, and Conio worse,
troubling to breed counts such as their sons.

The Pagani will do well when their devil   118
leaves them, though now there never will
be a clean testimony left of them.

Oh Ugolin de' Fantolini, your   121
name is safe, now no more may be looked for
whose degeneracy could blacken it further.

But go your way now, Tuscan, for at this time   124
I would far rather weep than go on talking,
our conversation has so wrung my mind."

We knew that those dear spirits could hear us   127
walking away, and so their saying nothing
led us to trust the way that we were taking.

Poi fummo fatti soli procedendo,   130
folgore parve quando l'aere fende,
voce che giunse di contra dicendo:

"Anciderammi qualunque m'apprende";   133
e fuggì come tuon che si dilegua,
se sùbito la nuvola scoscende.

Come da lei l'udir nostro ebbe triegua,   136
ed ecco l'altra con sì gran fracasso,
che somigliò tonar che tosto segua:

"Io sono Aglauro che divenni sasso";   139
e allor, per ristrignermi al poeta,
in destro feci, e non innanzi, il passo.

Già era l'aura d'ogne parte queta;   142
ed el mi disse: "Quel fu 'l duro camo
che dovria l'uom tener dentro a sua meta.

Ma voi prendete l'esca, sì che l'amo   145
de l'antico avversaro a sé vi tira;
e però poco val freno o richiamo.

Chiamavi 'l cielo e 'ntorno vi si gira,   148
mostrandovi le sue bellezze etterne,
e l'occhio vostro pur a terra mira;

onde vi batte chi tutto discerne."   151

When we were by ourselves then, traveling on,   130
like lightning when it splits the air a voice
coming the other way said as it reached us,

"Everyone who finds me will kill me,"   133
and fled as the thunder dies away
when the cloud bursts apart suddenly.

Our ears had hardly been relieved of it   136
when the next was there, the crash of it
was like the thunderclap coming close after:

"I am Aglauros who was turned to stone,"   139
and then, to draw closer to the poet
I stepped to the right instead of going on.

Now the breeze had fallen still on every side   142
and he said to me, "That was the hard bit
intended to keep a man within his measure.

But you take the bait, so that you are drawn   145
by his hook to the old adversary
and neither curb nor lure does much good then.

The heavens call to you and wheel around you,   148
revealing their eternal beauties to you,
and your eyes are fixed upon the earth,

and so he strikes you who sees everything."   151

CANTO XV

Quanto tra l'ultimar de l'ora terza
e 'l principio del dì par de la spera
che sempre a guisa di fanciullo scherza,

tanto pareva già inver' la sera   4
essere al sol del suo corso rimaso;
vespero là, e qui mezza notte era.

E i raggi ne ferien per mezzo 'l naso,   7
perché per noi girato era sì 'l monte,
che già dritti andavamo inver' l'occaso,

quand' io senti' a me gravar la fronte   10
a lo splendore assai più che di prima,
e stupor m'eran le cose non conte;

ond' io levai le mani inver' la cima   13
de le mie ciglia, e fecimi 'l solecchio,
che del soverchio visibile lima.

Come quando da l'acqua o da lo specchio   16
salta lo raggio a l'opposita parte,
salendo su per lo modo parecchio

a quel che scende, e tanto si diparte   19
dal cader de la pietra in igual tratta,
sì come mostra esperïenza e arte;

così mi parve da luce rifratta   22
quivi dinanzi a me esser percosso;
per che a fuggir la mia vista fu ratta.

"Che è quel, dolce padre, a che non posso   25
schermar lo viso tanto che mi vaglia,"
diss' io, "e pare inver' noi esser mosso?"

"Non ti maravigliar s'ancor t'abbaglia   28
la famiglia del cielo," a me rispuose:
"messo è che viene ad invitar ch'om saglia.

As much as is seen from the end of the third hour
to the beginning of the day of that sphere
which is forever playing like a child,

that was how much appeared to be remaining   4
now of the sun's course on its way to night.
There it was evening and here it was midnight.

And the beams were striking us full in the face,   7
for so far had the mountain been circled by us
that we were walking toward where the sun goes down,

when I felt weighing upon my forehead   10
a splendor far greater than before, and what
I did not know filled me with wonder at it

and with that I put my hand up over   13
my eyebrows and made for myself the shade
that files down the visible when it is too bright.

As when, off water or a mirror, the ray   16
leaps up in the opposite direction,
rising at the same angle that it comes down,

and at the same distance has moved as far   19
from the line of a plummeting stone,
as learning and experience have shown,

thus it appeared to me that I was struck by   22
light reflected from there before me
so that my sight fled from it instantly.

"What is it, gentle Father, from which I   25
cannot screen my eyes enough to see,"
I said, "and which seems to be moving toward us?"

"Do not wonder that the household of Heaven   28
dazzles you still," he answered me. "This is
a messenger come to invite us to ascend.

Tosto sarà ch'a veder queste cose 31
non ti fia grave, ma fieti diletto
quanto natura a sentir ti dispuose."

Poi giunti fummo a l'angel benedetto, 34
con lieta voce disse: "Intrate quinci
ad un scaleo vie men che li altri eretto."

Noi montavam, già partiti di linci, 37
e *"Beati misericordes!"* fue
cantato retro, e "Godi tu che vinci!"

Lo mio maestro e io soli amendue 40
suso andavamo; e io pensai, andando,
prode acquistar ne le parole sue;

e drizza'mi a lui sì dimandando: 43
"Che volse dir lo spirto di Romagna,
e 'divieto' e 'consorte' menzionando?"

Per ch'elli a me: "Di sua maggior magagna 46
conosce il danno; e però non s'ammiri
se ne riprende perché men si piagna.

Perché s'appuntano i vostri disiri 49
dove per compagnia parte si scema,
invidia move il mantaco a' sospiri.

Ma se l'amor de la spera supprema 52
torcesse in suso il disiderio vostro,
non vi sarebbe al petto quella tema;

ché, per quanti si dice più lì 'nostro,' 55
tanto possiede più di ben ciascuno,
e più di caritate arde in quel chiostro."

"Io son d'esser contento più digiuno," 58
diss' io, "che se mi fosse pria taciuto,
e più di dubbio ne la mente aduno.

Com' esser puote ch'un ben, distributo 61
in più posseditor, faccia più ricchi
di sé che se da pochi è posseduto?"

The sight of such things, in a little while,　　　　　31
will not trouble you, but will give you
whatever joy your nature lets you feel."

When we had come to the blessèd angel　　　　　34
he said with a glad voice, "Enter here
on a stairway less steep than the others were."

We were climbing up, already gone from there,　　　37
and *"Blessèd are the merciful"* behind us
was being sung, and "You that overcome, rejoice."

My master and I, we two alone, went on　　　　　40
upward, and I thought, as we walked, to gain
profit by attending to his words,

and I turned to him, asking, "What did he　　　　43
mean, that spirit from Romagna, when he
referred to exclusion and to 'partnership'?

Then he to me, "He knows the damage done　　　46
by his worst fault; therefore it is no wonder
he reproves it, to have less to mourn for.

Because your own desires are fastened where　　　49
if there is company each part is smaller,
envy works the bellows to your sighs.

But if the love of the highest sphere　　　　　52
had turned your longing upward you would not
have that fear in your breast any longer,

for the more they say 'ours' there, the more　　　55
good there is for each one, and the more
charity is burning in that cloister."

"I am more hungry to be satisfied,"　　　　　58
I said, "than if I had been silent, and
more doubt than ever gathers in my mind.

How can a good be shared out among many　　　61
so that each of them becomes richer in it
than if only a few divided it?"

Ed elli a me: "Però che tu rificchi   64
la mente pur a le cose terrene,
di vera luce tenebre dispicchi.

Quello infinito e ineffabil bene   67
che là sù è, così corre ad amore
com' a lucido corpo raggio vene.

Tanto si dà quanto trova d'ardore;   70
sì che, quantunque carità si stende,
cresce sovr' essa l'etterno valore.

E quanta gente più là sù s'intende,   73
più v'è da bene amare, e più vi s'ama,
e come specchio l'uno a l'altro rende.

E se la mia ragion non ti disfama,   76
vedrai Beatrice, ed ella pienamente
ti torrà questa e ciascun' altra brama.

Procaccia pur che tosto sieno spente,   79
come son già le due, le cinque piaghe,
che si richiudon per esser dolente."

Com' io voleva dicer "Tu m'appaghe,"   82
vidimi giunto in su l'altro girone,
sì che tacer mi fer le luci vaghe.

Ivi mi parve in una visïone   85
estatica di sùbito esser tratto,
e vedere in un tempio più persone;

e una donna, in su l'entrar, con atto   88
dolce di madre dicer: "Figliuol mio,
perché hai tu così verso noi fatto?

Ecco, dolenti, lo tuo padre e io   91
ti cercavamo." E come qui si tacque,
ciò che pareva prima, dispario.

Indi m'apparve un'altra con quell' acque   94
giù per le gote che 'l dolor distilla
quando di gran dispetto in altrui nacque,

And he to me, "Because your mind is set   64
upon nothing but terrestrial things,
you gather darkness out of light itself.

That infinite and indescribable good   67
which is there above races as swiftly
to love as a ray of light to a bright body.

It gives of itself according to the ardor   70
it finds, so that as charity spreads farther
the eternal good increases upon it,

and the more souls there are who love, up there,   73
the more there are to love well, and the more love
they reflect to each other, as in a mirror.

And if my talk does not ease your hunger,   76
you will see Beatrice, and she will wholly deliver
you from this and every other longing.

Devote yourself to having erased soon,   79
as two are gone already, the five wounds
that are healed by the pain that is in them."

As I was about to say "You content me,"   82
I saw that I had come to the next circle,
so that the yearning of my eyes silenced me.

Then it seemed to me that I was caught up, all   85
at once, out of myself, in a vision,
and was seeing in a temple many people,

and a woman in the doorway with the tender   88
expression of a mother saying, "My son,
why have you treated us as you have done?

See how your father and I have been looking   91
for you in sorrow." And as she said, afterward,
nothing, what had appeared first disappeared.

Then another woman appeared to me with those   94
waters running down her cheeks which grief distills
when it springs from great resentment of someone else,

e dir: "Se tu se' sire de la villa   97
del cui nome ne' dèi fu tanta lite,
e onde ogne scïenza disfavilla,

vendica te di quelle braccia ardite   100
ch'abbracciar nostra figlia, o Pisistràto."
E 'l segnor mi parea, benigno e mite,

risponder lei con viso temperato: 103
"Che farem noi a chi mal ne disira,
se quei che ci ama è per noi condannato?"

Poi vidi genti accese in foco d'ira   106
con pietre un giovinetto ancider, forte
gridando a sé pur: "Martira, martira!"

E lui vedea chinarsi, per la morte   109
che l'aggravava già, inver' la terra,
ma de li occhi facea sempre al ciel porte,

orando a l'alto Sire, in tanta guerra,   112
che perdonasse a' suoi persecutori,
con quello aspetto che pietà diserra.

Quando l'anima mia tornò di fori   115
a le cose che son fuor di lei vere,
io riconobbi i miei non falsi errori.

Lo duca mio, che mi potea vedere   118
far sì com' om che dal sonno si slega,
disse: "Che hai che non ti puoi tenere,

ma se' venuto più che mezza lega   121
velando li occhi e con le gambe avvolte,
a guisa di cui vino o sonno piega?"

"O dolce padre mio, se tu m'ascolte,   124
io ti dirò," diss' io, "ciò che m'apparve
quando le gambe mi furon sì tolte."

Ed ei: "Se tu avessi cento larve   127
sovra la faccia, non mi sarian chiuse
le tue cogitazion, quantunque parve.

and she said, "If you are the lord of the city 97
whose name the gods quarreled over so fiercely
and from which every form of knowledge shines,

take vengeance upon those impudent arms, 100
oh Pisistratus, that have embraced our daughter."
And it seemed to me that the lord answered her

kindly and gently, with a tranquil face, 103
"What shall we do to those who wish us ill
if one who loves us is condemned by us?"

Then I saw people inflamed with the fire of anger 106
killing a young man with stones. "Kill him, kill him,"
they kept shouting aloud to each other.

And I saw him sink down, for already death 109
was weighing upon him, toward the earth,
but he made of his eyes gates open to heaven,

praying to the Lord above, in such torment, 112
to pardon those who were persecuting him,
with that look which unlocks compassion.

When my soul returned again outside 115
to the things outside it that are real
I recognized my errors which were not false.

My leader who could see me behaving 118
as someone does throwing off the ties of sleep
said, "What is wrong with you? You can scarcely stand up

but have come more than half a league with your 121
eyes glazed and your feet tripping each other
like someone overcome with wine or sleep."

"Oh my kind Father, if you will listen to me 124
I will tell you," I said, "what appeared to me
when my legs were thus taken from me."

And he, "If there were a hundred masks upon 127
your face, they would be able to hide none,
even the slightest, of your thoughts from me.

Ciò che vedesti fu perché non scuse 130
d'aprir lo core a l'acque de la pace
che da l'etterno fonte son diffuse.

Non dimandai 'Che hai?' per quel che face 133
chi guarda pur con l'occhio che non vede,
quando disanimato il corpo giace;

ma dimandai per darti forza al piede: 136
così frugar conviensi i pigri, lenti
ad usar lor vigilia quando riede."

Noi andavam per lo vespero, attenti 139
oltre quanto potean li occhi allungarsi
contra i raggi serotini e lucenti.

Ed ecco a poco a poco un fummo farsi 142
verso di noi come la notte oscuro;
né da quello era loco da cansarsi.

Questo ne tolse li occhi e l'aere puro. 145

What you saw was shown to you so that you   130
would not refuse to open your heart to
the waters of peace poured from the eternal fountain.

    I did not ask 'What is wrong?' as one does   133
who looks only with the eye that does not see
at an insensible body where it lies,

    but I asked to give strength to your feet.   136
The sluggish have to be spurred on, who are
slow to use, when it returns, their waking hour."

    We were walking through the evening, straining   139
our eyes ahead as far as we could see
against those rays and their late shining,

    when there, little by little, a smoke was   142
coming toward us that was as dark as night,
nor was there anywhere to escape from it;

    this took from us our sight and the pure air.   145

CANTO XVI

Buio d'inferno e di notte privata
d'ogne pianeto, sotto pover cielo,
quant' esser può di nuvol tenebrata,

non fece al viso mio sì grosso velo   4
come quel fummo ch'ivi ci coperse,
né a sentir di così aspro pelo,

che l'occhio stare aperto non sofferse;   7
onde la scorta mia saputa e fida
mi s'accostò e l'omero m'offerse.

Sì come cieco va dietro a sua guida   10
per non smarrirsi e per non dar di cozzo
in cosa che 'l molesti, o forse ancida,

m'andava io per l'aere amaro e sozzo,   13
ascoltando il mio duca che diceva
pur: "Guarda che da me tu non sia mozzo."

Io sentia voci, e ciascuna pareva   16
pregar per pace e per misericordia
l'Agnel di Dio che le peccata leva.

Pur *"Agnus Dei"* eran le loro essordia;   19
una parola in tutte era e un modo,
sì che parea tra esse ogne concordia.

"Quei sono spirti, maestro, ch'i' odo?"   22
diss' io. Ed elli a me: "Tu vero apprendi,
e d'iracundia van solvendo il nodo."

"Or tu chi se' che 'l nostro fummo fendi,   25
e di noi parli pur come se tue
partissi ancor lo tempo per calendi?"

Così per una voce detto fue;   28
onde 'l maestro mio disse: "Rispondi,
e domanda se quinci si va sùe."

The murk of Hell and of a night empty
of every planet, under a bare sky
which clouds had made as dark as it could be,

never drew over my sight as heavy   4
a veil as that smoke which there covered us,
nor so rasping to the other senses,

for it would not let my eyes stay open,   7
and so my wise and faithful companion
came close to me and offered me his shoulder.

As a blind man goes along behind his guide   10
so that he does not lose his way or hit
something that could hurt or perhaps kill him,

so I walked through the bitter and foul air,   13
listening to my leader saying over
and over, "Be careful not to be cut off from me."

I heard voices, and each one seemed to be   16
praying for peace and for mercy
to the Lamb of God who takes sins away.

"Lamb of God" was the way they always began.   19
There was one word and one measure among them,
so there seemed to be concord among all of them.

"Are these spirits, Master, that I hear?"   22
I said. And he to me, "You have grasped the truth,
and they are untying the knot of anger."

"Who are you, then, by whom our smoke is parted   25
and who talk about us as though you counted
time according to the months' beginnings?"

This was spoken by one voice, and my master   28
at that said, "Answer, and ask whether
this is the right way to go up from here."

E io: "O creatura che ti mondi 31
per tornar bella a colui che ti fece,
maraviglia udirai, se mi secondi."

"Io ti seguiterò quanto mi lece," 34
rispuose; "e se veder fummo non lascia,
l'udir ci terrà giunti in quella vece."

Allora incominciai: "Con quella fascia 37
che la morte dissolve men vo suso,
e venni qui per l'infernale ambascia.

E se Dio m'ha in sua grazia rinchiuso, 40
tanto che vuol ch'i' veggia la sua corte
per modo tutto fuor del moderno uso,

non mi celar chi fosti anzi la morte, 43
ma dilmi, e dimmi s'i' vo bene al varco;
e tue parole fier le nostre scorte."

"Lombardo fui, e fu' chiamato Marco; 46
del mondo seppi, e quel valore amai
al quale ha or ciascun disteso l'arco.

Per montar sù dirittamente vai." 49
Così rispuose, e soggiunse: "I' ti prego
che per me prieghi quando sù sarai."

E io a lui: "Per fede mi ti lego 52
di far ciò che mi chiedi; ma io scoppio
dentro ad un dubbio, s'io non me ne spiego.

Prima era scempio, e ora è fatto doppio 55
ne la sentenza tua, che mi fa certo
qui, e altrove, quello ov' io l'accoppio.

Lo mondo è ben così tutto diserto 58
d'ogne virtute, come tu mi sone,
e di malizia gravido e coverto;

ma priego che m'addite la cagione, 61
sì ch'i' la veggia e ch'i' la mostri altrui;
ché nel cielo uno, e un qua giù la pone."

And I, "Oh creature making yourself pure 31
to go back to the one who made you in beauty,
you will hear a wonder if you come with me."

"I will follow you as far as I am allowed," 34
he answered, "and if the smoke keeps us from seeing
each other, hearing will hold us together instead."

Then I began, "With those swaddling bands 37
which death unfastens I am making my way
upward, and I came through Hell and its agony.

And if God has gathered me into His grace 40
so that He would have me behold His court
in a manner wholly outside modern use,

do not hide from me who you were before death, 43
but tell me, and tell me whether the pass
is this way, and your words will go with us."

"I was a Lombard, and my name was Marco. 46
I knew the world and I loved that virtue
toward which none any longer bends the bow.

To climb up you keep going straight ahead." 49
That was how he answered, and added,
"I pray you, when you are up there, pray for me."

And I to him, "I pledge my faith to you 52
to do what you asked me to, but I have in me
a doubt I must free myself of or it will burst me.

First it was single and now it has become 55
doubled by your words, which make me certain,
here and elsewhere, of what seems to go with it.

The world indeed is utterly deserted 58
by every virtue, as you have said to me,
pregnant with evil and overlaid with it,

but I beg you to show me what makes it so, 61
in a way I can see and point out to others,
for one puts it in heaven and another here below."

Alto sospir, che duolo strinse in "uhi!"   64
mise fuor prima; e poi cominciò: "Frate,
lo mondo è cieco, e tu vien ben da lui.

Voi che vivete ogne cagion recate   67
pur suso al cielo, pur come se tutto
movesse seco di necessitate.

Se così fosse, in voi fora distrutto   70
libero arbitrio, e non fora giustizia
per ben letizia, e per male aver lutto.

Lo cielo i vostri movimenti inizia;   73
non dico tutti, ma, posto ch'i' 'l dica,
lume v'è dato a bene e a malizia,

e libero voler; che, se fatica   76
ne le prime battaglie col ciel dura,
poi vince tutto, se ben si notrica.

A maggior forza e a miglior natura   79
liberi soggiacete; e quella cria
la mente in voi, che 'l ciel non ha in sua cura.

Però, se 'l mondo presente disvia,   82
in voi è la cagione, in voi si cheggia;
e io te ne sarò or vera spia.

Esce di mano a lui che la vagheggia   85
prima che sia, a guisa di fanciulla
che piangendo e ridendo pargoleggia,

l'anima semplicetta che sa nulla,   88
salvo che, mossa da lieto fattore,
volontier torna a ciò che la trastulla.

Di picciol bene in pria sente sapore;   91
quivi s'inganna, e dietro ad esso corre,
se guida o fren non torce suo amore.

Onde convenne legge per fren porre;   94
convenne rege aver, che discernesse
de la vera cittade almen la torre.

First he heaved a deep sigh, which grief wrung   64
to an "Ay," and then he began, "Brother,
the world is blind and surely you come from there.

You who are living ascribe every cause   67
only above, to Heaven, as though the only
mover of everything were necessity.

If that were true, freedom of will would be   70
destroyed in you, and it would not be just
to rejoice at goodness or grieve over evil.

The heavens set you going in your motions;   73
not in all of them, I mean, but if I did
you are given a light to know evil from good,

and free will which, if it can endure,   76
without weakening, the first bout with fixed Heaven,
if well nourished, conquers all it meets later.

To a greater power and a better nature   79
you are subject in your freedom, which creates
in you the mind which is not in the heavens' care.

So if the present world strays from its course,   82
the cause is in you; look for it in yourself
and I will be a true scout for you now in this.

Out of His hands who regards it tenderly   85
before it exists, in the form of a child
crying and laughing in a childish way,

comes the little simple soul that knows nothing   88
except that, moved by a joyful maker,
it turns happily to what gives it pleasure.

It tastes first the flavor of some slight good   91
and is deceived there and runs after it
if its love is not turned by curb or guide.

So that some law must be a curb for it;   94
there had to be a king who could see
at least the tower of the true city.

Le leggi son, ma chi pon mano ad esse?   97
Nullo, però che 'l pastor che procede,
rugumar può, ma non ha l'unghie fesse;

per che la gente, che sua guida vede   100
pur a quel ben fedire ond' ella è ghiotta,
di quel si pasce, e più oltre non chiede.

Ben puoi veder che la mala condotta   103
è la cagion che 'l mondo ha fatto reo,
e non natura che 'n voi sia corrotta.

Soleva Roma, che 'l buon mondo feo,   106
due soli aver, che l'una e l'altra strada
facean vedere, e del mondo e di Deo.

L'un l'altro ha spento; ed è giunta la spada   109
col pasturale, e l'un con l'altro insieme
per viva forza mal convien che vada;

però che, giunti, l'un l'altro non teme: 112
se non mi credi, pon mente a la spiga,
ch'ogn' erba si conosce per lo seme.

In sul paese ch'Adice e Po riga,   115
solea valore e cortesia trovarsi,
prima che Federigo avesse briga;

or può sicuramente indi passarsi   118
per qualunque lasciasse, per vergogna,
di ragionar coi buoni o d'appressarsi.

Ben v'èn tre vecchi ancora in cui rampogna   121
l'antica età la nova, e par lor tardo
che Dio a miglior vita li ripogna:

Currado da Palazzo e 'l buon Gherardo   124
e Guido da Castel, che mei si noma,
francescamente, il semplice Lombardo.

Dì oggimai che la Chiesa di Roma,   127
per confondere in sé due reggimenti,
cade nel fango, e sé brutta e la soma."

The laws exist, but who puts a hand to them?   *97*
None, because the shepherd who goes before
may chew the cud but his hooves are not cloven.

So the people, as they see their leader   *100*
snatch only that good they themselves are greedy for,
feed only on that and look for nothing more.

You can see clearly that the world has been made   *103*
evil by having been misled, and not
nature in you that is corrupted.

At one time Rome, which made the good world,   *106*
had two suns, each lighting up its road:
the way of the world and the way of God.

One has put out the other, and the sword   *109*
has joined the shepherd's crook, and both together
are forced to take their way into error,

for, joined, the one has no fear of the other.   *112*
If you do not believe me, think of the ear
of grain, for by its seed each plant is known.

In the country watered by the Adige and the Po   *115*
at one time you could find courtesy and valor,
before Frederick had run into trouble.

Now anyone can safely pass there   *118*
who does not want to talk to the good, for shame,
nor have to get too close to them.

Though in fact there are three old men in whom   *121*
the ancient times rebuke the new, and to them God seems
late in taking them to a better life.

Currado da Palazzo and the good Gherardo,   *124*
and Guido da Castel, who is better named
after the French fashion, the guileless Lombard.

From this time on say that the Church of Rome,   *127*
by confounding two governments in itself
falls in the mud and fouls itself and its burden."

"O Marco mio," diss' io, "bene argomenti;   130
e or discerno perché dal retaggio
li figli di Levì furono essenti.

Ma qual Gherardo è quel che tu per saggio   133
di' ch'è rimaso de la gente spenta,
in rimprovèro del secol selvaggio?"

"O tuo parlar m'inganna, o el mi tenta,"   136
rispuose a me; "ché, parlandomi tosco,
par che del buon Gherardo nulla senta.

Per altro sopranome io nol conosco,   139
s'io nol togliessi da sua figlia Gaia.
Dio sia con voi, ché più non vegno vosco.

Vedi l'albor che per lo fummo raia   142
già biancheggiare, e me convien partirmi
(l'angelo è ivi) prima ch'io li paia."

Così tornò, e più non volle udirmi.   145

"Oh my Marco," I said, "you reason well,   130
and now I understand why the sons
of Levi were exempted from the inheritance.

But what Gherardo is this, who you say   133
remains an example of the extinct race
in reproof of the barbarous present day?"

"Either your speech deceives me or it tests me,"   136
he answered me, "for you speak Tuscan to me
and seem to know nothing of the good Gherardo.

I know him by no other surname   139
unless I take it from Gaia, his daughter.
God be with you, for I come with you no farther.

You see shining through the smoke the brightness   142
turning it white already, and I must leave
before the angel sees me—there he is."

So he turned back and would hear me no more.   145

CANTO XVII

Ricorditi, lettor, se mai ne l'alpe
ti colse nebbia per la qual vedessi
non altrimenti che per pelle talpe,

come, quando i vapori umidi e spessi   4
a diradar cominciansi, la spera
del sol debilemente entra per essi;

e fia la tua imagine leggera   7
in giugnere a veder com' io rividi
lo sole in pria, che già nel corcar era.

Sì, pareggiando i miei co' passi fidi   10
del mio maestro, usci' fuor di tal nube
ai raggi morti già ne' bassi lidi.

O imaginativa che ne rube   13
talvolta sì di fuor, ch'om non s'accorge
perché dintorno suonin mille tube,

chi move te, se 'l senso non ti porge?   16
Moveti lume che nel ciel s'informa,
per sé o per voler che giù lo scorge.

De l'empiezza di lei che mutò forma   19
ne l'uccel ch'a cantar più si diletta,
ne l'imagine mia apparve l'orma;

e qui fu la mia mente sì ristretta   22
dentro da sé, che di fuor non venìa
cosa che fosse allor da lei ricetta.

Poi piovve dentro a l'alta fantasia   25
un crucifisso, dispettoso e fero
ne la sua vista, e cotal si moria;

intorno ad esso era il grande Assüero,   28
Estèr sua sposa e 'l giusto Mardoceo,
che fu al dire e al far così intero.

Remember, reader, if ever, high in
the mountains, the fog caught you, so you could see
only as moles do, looking through their skin,

how when the humid, dense vapors begin   4
to grow thinner the sphere of the sun
finds its way feebly in among them,

and your imagination will easily   7
picture how, at first, I came to see
the sun again, already going down.

So, keeping pace with my master's trusted   10
footsteps, out of a fog like that I came
when already the beams on the shore below were dead.

Oh imagination, who sometimes steal us   13
so from things outside us that we do not notice
if a thousand trumpets sound around us,

who moves you if the senses give you nothing?   16
A light moves you, in the heavens forming
by itself, or by some will that guides it downward.

Of her impious act who changed her own   19
shape to that bird's who most delights in singing
the form appeared in my imagination,

and at this my mind became so turned   22
upon itself that it took in nothing,
at the time, that came to it from outside it.

Then there rained down, in the high fantasy,   25
one who was crucified; scornful and fierce
he looked out, and so he was about to die.

Around him were the great Ahasuerus,   28
Esther his wife and Mordecai the just,
who in his words and what he did was faultless.

E come questa imagine rompeo 31
sé per sé stessa, a guisa d'una bulla
cui manca l'acqua sotto qual si feo,

surse in mia visïone una fanciulla 34
piangendo forte, e dicea: "O regina,
perché per ira hai voluto esser nulla?

Ancisa t'hai per non perder Lavina; 37
or m'hai perduta! Io son essa che lutto,
madre, a la tua pria ch'a l'altrui ruina."

Come si frange il sonno ove di butto 40
nova luce percuote il viso chiuso,
che fratto guizza pria che muoia tutto;

così l'imaginar mio cadde giuso 43
tosto che lume il volto mi percosse,
maggior assai che quel ch'è in nostro uso.

I' mi volgea per veder ov' io fosse, 46
quando una voce disse "Qui si monta,"
che da ogne altro intento mi rimosse;

e fece la mia voglia tanto pronta 49
di riguardar chi era che parlava,
che mai non posa, se non si raffronta.

Ma come al sol che nostra vista grava 52
e per soverchio sua figura vela,
così la mia virtù quivi mancava.

"Questo è divino spirito, che ne la 55
via da ir sù ne drizza sanza prego,
e col suo lume sé medesmo cela.

Sì fa con noi, come l'uom si fa sego; 58
ché quale aspetta prego e l'uopo vede,
malignamente già si mette al nego.

Or accordiamo a tanto invito il piede; 61
procacciam di salir pria che s'abbui,
ché poi non si poria, se 'l dì non riede."

And as this image broke up on its own   31
like a bubble when the water is gone
from under it, out of which it was made,

there rose into my vision a young girl weeping   34
bitterly, and she was saying, "Oh Queen,
why did your anger make you want to be nothing?

You have killed yourself not to lose Lavinia;   37
now you have lost me. I am the one, Mother,
who grieve that your ruin comes before another's."

As sleep is shattered when a sudden   40
new light strikes on the closed eyes and, though
broken, it flickers before it is all gone,

so my imagining fell away from me   43
the moment that a light greater than any
we are used to struck me in the face.

I was turning to see where I was   46
when a voice said, "The way up is here,"
recalling me from any other purpose,

and made my will full of such eagerness   49
to see who it was who had spoken,
as cannot rest until it is face to face.

But, as when the sun weighs our vision down   52
and veils its own image with excess,
so my own strength was not enough for this.

"This is a divine spirit guiding us   55
on the way upward without our asking him,
and with his own light keeping himself hidden.

He treats us as a man does his own kind,   58
for he who sees the need and waits to be asked
says 'No' already, unkindly, in his mind.

Now to such welcome let our feet comply;   61
let us try to go up before nightfall,
for we cannot, then, until the return of day."

Così disse il mio duca, e io con lui 64
volgemmo i nostri passi ad una scala;
e tosto ch'io al primo grado fui,

senti'mi presso quasi un muover d'ala 67
e ventarmi nel viso e dir: *"Beati*
pacifici, che son sanz' ira mala!"

Già eran sovra noi tanto levati 70
li ultimi raggi che la notte segue,
che le stelle apparivan da più lati.

'O virtù mia, perché sì ti dilegue?' 73
fra me stesso dicea, ché mi sentiva
la possa de le gambe posta in triegue.

Noi eravam dove più non saliva 76
la scala sù, ed eravamo affissi,
pur come nave ch'a la piaggia arriva.

E io attesi un poco, s'io udissi 79
alcuna cosa nel novo girone;
poi mi volsi al maestro mio, e dissi:

"Dolce mio padre, dì, quale offensione 82
si purga qui nel giro dove semo?
Se i piè si stanno, non stea tuo sermone."

Ed elli a me: "L'amor del bene, scemo 85
del suo dover, quiritta si ristora;
qui si ribatte il mal tardato remo.

Ma perché più aperto intendi ancora, 88
volgi la mente a me, e prenderai
alcun buon frutto di nostra dimora."

"Né creator né creatura mai," 91
cominciò el, "figliuol, fu sanza amore,
o naturale o d'animo; e tu 'l sai.

Lo naturale è sempre sanza errore, 94
ma l'altro puote errar per malo obietto
o per troppo o per poco di vigore.

So my leader said, and we turned our footsteps,   64
I along with him, toward a stairway,
and as soon as I was standing on the footstep

I felt close to me something like the moving   67
of a wing fanning my face, and heard *"Blessèd are
the peacemakers* who are without evil anger."

Already the last rays which night follows   70
had risen so far above us that the stars
were appearing on all sides around us.

"Oh my strength, why this melting away?"   73
I said in myself, feeling the force
of my legs becoming suspended.

We had come to where the stairs went no higher   76
and there we stopped, fixed, in the same way
a boat is when it arrives on the shore.

And for a little I listened, trying   79
to hear anything on the new circle;
then I turned and said to my master,

"My kind father, tell me what offense   82
is purged on the circle where we are?
Let your words not be still although our feet are."

And he to me, "The love of good which falls   85
short of what it owes is restored just here;
here the sinfully lax oar is plied again.

But in order that you may understand it   88
more clearly, turn your mind to me, so that you may
gather some good fruit from our delay.

Neither Creator nor creature ever,"   91
he began, "was without love, my son, whether
natural or of the mind, and you know this.

The natural is always without error,   94
but the other can err by choosing the wrong object
or having too much or too little vigor.

Mentre ch'elli è nel primo ben diretto,   97
e ne' secondi sé stesso misura,
esser non può cagion di mal diletto;

ma quando al mal si torce, o con più cura   100
o con men che non dee corre nel bene,
contra 'l fattore adovra sua fattura.

Quinci comprender puoi ch'esser convene   103
amor sementa in voi d'ogne virtute
e d'ogne operazion che merta pene.

Or, perché mai non può da la salute   106
amor del suo subietto volger viso,
da l'odio proprio son le cose tute;

e perché intender non si può diviso,   109
e per sé stante, alcuno esser dal primo,
da quello odiare ogne effetto è deciso.

Resta, se dividendo bene stimo,   112
che 'l mal che s'ama è del prossimo; ed esso
amor nasce in tre modi in vostro limo.

È chi, per esser suo vicin soppresso,   115
spera eccellenza, e sol per questo brama
ch'el sia di sua grandezza in basso messo;

è chi podere, grazia, onore e fama   118
teme di perder perch' altri sormonti,
onde s'attrista sì che 'l contrario ama;

ed è chi per ingiuria par ch'aonti,   121
sì che si fa de la vendetta ghiotto,
e tal convien che 'l male altrui impronti.

Questo triforme amor qua giù di sotto   124
si piange: or vo' che tu de l'altro intende,
che corre al ben con ordine corrotto.

Ciascun confusamente un bene apprende   127
nel qual si queti l'animo, e disira;
per che di giugner lui ciascun contende.

While it is turned toward the primal good,   97
controlling the secondary as it should,
it cannot be the cause of sinful pleasure,

but when it twists toward evil or pursues   100
the good with more or less zeal than it owes,
what is made labors against its maker.

Thus you can understand that love must be   103
the seed in you of every virtue and
of every act that deserves punishment.

Now, because love can never turn its face   106
from the well-being of its subject, there is
nothing that is able to hate itself.

And since a being by itself, cut off from   109
the First One, cannot be conceived,
all creatures are prevented from hating Him.

It follows, if I distinguish correctly,   112
that it is evil for the neighbor that is loved;
this love is born in three forms in your clay.

There is the one who hopes he will excel   115
by pushing down his neighbor, and for this
longs only to see him fallen from his greatness.

There is the one who fears losing power,   118
favor, honor, and fame, if surpassed by another,
which so grieves him that he loves the opposite,

and there is the one who feels such shame from   121
an insult that he turns greedy for vengeance;
such a one is impelled to plot another's harm.

For these three forms of love, they weep down there below,   124
I would have you think of the other now
which pursues the good in a corrupted way.

Everyone vaguely perceives a good   127
in which the mind may rest, and longs for it,
and so each one struggles to come to it.

Se lento amore a lui veder vi tira   130
o a lui acquistar, questa cornice,
dopo giusto penter, ve ne martira.

Altro ben è che non fa l'uom felice;   133
non è felicità, non è la buona
essenza, d'ogne ben frutto e radice.

L'amor ch'ad esso troppo s'abbandona,   136
di sovr' a noi si piange per tre cerchi;
ma come tripartito si ragiona,

tacciolo, acciò che tu per te ne cerchi."   139

If the love which draws you to see it or acquire it   130
is half-hearted, this is the terrace
that punishes you, after due repentance, for that.

There is another good that makes no one happy.   133
It is not happiness; it is not the Good
Essence, the fruit and root of every good.

The love that abandons itself to this excess   136
is wept for in three circles above us,
but as to how it is ordered in three ways

I say nothing, so you may find it for yourself."   139

CANTO XVIII

Posto avea fine al suo ragionamento
l'alto dottore, e attento guardava
ne la mia vista s'io parea contento;

e io, cui nova sete ancor frugava,   4
di fuor tacea, e dentro dicea: "Forse
lo troppo dimandar ch'io fo li grava."

Ma quel padre verace, che s'accorse   7
del timido voler che non s'apriva,
parlando, di parlare ardir mi porse.

Ond' io: "Maestro, il mio veder s'avviva   10
sì nel tuo lume, ch'io discerno chiaro
quanto la tua ragion parta o descriva.

Però ti prego, dolce padre caro,   13
che mi dimostri amore, a cui reduci
ogne buono operare e 'l suo contraro."

"Drizza," disse, "ver' me l'agute luci   16
de lo 'ntelletto, e fieti manifesto
l'error de' ciechi che si fanno duci.

L'animo, ch'è creato ad amar presto,   19
ad ogne cosa è mobile che piace,
tosto che dal piacere in atto è desto.

Vostra apprensiva da esser verace   22
tragge intenzione, e dentro a voi la spiega,
sì che l'animo ad essa volger face;

e se, rivolto, inver' di lei si piega,   25
quel piegare è amor, quell' è natura
che per piacer di novo in voi si lega.

Poi, come 'l foco movesi in altura   28
per la sua forma ch'è nata a salire
là dove più in sua matera dura,

The exalted teacher had finished his
exposition and was watching my face
carefully to see whether I was content,

and I, whom a new thirst was tormenting,   4
outwardly said nothing, and in myself,
"Maybe I annoy him with too much questioning."

But that true father, who had recognized   7
the wish too timid to disclose itself,
by speaking gave me courage to speak, myself.

So I said, "Master, my seeing is so enlivened   10
by your light that I am able to understand
clearly the outlines of your explanation.

Therefore I pray you, beloved, gentle father,   13
explain to me what love is, as you refer to it
every good action and its opposite."

"Turn toward me," he said, "the sharpened beams   16
of your intelligence, and you will see
the misleading way of the blind who say 'Follow me.'

The soul, as it is created quick to love,   19
is drawn by everything that pleases it
as soon as pleasure stirs to action in it.

Your apprehension takes from the real world   22
an image and unfolds it within you
so that it becomes what the soul turns to,

and if the soul, turned so, inclines to it,   25
that inclination is love, and it is nature,
which is bound to you every time by pleasure.

Then, as fire through its own form moves upward,   28
born as it is to rise in the very place
where it stays longest in its own matter,

così l'animo preso entra in disire,   31
ch'è moto spiritale, e mai non posa
fin che la cosa amata il fa gioire.

Or ti puote apparer quant' è nascosa   34
la veritate a la gente ch'avvera
ciascun amore in sé laudabil cosa;

però che forse appar la sua matera   37
sempre esser buona, ma non ciascun segno
è buono, ancor che buona sia la cera."

"Le tue parole e 'l mio seguace ingegno,"   40
rispuos' io lui, "m'hanno amor discoverto,
ma ciò m'ha fatto di dubbiar più pregno;

ché, s'amore è di fuori a noi offerto   43
e l'anima non va con altro piede,
se dritta o torta va, non è suo merto."

Ed elli a me: "Quanto ragion qui vede,   46
dir ti poss' io; da indi in là t'aspetta
pur a Beatrice, ch'è opra di fede.

Ogne forma sustanzïal, che setta   49
è da matera ed è con lei unita,
specifica vertute ha in sé colletta,

la qual sanza operar non è sentita,   52
né si dimostra mai che per effetto,
come per verdi fronde in pianta vita.

Però, là onde vegna lo 'ntelletto   55
de le prime notizie, omo non sape,
e de' primi appetibili l'affetto,

che sono in voi sì come studio in ape   58
di far lo mele; e questa prima voglia
merto di lode o di biasmo non cape.

Or perché a questa ogn' altra si raccoglia,   61
innata v'è la virtù che consiglia,
e de l'assenso de' tener la soglia.

so the caught soul enters into desire,   31
which is a movement of the spirit that never
rests until what it loves brings joy to it.

Now it may be apparent to you   34
how hidden the truth is from those who will tell you
that every love in itself is laudable,

perhaps because the substance of it always   37
seems to be good, but not every seal is good
merely because the wax itself is good."

"The words you said, and my mind as it followed,"   40
I answered him, "have revealed love to me
only to quicken a new question in me,

for if love is offered from outside us   43
and the soul moves with no other feet, it gets
no credit whether it goes straight or crooked."

And he to me, "As far as reason sees here   46
I can tell you; beyond that you must wait
for Beatrice alone, for faith is the fabric of it.

Every substantial form, which is at once   49
distinct from matter and united with it,
has a specific virtue stored within it

known only by its operation   52
and revealed by the effect it has,
as the green leaves reveal the life of a plant.

And so, nobody knows where they come from,   55
the understanding of the first ideas,
or the fondness for the first object of passion;

they are in you, as the need to make honey   58
is in the bee, and for this primary
urge there is no place either for praise or blame.

Now, so that every other will may be   61
caught up in this, there is a counseling virtue
in you that should guard the sill of what you agree to.

Quest' è 'l principio là onde si piglia 64
ragion di meritare in voi, secondo
che buoni e rei amori accoglie e viglia.

Color che ragionando andaro al fondo, 67
s'accorser d'esta innata libertate;
però moralità lasciaro al mondo.

Onde, poniam che di necessitate 70
surga ogne amor che dentro a voi s'accende,
di ritenerlo è in voi la podestate.

La nobile virtù Beatrice intende 73
per lo libero arbitrio, e però guarda
che l'abbi a mente, s'a parlar ten prende."

La luna, quasi a mezza notte tarda, 76
facea le stelle a noi parer più rade,
fatta com' un secchion che tuttor arda;

e correa contra 'l ciel per quelle strade 79
che 'l sole infiamma allor che quel da Roma
tra ' Sardi e ' Corsi il vede quando cade.

E quell' ombra gentil per cui si noma 82
Pietola più che villa mantoana,
del mio carcar diposta avea la soma;

per ch'io, che la ragione aperta e piana 85
sovra le mie quistioni avea ricolta,
stava com' om che sonnolento vana.

Ma questa sonnolenza mi fu tolta 88
subitamente da gente che dopo
le nostre spalle a noi era già volta.

E quale Ismeno già vide e Asopo 91
lungo di sé di notte furia e calca,
pur che i Teban di Bacco avesser uopo,

cotal per quel giron suo passo falca, 94
per quel ch'io vidi di color, venendo,
cui buon volere e giusto amor cavalca.

This is the principle in which one finds 64
the ground of merit in you, as it gathers
and sifts the good loves from the evil ones.

Those whose thought went into the deepest places 67
were aware of this innate liberty,
so they left the world rules of morality.

If we admit, then, that every love lit 70
in you rises from necessity,
within you is the power to restrain it.

That noble faculty is what Beatrice 73
means by free will; and so be sure to have it
in mind if she should speak to you about it."

The moon, late almost to midnight, taking 76
the form of a brazier, all of it glowing,
made the stars appear scarcer to us,

and ran against the sky along that track 79
which the sun sets alight when from Rome one sees it
go down between Sardinians and Corsicans,

and that noble shade who has made Pietola 82
be mentioned more often than any Mantuan town
had taken the burden I gave him and laid it down,

so that I who had gathered his clear and open 85
discourse in answer to my questions
wandered in thought like someone half-awake.

But this drifting toward sleep was snatched away 88
from me suddenly by people coming around
in back of us who had reached us from behind.

And as the Ismenus and the Asopus saw 91
the crowds and frenzy on their banks long ago
whenever the Thebans felt a need for Bacchus,

so, bending their course around the circle, 94
those came crowding who I could see were ridden
by the right kind of love and a good will.

Tosto fur sovr' a noi, perché correndo 97
si movea tutta quella turba magna;
e due dinanzi gridavan piangendo:

"Maria corse con fretta a la montagna"; 100
e: "Cesare, per soggiogare Ilerda,
punse Marsilia e poi corse in Ispagna."

"Ratto, ratto, che 'l tempo non si perda 103
per poco amor," gridavan li altri appresso,
"che studio di ben far grazia rinverda."

"O gente in cui fervore aguto adesso 106
ricompie forse negligenza e indugio
da voi per tepidezza in ben far messo,

questi che vive, e certo i' non vi bugio, 109
vuole andar sù, pur che 'l sol ne riluca;
però ne dite ond' è presso il pertugio."

Parole furon queste del mio duca; 112
e un di quelli spirti disse: "Vieni
di retro a noi, e troverai la buca.

Noi siam di voglia a muoverci sì pieni, 115
che restar non potem; però perdona,
se villania nostra giustizia tieni.

Io fui abate in San Zeno a Verona 118
sotto lo 'mperio del buon Barbarossa,
di cui dolente ancor Milan ragiona.

E tale ha già l'un piè dentro la fossa, 121
che tosto piangerà quel monastero,
e tristo fia d'avere avuta possa;

perché suo figlio, mal del corpo intero, 124
e de la mente peggio, e che mal nacque,
ha posto in loco di suo pastor vero."

Io non so se più disse o s'ei si tacque, 127
tant' era già di là da noi trascorso;
ma questo intesi, e ritener mi piacque.

They were soon upon us, because that   97
great crowd, all of it, was moved by their running,
and the two that were in front, in tears, cried out,

"Mary ran, hurrying to the mountain,"   100
and "Caesar, to subjugate Lerida,
struck at Marseille and then rushed on to Spain."

"Hurry, hurry, for fear of losing   103
time through lack of love," those behind were calling;
"zeal in doing right may make grace green again."

"Oh people in whom a whetted fervor now   106
repays, perhaps, negligence, and delay
that you made once, doing good half-heartedly,

this man who is alive—I am not lying—   109
wants to go up when the sun lights us again;
tell us where is the nearest opening."

These were my leader's words, and one of those   112
spirits said, "Come along behind us
and you will find where the opening is.

We are so full of the desire to be   115
moving that we cannot stop, so pardon us
if our penance seems like discourtesy.

I was the Abbot of San Zeno in   118
Verona, under the good Barbarossa,
whom they talk of, still grieving, in Milan.

And one with one foot in the grave already   121
soon will be weeping over that monastery,
sorry that it was ever in his power,

because he put his son, deformed in his   124
entire body, worse in his mind, and his
birth shameful, in place of its true shepherd."

I do not know whether he said more or not,   127
he had already run past us so far,
but this I heard and was glad to remember.

E quei che m'era ad ogne uopo soccorso   130
disse: "Volgiti qua: vedine due
venir dando a l'accidïa di morso."

Di retro a tutti dicean: "Prima fue   133
morta la gente a cui il mar s'aperse,
che vedesse Iordan le rede sue."

E: "Quella che l'affanno non sofferse   136
fino a la fine col figlio d'Anchise,
sé stessa a vita sanza gloria offerse."

Poi quando fuor da noi tanto divise   139
quell' ombre, che veder più non potiersi,
novo pensiero dentro a me si mise,

del qual più altri nacquero e diversi;   142
e tanto d'uno in altro vaneggiai,
che li occhi per vaghezza ricopersi,

e 'l pensamento in sogno trasmutai.   145

And he who helped in every need of mine
said, "Turn around here; see, there are two of them
who are biting down on sloth as they come."

130

Behind all the others they were saying, "Those
people for whom the sea parted were dead
before Jordan saw those who would inherit it."

133

And "Those who did not struggle the whole way
to the end, laboring with Anchises' son,
gave themselves up to a life without glory."

136

Then when those shades had gone so far away
from us that we could not see them any more,
a new thought took up its place in me

139

from which others of several kinds were born
and I wandered so from one to another of them
that my eyes hazed over and I closed them

142

and transformed what I was thinking into a dream.

145

CANTO XIX

Ne l'ora che non può 'l calor dïurno
intepidar più 'l freddo de la luna,
vinto da terra, e talor da Saturno

—quando i geomanti lor Maggior Fortuna   4
veggiono in orïente, innanzi a l'alba,
surger per via che poco le sta bruna—,

mi venne in sogno una femmina balba,   7
ne li occhi guercia, e sovra i piè distorta,
con le man monche, e di colore scialba.

Io la mirava; e come 'l sol conforta   10
le fredde membra che la notte aggrava,
così lo sguardo mio le facea scorta

la lingua, e poscia tutta la drizzava   13
in poco d'ora, e lo smarrito volto,
com' amor vuol, così le colorava.

Poi ch'ell' avea 'l parlar così disciolto,   16
cominciava a cantar sì, che con pena
da lei avrei mio intento rivolto.

"Io son," cantava, "io son dolce serena,   19
che' marinari in mezzo mar dismago;
tanto son di piacere a sentir piena!

Io volsi Ulisse del suo cammin vago   22
al canto mio; e qual meco s'ausa,
rado sen parte; sì tutto l'appago!"

Ancor non era sua bocca richiusa,   25
quand' una donna apparve santa e presta
lunghesso me per far colei confusa.

"O Virgilio, Virgilio, chi è questa?"   28
fieramente dicea; ed el venìa
con li occhi fitti pur in quella onesta.

At the hour when the heat of the day can warm
the cold of the moon no longer, overcome
by the earth, and now and then by Saturn,

when the geomancers see their *Major Fortune*   4
rise in the east before the dawn, along
a path that stays dark for it not for long,

there came to me in a dream a stammering   7
woman, cross-eyed, and her feet were crooked,
her hands mangled, and her color faded.

I looked at her, and as the sun revives   10
life in the cold limbs the night has deadened,
so that look of mine upon her loosened

her tongue, and then in a short time straightened   13
all that was twisted in her, and gave her color
to make her look as love would want to see her.

After speech thus had been set free in her   16
she began to sing, so that it would have been
hard for me to have turned my mind from her.

"I am," she sang, "I am the sweet siren   19
who lures sailors astray out on the sea
so full of pleasure they are when they hear me.

I turned Ulysses from his wandering course   22
with my singing, and he leaves me seldom
who is at home with me, so wholly I satisfy him."

She had not yet closed her mouth when beside her   25
appeared a watchful and holy lady
to put confusion in that other one.

"Oh Virgil, oh Virgil," she said in anger,   28
"who is this?" And he came, his eyes never
moving away from that truthful figure.

L'altra prendea, e dinanzi l'apria   31
fendendo i drappi, e mostravami 'l ventre;
quel mi svegliò col puzzo che n'uscia.

Io mossi li occhi, e 'l buon maestro: "Almen tre   34
voci t'ho messe!" dicea, "Surgi e vieni;
troviam l'aperta per la qual tu entre."

Sù mi levai, e tutti eran già pieni   37
de l'alto dì i giron del sacro monte,
e andavam col sol novo a le reni.

Seguendo lui, portava la mia fronte   40
come colui che l'ha di pensier carca,
che fa di sé un mezzo arco di ponte;

quand' io udi' "Venite; qui si varca"   43
parlare in modo soave e benigno,
qual non si sente in questa mortal marca.

Con l'ali aperte, che parean di cigno,   46
volseci in sù colui che sì parlonne
tra due pareti del duro macigno.

Mosse le penne poi e ventilonne,   49
"Qui lugent" affermando esser beati,
ch'avran di consolar l'anime donne.

"Che hai che pur inver' la terra guati?"   52
la guida mia incominciò a dirmi,
poco amendue da l'angel sormontati.

E io: "Con tanta sospeccion fa irmi   55
novella visïon ch'a sé mi piega,
sì ch'io non posso dal pensar partirmi."

"Vedesti," disse, "quell'antica strega   58
che sola sovr' a noi omai si piagne;
vedesti come l'uom da lei si slega.

Bastiti, e batti a terra le calcagne;   61
li occhi rivolgi al logoro che gira
lo rege etterno con le rote magne."

He took hold of the other, tearing what she wore   *31*
to open her in front and show me her belly,
and the stench that came out of it wakened me.

I turned to look, and "I have called you   *34*
at least three times," the good master said. "Rise and come.
Let us find the opening for you to go through."

I drew myself up, and on the mountain   *37*
all the circles were full of the high day,
and as we walked we had on our backs the new sun.

Following him, I bore my brow as he   *40*
does who has it weighed down with thought, making
half the arch of a bridge with his body,

when I heard, "Come. You can go through here,"   *43*
spoken in such a kind and gentle manner
as in this mortal bourn we never hear.

With wings that looked like the wings of a swan,   *46*
open, he who thus spoke to us had us turn
upward between two walls of the hard stone.

Then he moved the wings, stirring the air to us,   *49*
affirming that they are blessed who mourn,
for their souls shall have gentle consolation.

"What is it that makes you keep your eyes down   *52*
on the ground?" my guide began to say to me when
we had both climbed a little above the angel.

And I, "A strange vision is folding me   *55*
into itself, and makes me walk so cautiously
because I cannot take my mind from it."

"Did you see," he said, "that ancient witch, because   *58*
of whom alone they weep still, there above us?
Did you see how a man can free himself from her?

Let that be enough for you, and let your heels   *61*
strike the earth and your eyes return to the lure
which the Eternal King spins in the great wheels."

Quale 'l falcon, che prima a' piè si mira,   64
indi si volge al grido e si protende
per lo disio del pasto che là il tira,

tal mi fec' io; e tal, quanto si fende   67
la roccia per dar via a chi va suso,
n'andai infin dove 'l cerchiar si prende.

Com' io nel quinto giro fui dischiuso,   70
vidi gente per esso che piangea,
giacendo a terra tutta volta in giuso.

"Adhaesit pavimento anima mea"   73
sentia dir lor con sì alti sospiri,
che la parola a pena s'intendea.

"O eletti di Dio, li cui soffriri   76
e giustizia e speranza fa men duri,
drizzate noi verso li alti saliri."

"Se voi venite dal giacer sicuri,   79
e volete trovar la via più tosto,
le vostre destre sien sempre di fori."

Così pregò 'l poeta, e sì risposto   82
poco dinanzi a noi ne fu; per ch'io
nel parlare avvisai l'altro nascosto,

e volsi li occhi a li occhi al segnor mio: 85
ond'elli m'assentì con lieto cenno
ciò che chiedea la vista del disio.

Poi ch'io potei di me fare a mio senno,   88
trassimi sovra quella creatura
le cui parole pria notar mi fenno,

dicendo: "Spirto in cui pianger matura   91
quel sanza 'l quale a Dio tornar non pòssi,
sosta un poco per me tua maggior cura.

Chi fosti e perché vòlti avete i dossi   94
al sù, mi dì, e se vuo' ch'io t'impetri
cosa di là ond' io vivendo mossi."

Like the falcon that stares toward his feet before 64
he turns at the call and reaches forward
in his desire for the food that draws him there,

so I became, and so I went, as far 67
as the split in the rock that opens a way,
for whoever climbs, to where one starts around.

When I came out into the open 70
on the fifth circle I saw people lying
along it, all turned down to the ground, and weeping.

"*My soul holds on hard to the trodden dirt,*" 73
I heard them saying with such heavy sighs
that I could scarcely understand a word.

"Oh you whom God has chosen, so that hope 76
and justice make your sufferings less hard,
tell us where to find the steps that lead upward."

"If you have come here and do not have to lie here 79
and want to find the way most quickly, keep
your right hand toward the outside the whole time."

So the poet asked, and the answer came 82
from a little ahead of us, so that from
the words I made out the other who was hidden,

and turned my eyes toward the eyes of my lord, 85
whereon he gave a sign, assenting with pleasure
to what the craving in my look had asked for.

Then when I was free to act as I wished to 88
I drew myself to above that creature
whose words had made me take note of him before,

and said, "Spirit in whom weeping ripens 91
that without which there can be no return
to God, stay one moment, for me, your greater concern.

Who were you and why do you have your backs turned 94
upward, tell me, and whether you would have
me obtain something for you there where I came from, alive."

Ed elli a me: "Perché i nostri diretri 97
rivolga il cielo a sé, saprai; ma prima
scias quod ego fui successor Petri.

Intra Sïestri e Chiaveri s'adima 100
una fiumana bella, e del suo nome
lo titol del mio sangue fa sua cima.

Un mese e poco più prova' io come 103
pesa il gran manto a chi dal fango il guarda,
che piuma sembran tutte l'altre some.

La mia conversïone, omè! fu tarda; 106
ma, come fatto fui roman pastore,
così scopersi la vita bugiarda.

Vidi che lì non s'acquetava il core, 109
né più salir potiesi in quella vita;
per che di questa in me s'accese amore.

Fino a quel punto misera e partita 112
da Dio anima fui, del tutto avara;
or, come vedi, qui ne son punita.

Quel ch'avarizia fa, qui si dichiara 115
in purgazion de l'anime converse;
e nulla pena il monte ha più amara.

Sì come l'occhio nostro non s'aderse 118
in alto, fisso a le cose terrene,
così giustizia qui a terra il merse.

Come avarizia spense a ciascun bene 121
lo nostro amore, onde operar perdési,
così giustizia qui stretti ne tene,

ne' piedi e ne le man legati e presi; 124
e quanto fia piacer del giusto Sire,
tanto staremo immobili e distesi."

Io m'era inginocchiato e volea dire; 127
ma com' io cominciai ed el s'accorse,
solo ascoltando, del mio reverire,

And he to me, "Why Heaven turns our   97
backs to it you will know, but before that
know that I was a successor to Peter.

There flows between Siestri and Chiavari   100
a fair river, and the title of my
blood makes its crest from that current's name.

One month, barely more, I proved how heavy weighs   103
the great mantle on him who saves it from the mire,
making all other burdens seem a feather.

My conversion, alas, came late, but I was   106
made a shepherd of Rome, and it was then
that I was able to see the falseness in life.

I saw that the heart was not at rest there,   109
nor was it able, in that life, to rise;
that was what lit in me the love of this.

Until that moment I had been a soul   112
all greed: wretched and separate from God.
Now, as you see, here I am punished for it.

What avarice does is enacted here   115
for the purging of the souls that are turned over,
and no pain on the mountain is more bitter.

Just as our eyes fastened upon the things   118
of earth without looking above them, so
justice holds them here on the earth below.

As avarice put out the love we had   121
of every good, so that all that we did
was lost, so here justice holds us tight,

our feet and hands bound and imprisoned, and   124
we shall stay outstretched and without moving here
as long as it may please the just Sire."

I had knelt down and wanted to speak, but as   127
I began, and he understood, only from
listening, the reverence I did him,

"Qual cagion," disse, "in giù così ti torse?"   130
E io a lui: "Per vostra dignitate
mia cosc**ï**enza dritto mi rimorse."

"Drizza le gambe, lèvati sù, frate!"   133
rispuose; "non errar: conservo sono
teco e con li altri ad una podestate.

Se mai quel santo evangelico suono   136
che dice 'Neque nubent' intendesti,
ben puoi veder perch' io così ragiono.

Vattene omai: non vo' che più t'arresti;   139
ché la tua stanza mio pianger disagia,
col qual maturo ciò che tu dicesti.

Nepote ho io di là c'ha nome Alagia,   142
buona da sé, pur che la nostra casa
non faccia lei per essempro malvagia;

e questa sola di là m'è rimasa."   145

"Why," he said, "have you bent down like that?"   130
And I to him, "Because of your dignity,
as I was standing, my conscience stung me."

"Straighten your legs and stand up, brother,"   133
he answered. "Do not be mistaken. I am,
with you and others, a servant of one power.

If ever you have understood that holy   136
phrase of the Gospel 'They neither marry . . .'
you will see plainly why I speak as I do.

Now go your way. I would have you stay no longer,   139
because your staying interrupts my weeping,
by which I ripen what you spoke of before.

I have a niece back there named Alagia;   142
good in herself, if only by example
our household does not make her evil,

and she is all that remains to me there."   145

CANTO XX

Contra miglior voler voler mal pugna;
onde contra 'l piacer mio, per piacerli,
trassi de l'acqua non sazia la spugna.

Mossimi; e 'l duca mio si mosse per li   4
luoghi spediti pur lungo la roccia,
come si va per muro stretto a' merli;

ché la gente che fonde a goccia a goccia   7
per li occhi il mal che tutto 'l mondo occupa,
da l'altra parte in fuor troppo s'approccia.

Maladetta sie tu, antica lupa,   10
che più che tutte l'altre bestie hai preda
per la tua fame sanza fine cupa!

O ciel, nel cui girar par che si creda   13
le condizion di qua giù trasmutarsi,
quando verrà per cui questa disceda?

Noi andavam con passi lenti e scarsi,   16
e io attento a l'ombre, ch'i' sentia
pietosamente piangere e lagnarsi;

e per ventura udi' "Dolce Maria!"   19
dinanzi a noi chiamar così nel pianto
come fa donna che in parturir sia;

e seguitar: "Povera fosti tanto,   22
quanto veder si può per quello ospizio
dove sponesti il tuo portato santo."

Seguentemente intesi: "O buon Fabrizio,   25
con povertà volesti anzi virtute
che gran ricchezza posseder con vizio."

Queste parole m'eran sì piaciute,   28
ch'io mi trassi oltre per aver contezza
di quello spirto onde parean venute.

Against a better will the will fights poorly,
so to please him, against my own pleasure, I
drew the sponge, not yet full, from the water.

I went on, and my leader went, stepping
in the empty places along the rock, as one
walks along a wall close to the battlements,

for the people who pour from their eyes, drop by drop,
the evil with which the whole world is filled
were too close to the edge on the other side.

A curse light on you, ancient she-wolf, who have
preyed upon more beasts than any other,
for the bottomless deep of your hunger.

Oh heaven, from whose wheeling we can see,
it seems, conditions changing here below,
when will he come, before whom she will flee?

We went on with slow and frugal steps, and I
was intent upon the shades, listening
to their piteous weeping and lamenting,

and by chance I heard someone ahead of us
call out through his tears "Sweet Mary," as
a woman does when she is in labor,

and then go on, "How poor you were we can see
when we think of that hostelry
in which you laid your holy burden down!"

And following that I heard, "Oh good Fabrizio,
you chose to possess virtue with poverty
instead of great wealth with iniquity."

These words gave me such pleasure that I
pressed forward to learn anything that I
could of that spirit from whom they seemed to come.

4

7

10

13

16

19

22

25

28

Esso parlava ancor de la larghezza
che fece Niccolò a le pulcelle,
per condurre ad onor lor giovinezza.

31

"O anima che tanto ben favelle,
dimmi chi fosti," dissi, "e perché sola
tu queste degne lode rinovelle.

34

Non fia sanza mercé la tua parola,
s'io ritorno a compiér lo cammin corto
di quella vita ch'al termine vola."

37

Ed elli: "Io ti dirò, non per conforto
ch'io attenda di là, ma perché tanta
grazia in te luce prima che sie morto.

40

Io fui radice de la mala pianta
che la terra cristiana tutta aduggia,
sì che buon frutto rado se ne schianta.

43

Ma se Doagio, Lilla, Guanto e Bruggia
potesser, tosto ne saria vendetta;
e io la cheggio a lui che tutto giuggia.

46

Chiamato fui di là Ugo Ciappetta;
di me son nati i Filippi e i Luigi
per cui novellamente è Francia retta.

49

Figliuol fu' io d'un beccaio di Parigi:
quando li regi antichi venner meno
tutti, fuor ch'un renduto in panni bigi,

52

trova'mi stretto ne le mani il freno
del governo del regno, e tanta possa
di nuovo acquisto, e sì d'amici pieno,

55

ch'a la corona vedova promossa
la testa di mio figlio fu, dal quale
cominciar di costor le sacrate ossa.

58

Mentre che la gran dota provenzale
al sangue mio non tolse la vergogna,
poco valea, ma pur non facea male.

61

He went on to tell of the munificence   31
that Nicholas displayed toward the virgins
to lead their youth in the way of honor.

"Oh soul who talk about such goodness, tell me   34
who you were, and why it is that only
you restore this praise to what it should be.

Your words will not go unrewarded   37
if I return to finish the short road
of this life that flies on to its end."

And he, "I will tell you, not for any solace   40
I expect from there, but because such grace
is shining in you before you are dead.

I was the root of the evil plant   43
that overshadows the whole Christian land
so that good fruit is seldom gathered there.

But if Douai, Lille, Ghent, and Bruges could do it,   46
vengeance would soon descend upon it;
I beg this of Him who judges everything.

Back there my name was Hugh Capet. From me   49
are descended all the Philips and Louis
by whom France has been ruled recently.

I was the son of a Parisian butcher.   52
When all the ancient kings were gone but one
who was a monk with a gray garment on,

I found the reins that govern the kingdom   55
tight in my hands, and so much power, come
to so quickly, and so many friends

that the head of my son was raised up into   58
the widowed crown, and with him begins
the tracing of their consecrated bones.

As long as the great dowry of Provence   61
had not deprived my bloom of any sense
of shame, it came to little, yet did no harm.

Lì cominciò con forza e con menzogna   64
la sua rapina; e poscia, per ammenda,
Pontì e Normandia prese e Guascogna.

Carlo venne in Italia e, per ammenda,   67
vittima fé di Curradino; e poi
ripinse al ciel Tommaso, per ammenda.

Tempo vegg' io, non molto dopo ancoi,   70
che tragge un altro Carlo fuor di Francia,
per far conoscer meglio e sé e' suoi.

Sanz' arme n'esce e solo con la lancia   73
con la qual giostrò Giuda, e quella ponta
sì, ch'a Fiorenza fa scoppiar la pancia.

Quindi non terra, ma peccato e onta   76
guadagnerà, per sé tanto più grave,
quanto più lieve simil danno conta.

L'altro, che già uscì preso di nave,   79
veggio vender sua figlia e patteggiarne
come fanno i corsar de l'altre schiave.

O avarizia, che puoi tu più farne,   82
poscia c'ha' il mio sangue a te sì tratto,
che non si cura de la propria carne?

Perché men paia il mal futuro e 'l fatto,   85
veggio in Alagna intrar lo fiordaliso,
e nel vicario suo Cristo esser catto.

Veggiolo un'altra volta esser deriso;   88
veggio rinovellar l'aceto e 'l fiele,
e tra vivi ladroni esser anciso.

Veggio il novo Pilato sì crudele,   91
che ciò nol sazia, ma sanza decreto
porta nel Tempio le cupide vele.

O Segnor mio, quando sarò io lieto   94
a veder la vendetta che, nascosa,
fa dolce l'ira tua nel tuo secreto?

Then by force and falsehood it began its   64
plunder, and afterward, for amends, it
seized Ponthieu and Normandy and Gascony.

Charles came into Italy and, for amends,   67
made Conradin a victim, and after that
sent Thomas back to heaven, for amends.

I see a time not many days from this one   70
that will bring forth another Charles from France
to make both himself and his people better known.

He comes forth without arms except the lance   73
that Judas jousted with, but he levels it
so that it splits open the paunch of Florence.

He will gain by this no land, but sin and shame,   76
which will weigh upon him more heavily
the more he treats such evildoing lightly.

The other who left a ship as a prisoner   79
I see selling his daughter, haggling over her
as corsairs do over their women slaves.

Oh Avarice, what more harm to us can you do,   82
now you have drawn my blood so close to you
it cares not for its own flesh any more?

To make past and future evils appear   85
smaller, I see the fleur-de-lys enter
Anagni, and Christ imprisoned in His vicar.

I see him being mocked a second time;   88
I see the vinegar and the gall renewed,
and between living thieves I see them kill Him.

I see the new Pilate, so cruel   91
that this is not enough, without consent sail
his greedy sails into the Temple.

Oh my Lord, when will I know the joy   94
of beholding that vengeance which, from hiding,
sweetens your anger in its secrecy?

Ciò ch'io dicea di quell' unica sposa 97
de lo Spirito Santo e che ti fece
verso me volger per alcuna chiosa,

tanto è risposto a tutte nostre prece 100
quanto 'l dì dura; ma com' el s'annotta,
contrario suon prendemo in quella vece.

Noi repetiam Pigmalïon allotta, 103
cui traditore e ladro e paricida
fece la voglia sua de l'oro ghiotta;

e la miseria de l'avaro Mida, 106
che seguì a la sua dimanda gorda,
per la qual sempre convien che si rida.

Del folle Acàn ciascun poi si ricorda, 109
come furò le spoglie, sì che l'ira
di Iosüè qui par ch'ancor lo morda.

Indi accusiam col marito Saffira; 112
lodiamo i calci ch'ebbe Elïodoro;
e in infamia tutto 'l monte gira

Polinestòr ch'ancise Polidoro; 115
ultimamente ci si grida: 'Crasso,
dilci, che 'l sai: di che sapore è l'oro?'

Talor parla l'uno alto e l'altro basso, 118
secondo l'affezion ch'ad ir ci sprona
ora a maggiore e ora a minor passo:

però al ben che 'l dì ci si ragiona, 121
dianzi non era io sol; ma qui da presso
non alzava la voce altra persona."

Noi eravam partiti già da esso, 124
e brigavam di soverchiar la strada
tanto quanto al poder n'era permesso,

quand' io senti', come cosa che cada, 127
tremar lo monte; onde mi prese un gelo
qual prender suol colui ch'a morte vada.

What I was saying about that only 97
bride of the Holy Ghost, which made you turn
to me for some further commentary,

is the answer to all our prayers as long 100
as the day lasts, but when the night is come
we take up in its stead a countertheme.

At that time we recall Pygmalion, 103
whom the gluttonous desire for gold made
a traitor, a thief, and a parricide,

and the misery of avaricious Midas, 106
sequel to his insatiable wish
which will always be worth laughing at.

Then each recalls the folly of Achan, 109
how he stole the spoils so that the anger
of Joshua seems to bite him again.

Then we accuse Sapphira and her husband, 112
we praise the kicks that caught Heliodorus
and around the mountain circles the infamous

name of Polymestor, who killed Polydorus. 115
Finally the cry is 'Tell us, Crassus,
since you know it, what does gold taste of?'

One talks loudly and another softly, 118
according to the feeling that drives us
now with more urgency and now with less.

So, talking of goodness in the daytime, 121
as we do here, I was not alone before,
but no one else raised a voice so near."

We had moved beyond him by that time, and 124
were pressing on our way, trying to go
forward as fast as we were able to,

when I felt, as though it were something falling, 127
the mountain shake, and at that I was seized with
such a chill as one feels on the way to death.

Certo non si scoteo sì forte Delo,   130
pria che Latona in lei facesse 'l nido
a parturir li due occhi del cielo.

Poi cominciò da tutte parti un grido   133
tal, che 'l maestro inverso me si feo,
dicendo: "Non dubbiar, mentr' io ti guido."

"Glorïa in excelsis" tutti *"Deo"*   136
dicean, per quel ch'io da' vicin compresi,
onde intender lo grido si poteo.

No' istavamo immobili e sospesi   139
come i pastor che prima udir quel canto,
fin che 'l tremar cessò ed el compiési.

Poi ripigliammo nostro cammin santo,   142
guardando l'ombre che giacean per terra,
tornate già in su l'usato pianto.

Nulla ignoranza mai con tanta guerra   145
mi fé desideroso di sapere,
se la memoria mia in ciò non erra,

quanta pareami allor, pensando, avere;   148
né per la fretta dimandare er' oso,
né per me lì potea cosa vedere:

così m'andava timido e pensoso.   151

Surely Delos was not so shaken 130
before Latona made her nest in it
to give birth to the two eyes of Heaven.

Then on all sides such a shouting began 133
that my master drew close to me and said,
"Do not be afraid as long as I am your guide."

"Glory to God in the highest" was what they 136
were all saying, as I could tell where the cry
could be understood, from those closest to me.

We stood in suspense, and not moving, 139
as the shepherds did who first heard that song,
until the quaking was finished and the singing.

Then we set out on our sacred way again, 142
looking, along the ground, at the shades lying
already returned to their constant weeping.

Never did ignorance arouse in me 145
so vehement an urge to know, if my
memory in this does not mislead me,

as I felt at that moment in my mind, 148
nor because of our haste did I then dare
ask, nor could I myself see a thing there,

so I went on, timid and sunk in thought. 151

CANTO XXI

La sete natural che mai non sazia
se non con l'acqua onde la femminetta
samaritana domandò la grazia,

mi travagliava, e pungeami la fretta   4
per la 'mpacciata via dietro al mio duca,
e condoleami a la giusta vendetta.

Ed ecco, sì come ne scrive Luca   7
che Cristo apparve a' due ch'erano in via,
giù surto fuor de la sepulcral buca,

ci apparve un'ombra, e dietro a noi venìa,   10
dal piè guardando la turba che giace;
né ci addemmo di lei, sì parlò pria,

dicendo: "O frati miei, Dio vi dea pace."   13
Noi ci volgemmo sùbiti, e Virgilio
rendéli 'l cenno ch'a ciò si conface.

Poi cominciò: "Nel beato concilio   16
ti ponga in pace la verace corte
che me rilega ne l'etterno essilio."

"Come!" diss' elli, e parte andavam forte: 19
"se voi siete ombre che Dio sù non degni,
chi v'ha per la sua scala tanto scorte?"

E 'l dottor mio: "Se tu riguardi a' segni   22
che questi porta e che l'angel profila,
ben vedrai che coi buon convien ch'e' regni.

Ma perché lei che dì e notte fila   25
non li avea tratta ancora la conocchia
che Cloto impone a ciascuno e compila,

l'anima sua, ch'è tua e mia serocchia,   28
venendo sù, non potea venir sola,
però ch'al nostro modo non adocchia.

The natural thirst which is never satisfied
but by that water whose grace the poor woman
of Samaria begged to be given

tormented me, and our haste was driving me 4
after my leader along the crowded way,
grieving over the just retribution,

and there, as Christ, after he had risen 7
from his tomb in the cave, appeared to those
two on their way, as Luke writes for us,

a shade appeared that from behind us had come 10
while we were watching the crowd lying at our feet,
and until he spoke we did not notice him,

and he said, "Oh, my brothers, may God give you peace." 13
We turned at once and Virgil gave the sign
that was the answer to his salutation.

And then began, "May the true court that holds me 16
in everlasting exile convey
you in peace to the blessed assembly."

"How is that?" he said as we hurried on. "If you 19
are shades God has judged unworthy to be
above, who has brought you this far on His stairway?"

And my teacher said, "If you look at the marks 22
this one bears, which the angel printed,
you will see plainly that he must reign with the good.

But since she who spins day and night had not 25
drawn off the spun thread from the distaff yet
which Clotho settles there for everyone

his soul, which is a sister of yours and mine, 28
could not come on its way up here alone,
because it does not see things in our manner.

Ond' io fui tratto fuor de l'ampia gola   31
d'inferno per mostrarli, e mosterrolli
oltre, quanto 'l potrà menar mia scola.

Ma dimmi, se tu sai, perché tai crolli   34
diè dianzi 'l monte, e perché tutto ad una
parve gridare infino a' suoi piè molli."

Sì mi diè, dimandando, per la cruna   37
del mio disio, che pur con la speranza
si fece la mia sete men digiuna.

Quei cominciò: "Cosa non è che sanza   40
ordine senta la religïone
de la montagna, o che sia fuor d'usanza.

Libero è qui da ogne alterazione: 43
di quel che 'l ciel da sé in sé riceve
esser ci puote, e non d'altro, cagione.

Per che non pioggia, non grando, non neve,   46
non rugiada, non brina più sù cade
che la scaletta di tre gradi breve;

nuvole spesse non paion né rade,   49
né coruscar, né figlia di Taumante,
che di là cangia sovente contrade;

secco vapor non surge più avante   52
ch'al sommo d'i tre gradi ch'io parlai,
dov' ha 'l vicario di Pietro le piante.

Trema forse più giù poco o assai;   55
ma per vento che 'n terra si nasconda,
non so come, qua sù non tremò mai.

Tremaci quando alcuna anima monda   58
sentesi, sì che surga o che si mova
per salir sù; e tal grido seconda.

De la mondizia sol voler fa prova,   61
che, tutto libero a mutar convento,
l'alma sorprende, e di voler le giova.

And so I was brought forth out of the wide
throat of Hell to guide him, and will be his guide
as far onward as my school can lead him.

31

But tell me, if you know, why the mountain
shook so just now, and why everyone
down to its wet base seemed to shout at once."

34

With his question he threaded the needle
of my desire so that with hope alone
he made my thirst less fierce than it had been.

37

That one began, "The rule that binds the mountain
allows nothing that is without order
or that departs from the way things are done here.

40

This place is free from every kind of change.
Only what Heaven from itself takes into
itself can be the cause of anything.

43

And so it does not rain nor snow nor hail;
dew never forms; the hoar frost does not fall
above the small stairs with the three short steps;

46

clouds, heavy or thin, are never seen,
nor flashes of lightning, nor Thaumas's daughter
who keeps moving from place to place, back there;

49

dry vapor does not come up any farther
than the three steps that I spoke of before
upon which Peter's vicar rests his feet.

52

It may quake slightly, or heavily, down below there,
but, I do not know how, the wind that is hidden
in the earth never made it quake up here.

55

It quakes here when a soul feels that it has
become pure so that it may rise or start
on the way up, and then that shout follows.

58

The will alone is the proof of its purity,
taking the soul by surprise when it is wholly
free to change its convent, and giving it the will to.

61

Prima vuol ben, ma non lascia il talento 64
che divina giustizia, contra voglia,
come fu al peccar, pone al tormento.

E io, che son giaciuto a questa doglia 67
cinquecent' anni e più, pur mo sentii
libera volontà di miglior soglia:

però sentisti il tremoto e li pii 70
spiriti per lo monte render lode
a quel Segnor, che tosto sù li 'nvii."

Così ne disse; e però ch'el si gode 73
tanto del ber quant' è grande la sete,
non saprei dir quant' el mi fece prode.

E 'l savio duca: "Omai veggio la rete 76
che qui vi 'mpiglia e come si scalappia,
perché ci trema e di che congaudete.

Ora chi fosti, piacciati ch'io sappia, 79
e perché tanti secoli giaciuto
qui se,' ne le parole tue mi cappia."

"Nel tempo che 'l buon Tito, con l'aiuto 82
del sommo rege, vendicò le fóra
ond' uscì 'l sangue per Giuda venduto,

col nome che più dura e più onora 85
era io di là," rispuose quello spirto,
"famoso assai, ma non con fede ancora.

Tanto fu dolce mio vocale spirto, 88
che, tolosano, a sé mi trasse Roma,
dove mertai le tempie ornar di mirto.

Stazio la gente ancor di là mi noma: 91
cantai di Tebe, e poi del grande Achille;
ma caddi in via con la seconda soma.

Al mio ardor fuor seme le faville, 94
che mi scaldar, de la divina fiamma
onde sono allumati più di mille;

It had so willed before, but against that will   64
its desire would not consent, which the divine
justice had turned toward the torment, as once toward the sin.

And I, who have been lying in this pain   67
five hundred years and more, only now felt
freedom of will for a better threshold,

which is why you felt the earthquake and heard   70
the devout spirits praising that Lord
all around the mountain—may He soon send them above!"

So he spoke to us, and as the pleasure   73
of the drink is greater when the thirst is greater,
I cannot describe the good he did me.

And the wise leader: "Now I see the net   76
that snares you here, and how it is untangled,
why it quakes here and what you celebrate.

Now may I know who you were, if you please,   79
and from your own words gather the reason
why you lay there so many centuries?"

"In the time when the good Titus, aided   82
by the highest king, avenged the wounds
from which the blood that Judas sold had bled,

I bore the name there that lasts longest," that spirit   85
answered, "and that bears most honor with it;
I was famous indeed, yet was without the faith.

So sweet was the spirit of song in me   88
that from Toulouse, my home, Rome summoned me
and thought my brows worthy to be adorned with myrtle.

People still know me there by the name of Statius.   91
I sang of Thebes, and then of great Achilles,
but fell on the way with the second burden.

The sparks that sowed that ardor in me came,   94
and my own warmth was from the divine flame
from which more than a thousand have been kindled.

de l'Eneïda dico, la qual mamma   97
fummi, e fummi nutrice, poetando:
sanz' essa non fermai peso di dramma.

E per esser vivuto di là quando   100
visse Virgilio, assentirei un sole
più che non deggio al mio uscir di bando."

Volser Virgilio a me queste parole   103
con viso che, tacendo, disse "Taci";
ma non può tutto la virtù che vuole;

ché riso e pianto son tanto seguaci   106
a la passion di che ciascun si spicca,
che men seguon voler ne' più veraci.

Io pur sorrisi come l'uom ch'ammicca;   109
per che l'ombra si tacque, e riguardommi
ne li occhi ove 'l sembiante più si ficca;

e "Se tanto labore in bene assommi,"   112
disse, "perché la tua faccia testeso
un lampeggiar di riso dimostrommi?"

Or son io d'una parte e d'altra preso: 115
l'una mi fa tacer, l'altra scongiura
ch'io dica; ond' io sospiro, e sono inteso

dal mio maestro, e "Non aver paura,"   118
mi dice, "di parlar; ma parla e digli
quel ch'e' dimanda con cotanta cura."

Ond' io: "Forse che tu ti maravigli,   121
antico spirto, del rider ch'io fei;
ma più d'ammirazion vo' che ti pigli.

Questi che guida in alto li occhi miei,   124
è quel Virgilio dal qual tu togliesti
forte a cantar de li uomini e d'i dèi.

Se cagion altra al mio rider credesti,   127
lasciala per non vera, ed esser credi
quelle parole che di lui dicesti."

I mean the *Aeneid*, which was to me 97
my mother and my nurse in poetry.
I would not have enough left to weigh without it.

And to have lived back there during the time 100
when Virgil was alive I would agree
to one more sun than I owe in exile."

At these words Virgil turned to me, saying 103
with a look, silently, "Be silent,"
but the power to will cannot do everything,

for laughter and tears follow so closely 106
upon the passions that each springs from,
that they obey the will least in the most truthful.

All I did was to smile, the way one does 109
as a gesture, and the shade fell silent, looking
into my eyes where expression most clearly shows,

and, "So may such great labor end in good," 112
he said. "Why was it that your face showed,
a moment ago, the lightning flash of a smile?"

Now I am held on one side and the other, 115
the one says be silent, the other
conjures me to speak, so that I sigh

and am understood by my master. "Do not be 118
afraid to speak," he says, "but speak and tell him
what he is asking so earnestly."

So I: "Ancient spirit, you may wonder 121
at my having smiled, but I would have you
held in the grasp of a greater wonder.

This one, who is guiding my eyes upward, 124
is that Virgil from whom you acquired
the power to sing of men and of gods.

If you suppose I smiled for any other 127
reason, dismiss it as untrue. Be sure
it was because of those words you said of him."

Già s'inchinava ad abbracciar li piedi   *130*
al mio dottor, ma el li disse: "Frate,
non far, ché tu se' ombra e ombra vedi."

Ed ei surgendo: "Or puoi la quantitate   *133*
comprender de l'amor ch'a te mi scalda,
quand' io dismento nostra vanitate,

trattando l'ombre come cosa salda."   *136*

He had already stooped to embrace my teacher's   130
feet, but, "Brother, do not do that," he said,
"For you are a shade, and what you see is a shade."

And the other, rising, "Now you can tell how great   133
must be the love for you that burns in me
when it escapes my mind that we are empty

and I treat a shade as a solid thing."   136

CANTO XXII

Già era l'angel dietro a noi rimaso,
l'angel che n'avea vòlti al sesto giro,
avendomi dal viso un colpo raso;

e quei c'hanno a giustizia lor disiro   4
detto n'avea beati, e le sue voci
con *"sitiunt,"* sanz' altro, ciò forniro.

E io più lieve che per l'altre foci   7
m'andava, sì che sanz' alcun labore
seguiva in sù li spiriti veloci;

quando Virgilio incominciò: "Amore,   10
acceso di virtù, sempre altro accese,
pur che la fiamma sua paresse fore;

onde da l'ora che tra noi discese   13
nel limbo de lo 'nferno Giovenale,
che la tua affezion mi fé palese,

mia benvoglienza inverso te fu quale   16
più strinse mai di non vista persona,
sì ch'or mi parran corte queste scale.

Ma dimmi, e come amico mi perdona   19
se troppa sicurtà m'allarga il freno,
e come amico omai meco ragiona:

come poté trovar dentro al tuo seno   22
loco avarizia, tra cotanto senno
di quanto per tua cura fosti pieno?"

Queste parole Stazio mover fenno   25
un poco a riso pria; poscia rispuose:
"Ogne tuo dir d'amor m'è caro cenno.

Veramente più volte appaion cose   28
che danno a dubitar falsa matera
per le vere ragion che son nascose.

By this time the angel was behind us,
the angel who had turned us toward the sixth
circle, erasing one stroke from my face,

and had told us that they are blessèd whose   4
thirst is for justice, and he confined his
words to "thirst," without the rest of the text.

And I went on, lighter than I had been   7
at the other passageways, so that without
effort I climbed after the swift spirits,

when Virgil began, "Love that is set alight   10
by virtue always sets alight another
if only its flame can be seen shining out,

so, since the hour when Juvenal came down   13
among us, into the limbo of Hell,
and brought me tidings of your affection,

my good will toward you has been as great   16
as one can feel for a person never seen,
so that now this stairway will seem short.

But tell me, and as a friend forgive me   19
if excess of confidence prompts me
to loosen the rein, and speak now as a friend to me:

how could avarice ever have found a place   22
within your breast, taken up as it was
with all that wisdom your own zeal had put there?"

These words at first led Statius to smile   25
a little, and then he answered, "All
you say is a dear token of love,

but in truth, things have a way of appearing, often,   28
that provides misleading grounds for doubt
because the real cause of them is hidden.

La tua dimanda tuo creder m'avvera   31
esser ch'i' fossi avaro in l'altra vita,
forse per quella cerchia dov' io era.

Or sappi ch'avarizia fu partita   34
troppo da me, e questa dismisura
migliaia di lunari hanno punita.

E se non fosse ch'io drizzai mia cura,   37
quand' io intesi là dove tu chiame,
crucciato quasi a l'umana natura:

'Perché non reggi tu, o sacra fame   40
de l'oro, l'appetito de' mortali?'
voltando sentirei le giostre grame.

Allor m'accorsi che troppo aprir l'ali   43
potean le mani a spendere, e pente'mi
così di quel come de li altri mali.

Quanti risurgeran coi crini scemi   46
per ignoranza, che di questa pecca
toglie 'l penter vivendo e ne li stremi!

E sappie che la colpa che rimbecca   49
per dritta opposizione alcun peccato,
con esso insieme qui suo verde secca;

però, s'io son tra quella gente stato   52
che piange l'avarizia, per purgarmi,
per lo contrario suo m'è incontrato."

"Or quando tu cantasti le crude armi   55
de la doppia trestizia di Giocasta,"
disse 'l cantor de' buccolici carmi,

"per quello che Cliò teco lì tasta,   58
non par che ti facesse ancor fedele
la fede, sanza qual ben far non basta.

Se così è, qual sole o quai candele   61
ti stenebraron sì, che tu drizzasti
poscia di retro al pescator le vele?"

Your question shows me that you believe 31
I was avaricious in the other life,
no doubt because of that circle where I was.

Now you should know that avarice was too far 34
away from me, and this lack of measure
thousands of moons have been punishment for.

And if I had not righted my concerns 37
when I had understood the passage where
you cry out, as though enraged at human nature,

'To what, oh accursèd hunger for gold, 40
do you not drive the appetite of mortals?'
I would feel the jousts down where the weights are rolled.

Then I learned that our hands can spread their wings 43
too wide in spending, and I repented
of that as of my other wrongdoings.

How many will rise without most of their hair 46
through ignorance, that takes away repentance
of this sin through life and at the last hour!

And you should know that the counterfault, 49
in exact opposition to every sin,
here withers, along with it, from its green,

so that if for my cleansing I have stayed 52
among those people who lament avarice,
that happened to me because of its opposite."

"Now, when you sang about the cruel weapons 55
and of the twofold sorrow of Jocasta,"
said the singer of the bucolic songs,

"it does not seem, from the notes Clio touches 58
with you there, that you were yet made faithful
by the faith without which good works alone fail.

If that is so, what sun or candles lighted 61
the darkness for you so that from then on
you set your sails to follow the fisherman?"

Ed elli a lui: "Tu prima m'invïasti   64
verso Parnaso a ber ne le sue grotte,
e prima appresso Dio m'alluminasti.

Facesti come quei che va di notte,   67
che porta il lume dietro e sé non giova,
ma dopo sé fa le persone dotte,

quando dicesti: 'Secol si rinova;   70
torna giustizia e primo tempo umano,
e progenïe scende da ciel nova.'

Per te poeta fui, per te cristiano: 73
ma perché veggi mei ciò ch'io disegno,
a colorare stenderò la mano.

Già era 'l mondo tutto quanto pregno   76
de la vera credenza, seminata
per li messaggi de l'etterno regno;

e la parola tua sopra toccata   79
si consonava a' nuovi predicanti;
ond' io a visitarli presi usata.

Vennermi poi parendo tanto santi,   82
che, quando Domizian li perseguette,
sanza mio lagrimar non fur lor pianti;

e mentre che di là per me si stette,   85
io li sovvenni, e i lor dritti costumi
fer dispregiare a me tutte altre sette.

E pria ch'io conducessi i Greci a' fiumi   88
di Tebe poetando, ebb' io battesmo;
ma per paura chiuso cristian fu'mi,

lungamente mostrando paganesmo;   91
e questa tepidezza il quarto cerchio
cerchiar mi fé più che 'l quarto centesmo.

Tu dunque, che levato hai il coperchio   94
che m'ascondeva quanto bene io dico,
mentre che del salire avem soverchio,

And the other to him, "You first showed me the way   64
to Parnassus to drink from its grottoes,
and it was you, after God, who first enlightened me.

You did what someone does walking at night   67
holding the lantern behind him so that
it does him no good but makes wise those who follow

when you said, 'The age is growing new again.   70
Justice returns, and the first human time,
and a new progeny descends from Heaven.'

Because of you I was a poet, because of you   73
a Christian, but to show you better
what I am drawing, I will reach out to color it.

The whole world was already pregnant   76
with the true faith, which had been sown
by the messengers from the eternal kingdom

and those words of yours that I have just quoted   79
harmonized so well with the new preachers
that my visits to them became a habit.

In time they came to seem so holy that   82
when Domitian persecuted them
they never wept without my own tears falling,

and for the rest of the time that I was there   85
I helped them, and their upright behavior
led me to hold all the other sects in scorn.

And before I had brought the Greeks to the rivers   88
of Thebes, in my poem, I had been
baptized, but fear kept me a secret Christian,

pretending for a long time to be a pagan,   91
and this tepidness kept me circling
on the fourth circle more than four centuries.

You then, who had raised the cover hiding   94
from me that great good of which I am speaking,
now on the way up, while we have time,

dimmi dov' è Terrenzio nostro antico,   97
Cecilio e Plauto e Varro, se lo sai:
dimmi se son dannati, e in qual vico."

"Costoro e Persio e io e altri assai,"   100
rispuose il duca mio, "siam con quel Greco
che le Muse lattar più ch'altri mai,

nel primo cinghio del carcere cieco;   103
spesse fïate ragioniam del monte
che sempre ha le nutrice nostre seco.

Euripide v'è nosco e Antifonte,   106
Simonide, Agatone e altri piùe
Greci che già di lauro ornar la fronte.

Quivi si veggion de le genti tue   109
Antigone, Deïfile e Argia,
e Ismene sì trista come fue.

Védeisi quella che mostrò Langia;   112
èvvi la figlia di Tiresia, e Teti,
e con le suore sue Deïdamia."

Tacevansi ambedue già li poeti,   115
di novo attenti a riguardar dintorno,
liberi da saliri e da pareti;

e già le quattro ancelle eran del giorno   118
rimase a dietro, e la quinta era al temo,
drizzando pur in sù l'ardente corno,

quando il mio duca: "Io credo ch'a lo stremo   121
le destre spalle volger ne convegna,
girando il monte come far solemo."

Così l'usanza fu lì nostra insegna,   124
e prendemmo la via con men sospetto
per l'assentir di quell' anima degna.

Elli givan dinanzi, e io soletto   127
di retro, e ascoltava i lor sermoni,
ch'a poetar mi davano intelletto.

tell me, where is our ancient Terence, if   97
you know, and Caecilius, and Plautus and Varius?
Are they damned? And in what kind of place?"

"They, and Persius, and I, and many others,"   100
my leader answered, "are with that Greek to whom
the Muses gave more milk than to any other,

in the first circle of the blind prison.   103
Time and again we talk about the mountain
that has with it forever those who nursed us.

Euripedes and Antiphon are with us there,   106
Simonides and Agathon and many other
Greeks who once adorned their brows with laurel.

There one may see, of your own people,   109
Antigone, Deiphyle, and Argia,
and Ismene, with her old sorrow still.

She who pointed out Langia is seen there;   112
there is the daughter of Tiresias,
and Thetis, and Deidamia with her sisters."

After that, both of the poets were still,   115
intent once more upon gazing around them,
free of the ascent and of the walls.

And by that time four of the handmaidens   118
of day remained behind, and the fifth one
at the chariot shaft drove upward its burning horn,

when my leader said, "I believe we must turn   121
our right shoulders toward the edge, and go on
the way we were going, around the mountain."

So, taught by what we had already done,   124
we took our way, which was made less uncertain
by the assent of that elect soul.

They walked in front and I followed behind   127
by myself, and as they talked I listened
and learned from them about writing poetry.

Ma tosto ruppe le dolci ragioni   *130*
un alber che trovammo in mezza strada,
con pomi a odorar soavi e buoni;

e come abete in alto si digrada   *133*
di ramo in ramo, così quello in giuso,
cred' io, perché persona sù non vada.

Dal lato onde 'l cammin nostro era chiuso,   *136*
cadea de l'alta roccia un liquor chiaro
e si spandeva per le foglie suso.

Li due poeti a l'alber s'appressaro;   *139*
e una voce per entro le fronde
gridò: "Di questo cibo avrete caro."

Poi disse: "Più pensava Maria onde   *142*
fosser le nozze orrevoli e intere,
ch'a la sua bocca, ch'or per voi risponde.

E le Romane antiche, per lor bere,   *145*
contente furon d'acqua; e Danïello
dispregiò cibo e acquistò savere.

Lo secol primo, quant' oro fu bello,   *148*
fé savorose con fame le ghiande,
e nettare con sete ogne ruscello.

Mele e locuste furon le vivande   *151*
che nodriro il Batista nel diserto;
per ch'elli è glorïoso e tanto grande

quanto per lo Vangelio v'è aperto."   *154*

But before long their pleasant conversation   *130*
was cut short by a tree that we found in
mid-path with fruit that smelled sweet and good,

and as a fir tree, as it rises, grows   *133*
smaller from branch to branch, so this one does
going downward, I think so that no one can climb it.

On the side that blocked off our way there fell   *136*
from a high rock a clear water, to spill
outward from it into the upper leaves.

The two poets went closer to the tree   *139*
and a voice from among the branches cried,
"This is food that you come to dearly."

Then said, "Mary cared about the honor   *142*
and completeness of the wedding feast more
than her own mouth, which answers for you now,

and in the old days the women of Rome   *145*
drank water and were content, and Daniel
despised food and he acquired wisdom.

The first age was as beautiful as gold.   *148*
Hunger gave the acorns their savor,
and thirst turned every brook to nectar.

Honey and locusts were the food   *151*
that nourished the Baptist in the desert
and gave him that glory and greatness

which the Gospel makes apparent to you."   *154*

CANTO XXIII

Mentre che li occhi per la fronda verde
ficcava ïo sì come far suole
chi dietro a li uccellin sua vita perde,

lo più che padre mi dicea: "Figliuole,   4
vienne oramai, ché 'l tempo che n'è imposto
più utilmente compartir si vuole."

Io volsi 'l viso, e 'l passo non men tosto,   7
appresso i savi, che parlavan sìe,
che l'andar mi facean di nullo costo.

Ed ecco piangere e cantar s'udìe   10
"Labïa mëa, Domine" per modo
tal, che diletto e doglia parturìe.

"O dolce padre, che è quel ch'i' odo?"   13
comincia' io; ed elli: "Ombre che vanno
forse di lor dover solvendo il nodo."

Sì come i peregrin pensosi fanno,   16
giugnendo per cammin gente non nota,
che si volgono ad essa e non restanno,

così di retro a noi, più tosto mota,   19
venendo e trapassando ci ammirava
d'anime turba tacita e devota.

Ne li occhi era ciascuna oscura e cava,   22
palida ne la faccia, e tanto scema
che da l'ossa la pelle s'informava.

Non credo che così a buccia strema   25
Erisittone fosse fatto secco,
per digiunar, quando più n'ebbe tema.

Io dicea fra me stesso pensando: "Ecco   28
la gente che perdé Ierusalemme,
quando Maria nel figlio diè di becco!"

While I had my eyes focused among the leafy
green branches, as they are used to doing
who pursue birds and lose their lives that way,

"Son," my more than father said to me,   4
"come along now, for the time allowed us
will have to be put to better use."

I turned my face, and my steps as promptly,   7
following the sages, and such was their talk
that it took no effort to walk behind them.

And then we could hear *My lips, Lord . . .* being sung   10
with weeping in a way that gave birth
to joy, and at the same time to grieving.

"Oh, sweet father, what is it that I hear?"   13
I began. And he, "Shades, perhaps, on their
way to untie the knot of what they owe."

As pilgrims do when, deep in their thoughts, they   16
approach those they do not know, on the way,
and they turn toward them but do not stay,

so from behind us, moving more swiftly,   19
a crowd of souls, silent and devout,
came and stared at us in wonder as they passed by.

Each was dark and hollow about the eyes,   22
their faces were pallid, and they were shrunken
so that the bones were showing through the skin.

I do not believe that Erysichthon   25
was ever so withered to a crust
by hunger, which was what he dreaded most.

In my own mind I said to myself, "These are   28
the people who lost Jerusalem, then,
when Mary drove the beak into her son!"

Parean l'occhiaie anella sanza gemme: 31
chi nel viso de li uomini legge 'omo'
ben avria quivi conosciuta l'emme.

Chi crederebbe che l'odor d'un pomo   34
sì governasse, generando brama,
e quel d'un'acqua, non sappiendo como?

Già era in ammirar che sì li affama,   37
per la cagione ancor non manifesta
di lor magrezza e di lor trista squama,

ed ecco del profondo de la testa   40
volse a me li occhi un'ombra e guardò fiso;
poi gridò forte: "Qual grazia m'è questa?"

Mai non l'avrei riconosciuto al viso;   43
ma ne la voce sua mi fu palese
ciò che l'aspetto in sé avea conquiso.

Questa favilla tutta mi raccese   46
mia conoscenza a la cangiata labbia,
e ravvisai la faccia di Forese.

"Deh, non contendere a l'asciutta scabbia   49
che mi scolora," pregava, "la pelle,
né a difetto di carne ch'io abbia;

ma dimmi il ver di te, dì chi son quelle   52
due anime che là ti fanno scorta;
non rimaner che tu non mi favelle!"

"La faccia tua, ch'io lagrimai già morta,   55
mi dà di pianger mo non minor doglia,"
rispuos' io lui, "veggendola sì torta.

Però mi dì, per Dio, che sì vi sfoglia;   58
non mi far dir mentr' io mi maraviglio,
ché mal può dir chi è pien d'altra voglia."

Ed elli a me: "De l'etterno consiglio   61
cade vertù ne l'acqua e ne la pianta
rimasa dietro, ond' io sì m'assottiglio.

The eye sockets looked like rings that had no stone.　　　31
Whoever reads OMO in the human
face would have recognized the M clearly there.

Who would believe that the smell of an apple　　　34
and the smell of water could make that happen
by begetting longing, unless they knew the reason?

I was wondering then what it is that starves them,　　　37
since I had not seen yet what had made them
so thin, with that miserable crust on them,

and there, from deep in the hollow of his head,　　　40
a shade turned his eyes on me and kept them on me,
then shouted in a loud voice, "What grace has come to me?"

I would never have known him from his face,　　　43
but I was certain when I heard his voice
of what his countenance had erased of itself.

That spark lighted again everything　　　46
I had known once of those features that had changed,
and I recognized the face of Forese.

"Ah, do not stay contending with the withered　　　49
scab," he begged, "that discolors my skin,
nor with the absence of the flesh I had,

but tell me the truth about yourself, and who　　　52
are these two souls who are escorting you?
Do not wait any longer to tell me."

"Your face which I wept for once when it was dead　　　55
gives me no less cause now for weeping," I answered,
"when I come to see it so distorted.

Therefore, in God's name tell me, what strips your leaves so;　　　58
do not ask me to speak while I still wonder,
for no one can speak well whose will is elsewhere."

And he to me, "From the eternal guidance　　　61
virtue drops through the water and through the tree
now behind us, and that is what so thins me.

Tutta esta gente che piangendo canta 64
per seguitar la gola oltra misura,
in fame e 'n sete qui si rifà santa.

Di bere e di mangiar n'accende cura 67
l'odor ch'esce del pomo e de lo sprazzo
che si distende su per sua verdura.

E non pur una volta, questo spazzo 70
girando, si rinfresca nostra pena:
io dico pena, e dovria dir sollazzo,

ché quella voglia a li alberi ci mena 73
che menò Cristo lieto a dire 'Elì,'
quando ne liberò con la sua vena."

E io a lui: "Forese, da quel dì 76
nel qual mutasti mondo a miglior vita,
cinqu' anni non son vòlti infino a qui.

Se prima fu la possa in te finita 79
di peccar più, che sovvenisse l'ora
del buon dolor ch'a Dio ne rimarita,

come se' tu qua sù venuto ancora? 82
Io ti credea trovar là giù di sotto,
dove tempo per tempo si ristora."

Ond' elli a me: "Sì tosto m'ha condotto 85
a ber lo dolce assenzo d'i martìri
la Nella mia con suo pianger dirotto.

Con suoi prieghi devoti e con sospiri 88
tratto m'ha de la costa ove s'aspetta,
e liberato m'ha de li altri giri.

Tanto è a Dio più cara e più diletta 91
la vedovella mia, che molto amai,
quanto in bene operare è più soletta;

ché la Barbagia di Sardigna assai 94
ne le femmine sue più è pudica
che la Barbagia dov' io la lasciai.

All of these people weeping as they sing,   64
for having followed their appetites to excess,
here in hunger and thirst remake their holiness.

The fragrance of the apple and of the spray   67
over the tops of the green leaves spreading
inflames a longing for drinking and eating,

and not just once is our pain freshened   70
on this level as we come around;
pain, I say, and I should say comfort,

for the will that leads us to the tree   73
is the same that made Christ say 'My God' gladly
when out of his own vein he set us free."

﹒ And I to him, "Forese, from that day   76
when you exchanged the world for a better life,
to this, five years have not turned all the way.

If you no longer had the power to sin   79
before the hour when that good suffering
overtook you that weds us to God again,

how is it that you have come up here so soon?   82
I had thought I would find you lower down
there where time is made good again with time."

Then he to me, "It is my Nella who   85
with the pouring of her tears has led me
to drink so soon the sweet wormwood of the torments.

With her devout prayers and sighs she has brought me 88
from the hillside where they are waiting,
and from the other circles has set me free.

My dear widow, whom I loved deeply,   91
is all the dearer and more to be cherished
by God because her good works are solitary,

for the women of the Barbagia   94
of Sardinia are more modest by far
than those of the Barbagia where I left her.

O dolce frate, che vuo' tu ch'io dica?   97
Tempo futuro m'è già nel cospetto,
cui non sarà quest' ora molto antica,

nel qual sarà in pergamo interdetto   100
a le sfacciate donne fiorentine
l'andar mostrando con le poppe il petto.

Quai barbare fuor mai, quai saracine,   103
cui bisognasse, per farle ir coperte,
o spiritali o altre discipline?

Ma se le svergognate fosser certe   106
di quel che 'l ciel veloce loro ammanna,
già per urlare avrian le bocche aperte;

ché, se l'antiveder qui non m'inganna,   109
prima fien triste che le guance impeli
colui che mo si consola con nanna.

Deh, frate, or fa che più non mi ti celi!   112
vedi che non pur io, ma questa gente
tutta rimira là dove 'l sol veli."

Per ch'io a lui: "Se tu riduci a mente   115
qual fosti meco, e qual io teco fui,
ancor fia grave il memorar presente.

Di quella vita mi volse costui   118
che mi va innanzi, l'altr' ier, quando tonda
vi si mostrò la suora di colui,"

e 'l sol mostrai; "costui per la profonda   121
notte menato m'ha d'i veri morti
con questa vera carne che 'l seconda.

Indi m'han tratto sù li suoi conforti,   124
salendo e rigirando la montagna
che drizza voi che 'l mondo fece torti.

Tanto dice di farmi sua compagna   127
che io sarò là dove fia Beatrice;
quivi convien che sanza lui rimagna.

Oh, sweet brother, what would you have me say? 97
A future time appears to me already
from which this hour will not seem very old

when from the pulpit the impudent women 100
of Florence will be forbidden
to go showing the nipples of their breasts.

What barbarian women, what Saracens 103
ever needed spiritual disciplines
or any other to make them keep covered?

But, shameless as they are, if they really 106
knew what swift heaven is preparing for them
their mouths would be open to howl already,

for if our foresight here does not deceive me 109
they will come to sorrow before his cheeks
grow hair who now is lulled with a lullaby.

Oh, brother, do not hide your story from me 112
any longer. See, not only I, but all these
people are staring at where you veil the sun."

So I said to him, "If you bring back to mind 115
what you were with me, and what I was with you,
the present memory will still be a sorrow.

That one before me turned me from that life only 118
a few days ago when," and I pointed to
the sun, "his sister appeared round to you.

He is the one who has conducted me 121
through the deep night of the truly dead,
with this true flesh following behind him.

He has given me heart, which has brought me up here, 124
climbing and turning around the mountain
that makes you, whom the world twisted, straight again.

He will be a companion to me, he says, 127
until I come to where Beatrice is,
where I will have to be left without him.

Virgilio è questi che così mi dice,"   130
e addita'lo; "e quest' altro è quell' ombra
per cuï scosse dianzi ogne pendice

lo vostro regno, che da sé lo sgombra."   133

It is Virgil who speaks so to me,"
and I pointed to him, "and that other is
the shade for whom all the slopes, just now,

130

of your kingdom shook, as they let him go."

133

CANTO XXIV

Né 'l dir l'andar, né l'andar lui più lento
facea, ma ragionando andavam forte,
sì come nave pinta da buon vento;

e l'ombre, che parean cose rimorte,   4
per le fosse de li occhi ammirazione
traean di me, di mio vivere accorte.

E io, continüando al mio sermone,   7
dissi: "Ella sen va sù forse più tarda
che non farebbe, per altrui cagione.

Ma dimmi, se tu sai, dov' è Piccarda;   10
dimmi s'io veggio da notar persona
tra questa gente che sì mi riguarda."

"La mia sorella, che tra bella e buona   13
non so qual fosse più, trïunfa lieta
ne l'alto Olimpo già di sua corona."

Sì disse prima; e poi: "Qui non si vieta   16
di nominar ciascun, da ch'è sì munta
nostra sembianza via per la dïeta.

Questi," e mostrò col dito, "è Bonagiunta,   19
Bonagiunta da Lucca; e quella faccia
di là da lui più che l'altre trapunta

ebbe la Santa Chiesa in le sue braccia: 22
dal Torso fu, e purga per digiuno
l'anguille di Bolsena e la vernaccia."

Molti altri mi nomò ad uno ad uno;   25
e del nomar parean tutti contenti,
sì ch'io però non vidi un atto bruno.

Vidi per fame a vòto usar li denti   28
Ubaldin da la Pila e Bonifazio
che pasturò col rocco molte genti.

The words neither slowed the walking nor the going
the words, but as we talked we went on walking
hard, like a ship driven by a good wind

and the shades, which seemed things that had died twice, into   4
the holes that they had for eyes drew
amazement at me when they learned I was alive.

And I continued my subject from before,   7
saying, "It may be that he is going more
slowly than he might because of the other.

But tell me, if you know, where Piccarda is;   10
tell me whether I am seeing, among these
who stare at me so, someone I should notice."

"I do not know whether my sister was   13
more beautiful or good. On high Olympus
she triumphs now, rejoicing in her crown."

He said that first, and then, "Here it is not   16
forbidden to name each other, since our
faces have been wrung out with hunger.

That one," and he pointed with his finger, "is   19
Bonagiunta, Bonagiunta da Lucca,
and behind him that most quilted of the faces

held the Holy Church in his embrace;   22
he is from Tours, and with fasting purges
the eels of Bolsena and wines of Vernaccio."

He named many others to me, one by one,   25
and all seemed happy to be named, and none
gave a dark look when he told who they were.

I saw, clamping his teeth in hunger on   28
nothing, Ubaldin de la Pila, and
Bonifazio whose rod led many to pasture.

Vidi messer Marchese, ch'ebbe spazio
già di bere a Forlì con men secchezza,
e sì fu tal, che non si sentì sazio.

31

Ma come fa chi guarda e poi s'apprezza
più d'un che d'altro, fei a quel da Lucca,
che più parea di me voler contezza.

34

El mormorava; e non so che "Gentucca"
sentiv' io là, ov' el sentia la piaga
de la giustizia che sì li pilucca.

37

"O anima," diss' io, "che par sì vaga
di parlar meco, fa sì ch'io t'intenda,
e te e me col tuo parlare appaga."

40

"Femmina è nata, e non porta ancor benda,"
cominciò el, "che ti farà piacere
la mia città, come ch'om la riprenda.

43

Tu te n'andrai con questo antivedere:
se nel mio mormorar prendesti errore,
dichiareranti ancor le cose vere.

46

Ma dì s'i' veggio qui colui che fore
trasse le nove rime, cominciando
'Donne ch'avete intelletto d'amore.' "

49

E io a lui: "I' mi son un che, quando
Amor mi spira, noto, e a quel modo
ch'e' ditta dentro vo significando."

52

"O frate, issa vegg' io," diss' elli, "il nodo
che 'l Notaro e Guittone e me ritenne
di qua dal dolce stil novo ch'i' odo!

55

Io veggio ben come le vostre penne
di retro al dittator sen vanno strette,
che de le nostre certo non avvenne;

58

e qual più a gradire oltre si mette,
non vede più da l'uno a l'altro stilo";
e, quasi contentato, si tacette.

61

I saw Messer Marchese, who, with less 31
thirst, once at Forlì drank as he pleased,
never feeling he had enough then, as he was.

But as a person will look and then notice one 34
more than the others, I noticed the one
from Lucca, who seemed most eager to know about me.

He murmured—I do not know what. I heard something 37
like *"Gentucca"* at the place where he was feeling
the pang of the justice that so plucks at them.

"Oh soul," I said, "who seem to want so much 40
to speak to me, do it so that I can hear you,
and satisfy both yourself and me with your speech."

"A woman has been born," he began, "and is not 43
yet veiled in marriage, who will make my city
pleasant to you, though men speak evil of it.

You will go on taking this prophecy with you. 46
If in my murmuring you misunderstand me,
in time things themselves will make it clear to you.

But tell me if I am seeing here the one 49
who brought forth the new poems: one
beginning *'Ladies who have understanding of love.'* "

And I to him, "I am one who, when 52
Love breathes in me, take note, and as it is
dictated within, go setting it down."

"Oh brother, now I see the knot that was keeping 55
the Notary and Guittone," he said, "and me
back from the sweet new style that I am hearing.

It is clear to me how closely behind 58
the one who dictates to them your pens follow,
while ours surely did nothing of the kind,

and if anyone looks beyond this for differences 61
between the styles, he will not find them."
And, as though content with that, he was silent.

Come li augei che vernan lungo 'l Nilo,   64
alcuna volta in aere fanno schiera,
poi volan più a fretta e vanno in filo,

così tutta la gente che lì era,   67
volgendo 'l viso, raffrettò suo passo,
e per magrezza e per voler leggera.

E come l'uom che di trottare è lasso,   70
lascia andar li compagni, e sì passeggia
fin che si sfoghi l'affollar del casso,

sì lasciò trapassar la santa greggia   73
Forese, e dietro meco sen veniva,
dicendo: "Quando fia ch'io ti riveggia?"

"Non so," rispuos' io lui, "quant' io mi viva;   76
ma già non fïa il tornar mio tantosto,
ch'io non sia col voler prima a la riva;

però che 'l loco u' fui a viver posto,   79
di giorno in giorno più di ben si spolpa,
e a trista ruina par disposto."

"Or va," diss' el; "che quei che più n'ha colpa,   82
vegg' ïo a coda d'una bestia tratto
inver' la valle ove mai non si scolpa.

La bestia ad ogne passo va più ratto,   85
crescendo sempre, fin ch'ella il percuote,
e lascia il corpo vilmente disfatto.

Non hanno molto a volger quelle ruote,"   88
e drizzò li occhi al ciel, "che ti fia chiaro
ciò che 'l mio dir più dichiarar non puote.

Tu ti rimani omai; ché 'l tempo è caro   91
in questo regno, sì ch'io perdo troppo
venendo teco sì a paro a paro."

Qual esce alcuna volta di gualoppo   94
lo cavalier di schiera che cavalchi,
e va per farsi onor del primo intoppo,

As the birds that winter along the Nile   64
gather into a flock, sometimes, in the air
and fly faster then, going in single file,

so all of the people who were there   67
turned their faces, and their pace quickened again,
light with thinness and longing as they were.

And as someone who is tired of running   70
lets his companions go on, and walks
until his chest has eased its heaving,

so Forese let the holy flock go by   73
and came along behind them with me,
saying, "When will I see you again?"

"I do not know," I answered him, "how long   76
I will live, but however soon I return here
my desire will already be at the shore,

because the place I was put to live in   79
day by day is stripped of any good
and seems headed for miserable ruin."

"Go with this," he said: "I can see the one who is most   82
to be blamed for it dragged at the tail of a beast
toward that valley where there is no pardon.

The beast goes faster at every step, gathering   85
speed all the time, and finally smashing
and leaving his body hideously mangled.

Those wheels do not have long to turn," and he   88
raised his eyes to the sky, "before that will be
clear to you which my words cannot tell more clearly.

Now you stay here behind, because time is precious   91
in this realm, and I lose too much of it
coming with you at your own pace, like this."

And as a horseman sometimes comes galloping   94
forth out of a company as it is riding
and goes to win the honor of the first encounter,

tal si partì da noi con maggior valchi;   97
e io rimasi in via con esso i due
che fuor del mondo sì gran marescalchi.

E quando innanzi a noi intrato fue,   100
che li occhi miei si fero a lui seguaci,
come la mente a le parole sue,

parvermi i rami gravidi e vivaci   103
d'un altro pomo, e non molto lontani
per esser pur allora vòlto in laci.

Vidi gente sott' esso alzar le mani   106
e gridar non so che verso le fronde,
quasi bramosi fantolini e vani

che pregano, e 'l pregato non risponde,   109
ma, per fare esser ben la voglia acuta,
tien alto lor disio e nol nasconde.

Poi si partì sì come ricreduta;   112
e noi venimmo al grande arbore adesso,
che tanti prieghi e lagrime rifiuta.

"Trapassate oltre sanza farvi presso: 115
legno è più sù che fu morso da Eva,
e questa pianta si levò da esso."

Sì tra le frasche non so chi diceva;   118
per che Virgilio e Stazio e io, ristretti,
oltre andavam dal lato che si leva.

"Ricordivi," dicea, "d'i maladetti   121
nei nuvoli formati, che, satolli,
Tesëo combatter co' doppi petti;

e de li Ebrei ch'al ber si mostrar molli,   124
per che no i volle Gedeon compagni,
quando inver' Madïan discese i colli."

Sì accostati a l'un d'i due vivagni   127
passammo, udendo colpe de la gola
seguite già da miseri guadagni.

so with longer strides he drew away from us   97
and I remained on the way with those two
who were such great marshals of the world.

And when he had gone so far ahead of us   100
that my eyes were left trying to follow him
as my mind was trying to follow words of his,

there appeared to me the laden green boughs   103
of another fruit tree, and it was not far,
for we had just come around the bend there.

I saw people under it reaching   106
their hands up toward the leaves and shouting
I do not know what, like silly greedy children

who beg, and the one they beg from does not answer,   109
but to sharpen their wanting of it
holds up what they want and lets them see it.

Then they went away as though they had come to see   112
that they were wrong, and we came to the great tree
that refuses so many prayers and tears.

"Go on your way without getting close to it.   115
There is a tree above from which Eve ate
and this plant has been reared up from that."

So through the leaves spoke I do not know who,   118
whereupon Virgil and Statius and I drew
together, moving along the rising side.

"Remember," the voice said, "those accursèd ones who were   121
formed in the clouds and, when they could eat no more,
fought with both of their breasts against Theseus,

and the Hebrews whose drinking showed they were soft   124
so that Gideon would not have them with him
when he went down the hills against Midian."

So, staying close to one of the edges,   127
we went on, hearing sins of gluttony
followed, in the past, by miserable wages.

Poi, rallargati per la strada sola,   *130*
ben mille passi e più ci portar oltre,
contemplando ciascun sanza parola.

"Che andate pensando sì voi sol tre?"   *133*
sùbita voce disse; ond' io mi scossi
come fan bestie spaventate e poltre.

Drizzai la testa per veder chi fossi;   *136*
e già mai non si videro in fornace
vetri o metalli sì lucenti e rossi,

com' io vidi un che dicea: "S'a voi piace   *139*
montare in sù, qui si convien dar volta;
quinci si va chi vuole andar per pace."

L'aspetto suo m'avea la vista tolta;   *142*
per ch'io mi volsi dietro a' miei dottori,
com' om che va secondo ch'elli ascolta.

E quale, annunziatrice de li albori,   *145*
l'aura di maggio movesi e olezza,
tutta impregnata da l'erba e da' fiori;

tal mi senti' un vento dar per mezza   *148*
la fronte, e ben senti' mover la piuma,
che fé sentir d'ambrosïa l'orezza.

E senti' dir: "Beati cui alluma   *151*
tanto di grazia, che l'amor del gusto
nel petto lor troppo disir non fuma,

esurïendo sempre quanto è giusto!"   *154*

Then, spread out as before on the solitary way,
more than a thousand steps carried us onward,
each in contemplation without a word.

130

"What are you thinking of as you go, you three
by yourselves?" a voice asked suddenly, so that I
started as frightened surprised animals shy.

133

I raised my head to see who it could be,
and never did glass or metal burning
in any furnace appear as red and glowing

136

as the one I saw, who said, "If it would please
you to go up, here is where you should turn.
Here is where one goes on the way to peace."

139

His countenance had taken away my sight
so that I turned and followed my teachers
like someone who is guided by what he hears.

142

And as the breeze of May that heralds dawn
stirs, bringing along with it the odors
it carries in itself of the grass and flowers,

145

such was the wind I felt then touch the center
of my forehead, and I felt the wing stir,
bringing to me the scent of ambrosia.

148

And I heard it say, "Blessèd are they whom grace
so illumines that the love of taste
does not smoke with too much longing in the breast,

151

but they hunger only for what is just."

154

Ora era onde 'l salir non volea storpio;
ché 'l sole avëa il cerchio di merigge
lasciato al Tauro e la notte a lo Scorpio:

per che, come fa l'uom che non s'affigge   4
ma vassi a la via sua, che che li appaia,
se di bisogno stimolo il trafigge,

così intrammo noi per la callaia,   7
uno innanzi altro prendendo la scala
che per artezza i salitor dispaia.

E quale il cicognin che leva l'ala   10
per voglia di volare, e non s'attenta
d'abbandonar lo nido, e giù la cala;

tal era io con voglia accesa e spenta   13
di dimandar, venendo infino a l'atto
che fa colui ch'a dicer s'argomenta.

Non lasciò, per l'andar che fosse ratto,   16
lo dolce padre mio, ma disse: "Scocca
l'arco del dir, che 'nfino al ferro hai tratto."

Allor sicuramente apri' la bocca   19
e cominciai: "Come si può far magro
là dove l'uopo di nodrir non tocca?"

"Se t'ammentassi come Meleagro   22
si consumò al consumar d'un stizzo,
non fora," disse, "a te questo sì agro;

e se pensassi come, al vostro guizzo,   25
guizza dentro a lo specchio vostra image,
ciò che par duro ti parrebbe vizzo.

Ma perché dentro a tuo voler t'adage,   28
ecco qui Stazio; e io lui chiamo e prego
che sia or sanator de le tue piage."

It was an hour when the climb could allow
no delay, for the sun had left the meridian ring
to Taurus, as night had to Scorpio,

so, as someone does who makes his way   4
without stopping, whatever he sees before him,
if the spur of necessity pierces him,

we went ahead into the passage,   7
one after the other, starting up the stairs
that are too narrow for climbers to go in pairs.

And as a fledgling stork raises a wing,   10
wanting to fly and not venturing
to leave the nest, and lowers it again,

so I was, with the wish to question   13
lighted and put out again, reaching
the point of someone about to say something.

My gentle father did not refrain,   16
for all the haste of our steps, from saying, "Loose
the arrow of speech which you have drawn to the iron."

Then I opened my mouth confidently   19
and said first, "How is it they can become thin
where the need of nourishment touches no one?"

"If you recall how Meleager   22
was consumed with the consuming of a burning
log," he said, "you will get the taste of it better,

and if you would think of the way, however   25
you move, your image moves in a mirror,
what seems hard to you would resist you no longer.

But so that you may find rest in your desire,   28
here is Statius, on whom I call, begging
him now to be your healer where you are sore."

"Se la veduta etterna li dislego,"
rispuose Stazio, "là dove tu sie,
discolpi me non potert' io far nego."

31

Poi cominciò: "Se le parole mie,
figlio, la mente tua guarda e riceve,
lume ti fiero al come che tu die.

34

Sangue perfetto, che poi non si beve
da l'assetate vene, e si rimane
quasi alimento che di mensa leve,

37

prende nel core a tutte membra umane
virtute informativa, come quello
ch'a farsi quelle per le vene vane.

40

Ancor digesto, scende ov' è più bello
tacer che dire; e quindi poscia geme
sovr' altrui sangue in natural vasello.

43

Ivi s'accoglie l'uno e l'altro insieme,
l'un disposto a patire, e l'altro a fare
per lo perfetto loco onde si preme;

46

e, giunto lui, comincia ad operare
coagulando prima, e poi avviva
ciò che per sua matera fé constare.

49

Anima fatta la virtute attiva
qual d'una pianta, in tanto differente,
che questa è in via e quella è già a riva,

52

tanto ovra poi, che già si move e sente,
come spungo marino; e indi imprende
ad organar le posse ond' è semente.

55

Or si spiega, figliuolo, or si distende
la virtù ch'è dal cor del generante,
dove natura a tutte membra intende.

58

Ma come d'animal divegna fante,
non vedi tu ancor: quest' è tal punto,
che più savio di te fé già errante,

61

"If I open to him the eternal   31
vision," Statius answered, "in the presence of you,
my excuse is that I cannot refuse you."

Then he began, "Son, if your mind attends   34
to my words, and takes them in, they will
shed light for you on how this is possible.

Perfect blood, which the thirsty veins never   37
drink, remains as it was before,
like food that you take away from the table.

It acquires in the heart power to inform   40
all of the human members, like that blood
which flows into the members to become them.

Further digested, it descends to where   43
it is better not to speak of, and falls from there
into another's blood in a natural vessel.

There the one makes the other welcome,   46
the one disposed to undergo, and the other
to act, because of the perfect place it is pressed from.

And when the second has joined with the first, it begins   49
to function: first it coagulates, then quickens
the matter to which it has given consistency.

When the active virtue has turned into a soul,   52
like that of a plant, except that the former
is on the way, the latter already at the shore,

it works on until it sees and feels,   55
like a sea fungus, then goes on forming
organs for the faculties it germinates.

Now, my son, it unfurls, now it extends   58
that virtue from the begetter's heart, where
nature provides for all the members.

But how it turns from being an animal into   61
being a child you cannot see yet; that is the point
that once misled someone wiser than you,

sì che per sua dottrina fé disgiunto   64
da l'anima il possibile intelletto,
perché da lui non vide organo assunto.

Apri a la verità che viene il petto;   67
e sappi che, sì tosto come al feto
l'articular del cerebro è perfetto,

lo motor primo a lui si volge lieto   70
sovra tant' arte di natura, e spira
spirito novo, di vertù repleto,

che ciò che trova attivo quivi, tira   73
in sua sustanzia, e fassi un'alma sola,
che vive e sente e sé in sé rigira.

E perché meno ammiri la parola,   76
guarda il calor del sol che si fa vino,
giunto a l'omor che de la vite cola.

Quando Làchesis non ha più del lino,   79
solvesi da la carne, e in virtute
ne porta seco e l'umano e 'l divino:

l'altre potenze tutte quante mute;   82
memoria, intelligenza e volontade
in atto molto più che prima agute.

Sanza restarsi, per sé stessa cade   85
mirabilmente a l'una de le rive;
quivi conosce prima le sue strade.

Tosto che loco lì la circunscrive,   88
la virtù formativa raggia intorno
così e quanto ne le membra vive.

E come l'aere, quand' è ben pïorno,   91
per l'altrui raggio che 'n sé si reflette,
di diversi color diventa addorno;

così l'aere vicin quivi si mette   94
in quella forma che in lui suggella
virtüalmente l'alma che ristette;

so that in his teaching he separated   64
the functioning intelligence from the soul,
because he could see no organ in charge of it.

Open your breast to the truth you are about   67
to hear, and know that, once the articulate
form of the brain is perfect in the embryo,

the Prime Mover turns to it, rejoicing   70
over such art of nature, breathing
into it a new spirit filled with virtue

which draws into its own substance what   73
it finds active there, and makes a single soul
that lives and feels and revolves in its own orbit.

And so that what I say may seem less strange to you, 76
think how the sun's heat turns into wine
when it combines with the juice which flows from the vine.

When Lachesis has no more flax, the soul is set   79
free of the flesh, and it takes with it
its latent self, human and divine.

All the other faculties remain mute,   82
but memory, intelligence, and will are far
sharper in acting than they were before.

It does not stay, but of itself it falls   85
in a way to marvel at, to one shore or the other,
and for the first time knows its own way there.

As soon as the place closes around it there,   88
the formative power radiates about it
in form and size like the living members.

And as the air when it is heavy with rain   91
becomes adorned with many colors
by reflecting in itself rays that are another's,

so the neighboring air turns into   94
the form imprinted on it by that virtue
of the soul which, at the time, remains there,

e simigliante poi a la fiammella 97
che segue il foco là 'vunque si muta,
segue lo spirto sua forma novella.

Però che quindi ha poscia sua paruta, 100
è chiamata ombra; e quindi organa poi
ciascun sentire infino a la veduta.

Quindi parliamo e quindi ridiam noi; 103
quindi facciam le lagrime e ' sospiri
che per lo monte aver sentiti puoi.

Secondo che ci affliggono i disiri 106
e li altri affetti, l'ombra si figura;
e quest' è la cagion di che tu miri."

E già venuto a l'ultima tortura 109
s'era per noi, e vòlto a la man destra,
ed eravamo attenti ad altra cura.

Quivi la ripa fiamma in fuor balestra, 112
e la cornice spira fiato in suso
che la reflette e via da lei sequestra;

ond' ir ne convenia dal lato schiuso 115
ad uno ad uno; e io temëa 'l foco
quinci, e quindi temeva cader giuso.

Lo duca mio dicea: "Per questo loco 118
si vuol tenere a li occhi stretto il freno,
però ch'errar potrebbesi per poco."

"Summae Deus clementïae" nel seno 121
al grande ardore allora udi' cantando,
che di volger mi fé caler non meno;

e vidi spirti per la fiamma andando; 124
per ch'io guardava a loro e a' miei passi,
compartendo la vista a quando a quando.

Appresso il fine ch'a quell' inno fassi, 127
gridavano alto: "Virum non cognosco";
indi ricominciavan l'inno bassi.

and then, in a way like that which makes the flame   97
follow the fire wherever it may go,
the spirit follows after the new form.

Then, since its appearance comes from that,   100
it is called a shade, and for every sense
it then develops organs, even for sight.

So we come to speech and so to smiling,   103
so we make the tears and the sighing
that you may have heard around the mountain.

As desire and the other affections   106
move us, the shade takes on its appearance;
this is how what you marveled at comes to be."

And now we had arrived at the last torment   109
and we had turned to the right hand
and on another care we were intent.

Here the bank sends flames shooting outward   112
and the edge of the terrace sends a blast upward
that throws it back and shields from it a pathway,

so that we had to follow the open side,   115
one by one, and on one side I was afraid
of the fire, and on the other, of falling.

My leader said, "This is a place where   118
one must keep a tight rein on the eyes,
for it would be easy to take a false step here."

"God of the highest mercy . . ." I heard singing   121
then within the heart of the great burning,
which also made me want, no less, to turn,

and I saw spirits walking in the flame,   124
so that I went on, dividing my sight
between them and my own steps, from moment to moment.

After they had sung to the end of that hymn   127
they shouted, "I know not a man," and then
softly started to sing the hymn again.

Finitolo, anco gridavano: "Al bosco 130
si tenne Diana, ed Elice caccionne
che di Venere avea sentito il tòsco."

Indi al cantar tornavano; indi donne 133
gridavano e mariti che fuor casti
come virtute e matrimonio imponne.

E questo modo credo che lor basti 136
per tutto il tempo che 'l foco li abbruscia:
con tal cura conviene e con tai pasti

che la piaga da sezzo si ricuscia. 139

When it was finished, afterward they shouted,   130
"Diana kept to the woods and drove out
Helice, who had felt the poison of Venus."

Then they went back to singing and then calling out   133
about wives and husbands who had kept chaste,
as virtue and marriage say they must.

And I think this custom is enough for them   136
all through the time the fire is burning them;
with such treatment and such nourishment

must the wound come to be healed at last.   139

CANTO XXVI

Mentre che sì per l'orlo, uno innanzi altro,
ce n'andavamo, e spesso il buon maestro
diceami: "Guarda: giovi ch'io ti scaltro";

feriami il sole in su l'omero destro,   4
che già, raggiando, tutto l'occidente
mutava in bianco aspetto di cilestro;

e io facea con l'ombra più rovente   7
parer la fiamma; e pur a tanto indizio
vidi molt' ombre, andando, poner mente.

Questa fu la cagion che diede inizio   10
loro a parlar di me; e cominciarsi
a dir: "Colui non par corpo fittizio";

poi verso me, quanto potëan farsi,   13
certi si fero, sempre con riguardo
di non uscir dove non fosser arsi.

"O tu che vai, non per esser più tardo,   16
ma forse reverente, a li altri dopo,
rispondi a me che 'n sete e 'n foco ardo.

Né solo a me la tua risposta è uopo;   19
ché tutti questi n'hanno maggior sete
che d'acqua fredda Indo o Etïopo.

Dinne com' è che fai di te parete   22
al sol, pur come tu non fossi ancora
di morte intrato dentro da la rete."

Sì mi parlava un d'essi; e io mi fora   25
già manifesto, s'io non fossi atteso
ad altra novità ch'apparve allora;

ché per lo mezzo del cammino acceso   28
venne gente col viso incontro a questa,
la qual mi fece a rimirar sospeso.

As we went on walking along the edge,
one before the other, many times there
the good teacher said, "Watch. Learn from my knowledge."

The sun struck me above the right shoulder   4
already with its rays, turning the whole
face of the west from celestial blue to white

and I with my shadow made the flames appear   7
a deeper red, and I saw it was something
that many shades noticed as we were passing.

It was this that started them speaking   10
about me, and to each other saying,
"This body does not look like an illusion."

Then certain of them came toward me as near   13
as they could venture while still taking care
not to come out where they would not be burned.

"Oh you that go, not from slowness but rather   16
perhaps from reverence, behind the others,
answer me who in thirst and fire am burning,

nor am I the only one longing for your   19
answer, but all these have a thirst for it greater
than Indian's or Ethiopian's for cold water.

Tell us how you make of yourself a wall   22
to the sun, as though you were one who still
had not made your way into the net of death,"

one of them said to me, and I would have made plain   25
to him who I was if my attention
had not been caught by a strange thing I saw then,

for in the middle of the burning path   28
people were coming facing the other
way so that I stared at them in wonder.

Lì veggio d'ogne parte farsi presta   31
ciascun' ombra e basciarsi una con una
sanza restar, contente a brieve festa;

    così per entro loro schiera bruna   34
s'ammusa l'una con l'altra formica,
forse a spïar lor via e lor fortuna.

    Tosto che parton l'accoglienza amica,   37
prima che 'l primo passo lì trascorra,
sopragridar ciascuna s'affatica:

    la nova gente: "Soddoma e Gomorra";   40
e l'altra: "Ne la vacca entra Pasife,
perché 'l torello a sua lussuria corra."

    Poi, come grue ch'a le montagne Rife   43
volasser parte, e parte inver' l'arene,
queste del gel, quelle del sole schife,

    l'una gente sen va, l'altra sen vene;   46
e tornan, lagrimando, a' primi canti
e al gridar che più lor si convene;

    e raccostansi a me, come davanti,   49
essi medesmi che m'avean pregato,
attenti ad ascoltar ne' lor sembianti.

    Io, che due volte avea visto lor grato,   52
incominciai: "O anime sicure
d'aver, quando che sia, di pace stato,

    non son rimase acerbe né mature   55
le membra mie di là, ma son qui meco
col sangue suo e con le sue giunture.

    Quinci sù vo per non esser più cieco;   58
donna è di sopra che m'acquista grazia,
per che 'l mortal per vostro mondo reco.

    Ma se la vostra maggior voglia sazia   61
tosto divegna, sì che 'l ciel v'alberghi
ch'è pien d'amore e più ampio si spazia,

Then I see each shade going one way hurry 31
to kiss each shade going the other way,
not stopping, content with the brief greeting,

as in their dark company ant will touch 34
ant, muzzle to muzzle, looking perhaps
to learn the way or find out their fortune.

Once they have greeted each other as friends 37
and before they take the first step onward
each tries to shout louder than the others:

those that just came shout, "Sodom and Gomorrah," 40
and the others, "Pasiphaë enters the cow
to make the young bull charge into her lust."

Then like cranes, some toward the Riphaean Mountains 43
flying and some toward the desert fleeing
from the frost as the others flee from the sun,

one group goes away and the other comes on, 46
and they return in tears to what they were singing
and to whichever cry is right for them,

and the same ones who had asked me the question 49
came over to me as they had before,
their faces full of their desire to listen.

I for the second time seeing their longing 52
began, "Oh souls certain of being
at peace whenever the time for that shall be,

I have not left my limbs, either 55
green or ripe, back there, but they are with me here
with their own blood and their own jointed bones.

I am on my way up to be blind no longer. 58
There above, a lady has won for me
the grace to pass, still mortal, through your world.

But so may your greatest longing come to be 61
fulfilled soon, and that Heaven harbor you
that is most spacious and is filled with love,

ditemi, acciò ch'ancor carte ne verghi,
chi siete voi, e chi è quella turba
che se ne va di retro a' vostri terghi." 64

Non altrimenti stupido si turba
lo montanaro, e rimirando ammuta,
quando rozzo e salvatico s'inurba, 67

che ciascun' ombra fece in sua paruta;
ma poi che furon di stupore scarche,
lo qual ne li alti cuor tosto s'attuta, 70

"Beato te, che de le nostre marche,"
ricominciò colei che pria m'inchiese,
"per morir meglio, esperïenza imbarche! 73

La gente che non vien con noi, offese
di ciò per che già Cesar, trïunfando,
'Regina' contra sé chiamar s'intese: 76

però si parton 'Soddoma' gridando,
rimproverando a sé com' hai udito,
e aiutan l'arsura vergognando. 79

Nostro peccato fu ermafrodito;
ma perché non servammo umana legge,
seguendo come bestie l'appetito, 82

in obbrobrio di noi, per noi si legge,
quando partinci, il nome di colei
che s'imbestiò ne le 'mbestiate schegge. 85

Or sai nostri atti e di che fummo rei:
se forse a nome vuo' saper chi semo,
tempo non è di dire, e non saprei. 88

Farotti ben di me volere scemo:
son Guido Guinizzelli, e già mi purgo
per ben dolermi prima ch'a lo stremo." 91

Quali ne la tristizia di Ligurgo
si fer due figli a riveder la madre,
tal mi fec' io, ma non a tanto insurgo, 94

tell me, so I may write it later, who 64
are you, and who are they in that assembly
that is going away from behind you?"

No different from someone out of the mountains, 67
amazed, open-mouthed, turning and looking, speechless,
on entering, rough and wild, into the city,

was the way each of the shades appeared to be, 70
but when they were free of their astonishment,
a thing soon quieted in noble hearts,

"Blessèd are you," he that had spoken to me 73
began again, "who to die better come
to be laden with knowledge of our region.

The offense of the people who are 76
not coming with us is the one that made Caesar hear
himself called 'Queen' as he passed in triumph.

That is why they shout 'Sodom' when they leave, 79
to reproach themselves, as you have heard, and their
shame adds to the burning of the fire.

Our sin was the performance as both sexes, 82
but because we did not uphold human law,
pursuing appetite like animals,

when we leave them, we call opprobrium 85
upon ourselves, her name is repeated by us
who was a beast inside the wooden beast.

Now you know what we did and what our guilt is. 88
Though you may wish to know us each by name
there is no time for that, nor could I tell you,

but for my part I will grant your wish: I am 91
Guido Guinizzelli, purifying myself
already because I repented before the end."

As the two sons became during the sorrow 94
of Lycurgus, when they saw their mother again,
I became, without rising to their expression,

quand' io odo nomar sé stesso il padre 97
mio e de li altri miei miglior che mai
rime d'amor usar dolci e leggiadre;

e sanza udire e dir pensoso andai 100
lunga fïata rimirando lui,
né, per lo foco, in là più m'appressai.

Poi che di riguardar pasciuto fui, 103
tutto m'offersi pronto al suo servigio
con l'affermar che fa credere altrui.

Ed elli a me: "Tu lasci tal vestigio, 106
per quel ch'i' odo, in me, e tanto chiaro,
che Letè nol può tòrre né far bigio.

Ma se le tue parole or ver giuraro, 109
dimmi che è cagion per che dimostri
nel dire e nel guardar d'avermi caro."

E io a lui: "Li dolci detti vostri, 112
che, quanto durerà l'uso moderno,
faranno cari ancora i loro incostri."

"O frate," disse, "questi ch'io ti cerno 115
col dito," e additò un spirto innanzi,
"fu miglior fabbro del parlar materno.

Versi d'amore e prose di romanzi 118
soverchiò tutti; e lascia dir li stolti
che quel di Lemosì credon ch'avanzi.

A voce più ch'al ver drizzan li volti, 121
e così ferman sua oppinïone
prima ch'arte o ragion per lor s'ascolti.

Così fer molti antichi di Guittone, 124
di grido in grido pur lui dando pregio,
fin che l'ha vinto il ver con più persone.

Or se tu hai sì ampio privilegio, 127
che licito ti sia l'andare al chiostro
nel quale è Cristo abate del collegio,

hearing my father and the father of others 97
my betters and whoever has come to use
sweet graceful rhymes of love say his own name,

and without hearing or speaking I walked on 100
a long way, thoughtful, gazing at him,
but because of the fire went no closer.

When my sight had feasted enough upon him 103
I offered my whole self at once to his service
with that earnestness that makes others believe.

And he to me, "You leave a mark so deep, 106
through what I hear, and see clearly, in me
that Lethe cannot wash it out nor fade it.

But if it is the truth which you have promised, 109
tell why it is that your face and speech
make it apparent that you hold me dear."

And I to him, "The sweet songs of yours 112
that so long as our present words endure
will make precious the ink in which they were written."

"Oh brother," he said, "the one at whom I am pointing 115
with my finger," indicating a spirit before him,
"was a better workman in the mother tongue:

verses of love and stories of romance, 118
he was peerless in all of them, and let the fools babble
who believe that the Limousin writes better.

They attend fashion rather than the truth, 121
and in that way they make up their opinion
before they give heed to art or reason.

That was the way many did with Guittone, 124
shout after shout all giving the prize to him
until the truth overcame most of them.

Now if so vast a privilege is yours 127
that you are free to walk on to the cloister
in which Christ is the abbot of the college,

falli per me un dir d'un paternostro,   130
quanto bisogna a noi di questo mondo,
dove poter peccar non è più nostro."

Poi, forse per dar luogo altrui secondo   133
che presso avea, disparve per lo foco,
come per l'acqua il pesce andando al fondo.

Io mi fei al mostrato innanzi un poco,   136
e dissi ch'al suo nome il mio disire
apparecchiava grazïoso loco.

El cominciò liberamente a dire: 139
"Tan m'abellis vostre cortes deman,
qu'ieu no me puesc ni voill a vos cobrire.

Ieu sui Arnaut, que plor e vau cantan;   142
consiros vei la passada folor,
e vei jausen lo joi qu'esper, denan.

Ara vos prec, per aquella valor   145
que vos guida al som de l'escalina,
sovenha vos a temps de ma dolor!"

Poi s'ascose nel foco che li affina.   148

recite to Him there a Paternoster for me,   *130*
insofar as we need one in this world
where the power to sin is ours no longer."

Then, it may be to make room for another   *133*
who was close to him, he vanished through the fire
like a fish going into the deepest water.

I moved forward a little toward the one   *136*
who had been pointed out and said to him
that my wish had made a welcome for his name.

Freely he began to speak to me: *139*
"Your courteous question gives such pleasure to me*
that I will not and cannot conceal myself from you.

I am Arnaut who weep and go singing.   *142*
With anguish of mind I see my old folly
and with joy see before me the hoped-for day.

Now I beg of you by that power   *145*
that is leading you to the top of the stair,
while there is time remember how I suffer!"

Then hid himself in the fire that refines them.   *148*

*In the original, Arnaut's speech is in Provençal.

CANTO XXVII

Sì come quando i primi raggi vibra
là dove il suo fattor lo sangue sparse,
cadendo Ibero sotto l'alta Libra,

e l'onde in Gange da nona rïarse,   4
sì stava il sole; onde 'l giorno sen giva,
come l'angel di Dio lieto ci apparse.

Fuor de la fiamma stava in su la riva,   7
e cantava *"Beati mundo corde!"*
in voce assai più che la nostra viva.

Poscia "Più non si va, se pria non morde,   10
anime sante, il foco: intrate in esso,
e al cantar di là non siate sorde,"

ci disse come noi li fummo presso;   13
per ch'io divenni tal, quando lo 'ntesi,
qual è colui che ne la fossa è messo.

In su le man commesse mi protesi,   16
guardando il foco e imaginando forte
umani corpi già veduti accesi.

Volsersi verso me le buone scorte;   19
e Virgilio mi disse: "Figliuol mio,
qui può esser tormento, ma non morte.

Ricorditi, ricorditi! E se io   22
sovresso Gerïon ti guidai salvo,
che farò ora presso più a Dio?

Credi per certo che se dentro a l'alvo   25
di questa fiamma stessi ben mille anni,
non ti potrebbe far d'un capel calvo.

E se tu forse credi ch'io t'inganni,   28
fatti ver' lei, e fatti far credenza
con le tue mani al lembo d'i tuoi panni.

As when the first rays are quivering
there where its Creator shed His blood,
the Ebro under high Libra lying,

and noon scorching the waves of the Ganges,   4
so the sun stood, and so the day was going
when the joyful angel of God appeared to us.

Outside the flames, above the bank he stood   7
and he sang *"Blessèd are the pure in heart"*
in a voice that was more alive than ours.

Then, "There is no going past here without   10
the bite of the fire first, holy souls. Enter it
without being deaf to the singing beyond it,"

he said to us when we had come near him,   13
so that when I heard him I became
like someone who is put into the grave.

I bent over my hands clasped together,   16
looking at the fire and intensely imagining
human bodies that I had seen burning.

The good escorts turned to face me   19
and Virgil said to me, "There may be
torment here, my son, but not death.

Remember, remember: if even upon   22
Geryon I guided you safely, what
shall I do now that we are nearer to God?

Believe beyond doubt that even if you were   25
to spend a full thousand years in the womb of this fire
it could not make you bald by a single hair.

And if you think I may not be telling you   28
the truth, go over to it and find out
for yourself: hold out the edge of your robe to it.

Pon giù omai, pon giù ogne temenza;   *31*
volgiti in qua e vieni: entra sicuro!"
E io pur fermo e contra cosci̇enza.

Quando mi vide star pur fermo e duro,   *34*
turbato un poco disse: "Or vedi, figlio:
tra Bëatrice e te è questo muro."

Come al nome di Tisbe aperse il ciglio   *37*
Piramo in su la morte, e riguardolla,
allor che 'l gelso diventò vermiglio;

così, la mia durezza fatta solla,   *40*
mi volsi al savio duca, udendo il nome
che ne la mente sempre mi rampolla.

Ond' ei crollò la fronte e disse: "Come!   *43*
volenci star di qua?"; indi sorrise
come al fanciul si fa ch'è vinto al pome.

Poi dentro al foco innanzi mi si mise,   *46*
pregando Stazio che venisse retro,
che pria per lunga strada ci divise.

Sì com' fui dentro, in un bogliente vetro   *49*
gittato mi sarei per rinfrescarmi,
tant' era ivi lo 'ncendio sanza metro.

Lo dolce padre mio, per confortarmi,   *52*
pur di Beatrice ragionando andava,
dicendo: "Li occhi suoi già veder parmi."

Guidavaci una voce che cantava   *55*
di là; e noi, attenti pur a lei,
venimmo fuor là ove si montava.

"Venite, benedicti Patris mei,"   *58*
sonò dentro a un lume che lì era,
tal che mi vinse e guardar nol potei.

"Lo sol sen va," soggiunse, "e vien la sera;   *61*
non v'arrestate, ma studiate il passo,
mentre che l'occidente non si annera."

From here on put away, put away all fear.   31
Turn this way, and with confidence enter here."
And I still stood there, and against my conscience.

When he saw that I remained there, stubborn,   34
he said, somewhat vexed, "Now look, my son,
this wall is between you and Beatrice."

As at the name of Thisbe, Pyramus,   37
when he was dying, opened his eyes to gaze
upon her, when the mulberry turned red,

so as my rigidity melted I   40
turned to my wise leader at the sound
of the name that wells up always in my mind.

At that he shook his head and said, "Well,   43
do we want to stay on this side?" and then smiled
as at a child who has been won with an apple.

Then he put himself into the fire before me,   46
asking Statius, who for a long way
had been between us, to come behind him.

As soon as I was in it I would have thrown   49
myself into boiling glass to be cooler,
the burning there was so beyond measure.

My kind father, to comfort me, kept talking   52
of Beatrice as he went, saying,
"I seem to see her eyes already."

There was a voice singing, on the other side,   55
guiding us, and listening only to that
we came out where the way begins to climb.

"Come, blessèd of my Father" sounded within   58
a light there; and it was such that it
overcame me, and I could not look at it.

"The sun is going," it went on, "and evening   61
is coming; do not stop, but keep pressing
your steps onward while the west is not yet dark."

Dritta salia la via per entro 'l sasso   64
verso tal parte ch'io toglieva i raggi
dinanzi a me del sol ch'era già basso.

E di pochi scaglion levammo i saggi,   67
che 'l sol corcar, per l'ombra che si spense,
sentimmo dietro e io e li miei saggi.

E pria che 'n tutte le sue parti immense   70
fosse orizzonte fatto d'uno aspetto,
e notte avesse tutte sue dispense,

ciascun di noi d'un grado fece letto;   73
ché la natura del monte ci affranse
la possa del salir più e 'l diletto.

Quali si stanno ruminando manse   76
le capre, state rapide e proterve
sovra le cime avante che sien pranse,

tacite a l'ombra, mentre che 'l sol ferve,   79
guardate dal pastor, che 'n su la verga
poggiato s'è e lor di posa serve;

e quale il mandrïan che fori alberga,   82
lungo il peculio suo queto pernotta,
guardando perché fiera non lo sperga;

tali eravamo tutti e tre allotta,   85
io come capra, ed ei come pastori,
fasciati quinci e quindi d'alta grotta.

Poco parer potea lì del di fori;   88
ma, per quel poco, vedea io le stelle
di lor solere e più chiare e maggiori.

Sì ruminando e sì mirando in quelle,   91
mi prese il sonno; il sonno che sovente,
anzi che 'l fatto sia, sa le novelle.

Ne l'ora, credo, che de l'orïente   94
prima raggiò nel monte Citerea,
che di foco d'amor par sempre ardente,

The way went straight up through the rock,   64
in such a direction that I cut off, before me,
the rays of the sun which was low already.

And we had tried only a few of the steps   67
when, from the disappearance of my shadow,
I and my sages knew the sun had set behind us.

And before the vastnesses of the horizon   70
on all sides came to appear the same,
and night had all of her dominion,

each of us made one of the steps a bed,   73
since the nature of the mountain took from us
the strength to climb farther, rather than the wish.

As goats remain still, quietly chewing,   76
that along the tops of the hills were racing
and wild, until they had finished eating,

silent in the shade, while the sun is hot,   79
guarded by the shepherd who leans on his rod
and as he leans watches over them,

and as the herdsman who lodges out   82
in the open, spending the night beside his quiet
flock, watching for a wild beast that would scatter them,

so were we at that time, all three of us,   85
I like the goats, and they like shepherds, shut
in by the high rock wall on this side and on that.

Little of what was outside could be seen there,   88
but in that little space I saw the stars
larger than was usual, and brighter.

So, as I was ruminating and gazing at them,   91
sleep took hold of me, sleep which often
knows the tidings of things before they happen.

At the hour, I think, when Cytherea shone   94
first, out of the east, upon the mountain,
she who seems always burning with the fire of love,

giovane e bella in sogno mi parea 97
donna vedere andar per una landa
cogliendo fiori; e cantando dicea:

"Sappia qualunque il mio nome dimanda 100
ch'i' mi son Lia, e vo movendo intorno
le belle mani a farmi una ghirlanda.

Per piacermi a lo specchio, qui m'addorno; 103
ma mia suora Rachel mai non si smaga
dal suo miraglio, e siede tutto giorno.

Ell' è d'i suoi belli occhi veder vaga 106
com' io de l'addornarmi con le mani;
lei lo vedere, e me l'ovrare appaga."

E già per li splendori antelucani, 109
che tanto a' pellegrin surgon più grati,
quanto, tornando, albergan men lontani,

le tenebre fuggian da tutti lati, 112
e 'l sonno mio con esse; ond' io leva'mi,
veggendo i gran maestri già levati.

"Quel dolce pome che per tanti rami 115
cercando va la cura de' mortali,
oggi porrà in pace le tue fami."

Virgilio inverso me queste cotali 118
parole usò; e mai non furo strenne
che fosser di piacere a queste iguali.

Tanto voler sopra voler mi venne 121
de l'esser sù, ch'ad ogne passo poi
al volo mi sentia crescer le penne.

Come la scala tutta sotto noi 124
fu corsa e fummo in su 'l grado superno,
in me ficcò Virgilio li occhi suoi,

e disse: "Il temporal foco e l'etterno 127
veduto hai, figlio; e se' venuto in parte
dov' io per me più oltre non discerno.

In a dream I seemed to see a beautiful young   97
lady walking in a clearing, picking
flowers, and this is what she was singing:

"Whoever asks my name may know that I   100
am Leah, and as I go turning my
beautiful hands, making myself a garland,

I adorn myself for my pleasure at the mirror,   103
but my sister Rachel never turns from her
mirror, and she sits all day long.

She is as happy to see her own beautiful eyes   106
as I am to adorn myself with my hands.
For her, seeing, and for me, doing satisfies."

And now through the reflected light that comes   109
before dawn, whose rising is to pilgrims
ever more welcome as they sleep nearer home,

the darknesses on every side were fleeing   112
and my sleep with them, and so I rose, seeing
that the great masters had already risen.

"That sweet fruit which the care of mortals   115
through so many branches goes looking for
will bring peace today to all your hunger."

It was such words as these that Virgil   118
said to me, and there was no gift ever
that had given so great a pleasure.

Such a desire upon desire to be up there   121
came to me that with each step after that
I felt my feathers growing for the flight.

When under us the whole of the stairway   124
had run and we were on the highest step
of all, Virgil fixed his eyes upon me

and said, "You have seen the temporal fire   127
and the eternal, my son, and you have come
to where I, by myself, can see no farther.

Tratto t'ho qui con ingegno e con arte;   130
lo tuo piacere omai prendi per duce;
fuor se' de l'erte vie, fuor se' de l'arte.

Vedi lo sol che 'n fronte ti riluce;   133
vedi l'erbette, i fiori e li arbuscelli
che qui la terra sol da sé produce.

Mentre che vegnan lieti li occhi belli   136
che, lagrimando, a te venir mi fenno,
seder ti puoi e puoi andar tra elli.

Non aspettar mio dir più né mio cenno;   139
libero, dritto e sano è tuo arbitrio,
e fallo fora non fare a suo senno:

per ch'io te sovra te corono e mitrio."   142

I have brought you here with understanding   130
and art. From here on your own pleasure must guide you.
You have emerged from the steep ways and the narrow.

Look at the sun which shines on your forehead,   133
look at the young grass, the flowers, the trees
that the earth here, all by itself, grows.

Until those lovely eyes have come to you   136
in joy, whose weeping made me come to you,
you may sit here or wander among these.

Expect no further word or sign from me.   139
Your own will is whole, upright, and free,
and it would be wrong not to do as it bids you,

therefore I crown and miter you over yourself."   142

CANTO XXVIII

Vago già di cercar dentro e dintorno
la divina foresta spessa e viva,
ch'a li occhi temperava il novo giorno,

sanza più aspettar, lasciai la riva,   4
prendendo la campagna lento lento
su per lo suol che d'ogne parte auliva.

Un'aura dolce, sanza mutamento   7
avere in sé, mi feria per la fronte
non di più colpo che soave vento;

per cui le fronde, tremolando, pronte   10
tutte quante piegavano a la parte
u' la prim' ombra gitta il santo monte;

non però dal loro esser dritto sparte   13
tanto, che li augelletti per le cime
lasciasser d'operare ogne lor arte;

ma con piena letizia l'ore prime,   16
cantando, ricevieno intra le foglie,
che tenevan bordone a le sue rime,

tal qual di ramo in ramo si raccoglie   19
per la pineta in su 'l lito di Chiassi,
quand' Ëolo scilocco fuor discioglie.

Già m'avean trasportato i lenti passi   22
dentro a la selva antica tanto, ch'io
non potea rivedere ond' io mi 'ntrassi;

ed ecco più andar mi tolse un rio,   25
che 'nver' sinistra con sue picciole onde
piegava l'erba che 'n sua ripa uscìo.

Tutte l'acque che son di qua più monde,   28
parrieno avere in sé mistura alcuna
verso di quella, che nulla nasconde,

Now, eager to look into and around
the divine forest, dense and luxuriant,
that tempered to my eyes the new daylight,

I left the bank, delaying no longer,   4
and wandered through the meadow slowly, slowly,
over the ground that was fragrant everywhere.

A sweet air that within itself was   7
unvarying struck me on the forehead,
a stroke no rougher than a gentle breeze,

at which the trembling branches all together   10
bent at once in that direction where
the holy mountain casts its first shadow,

without ever leaning over so far from   13
the upright as to make the small birds stop
the practice of their art in the treetops,

but full of joy they welcomed the first hour,   16
singing among the leaves, which went on humming
a continuo under their rhyming,

like that which gathers from branch to branch through   19
the pine wood above the shore at Chiassi
when Aeolus releases the sirocco.

My slow steps had already taken me   22
so far into the ancient wood that I
could not see back to where I had come in

and there I was stopped from going forward   25
by a stream whose small waves were bending toward
the left the grasses growing along it.

All the waters that are purest here   28
would seem to have something in them that was impure
compared to that, which does not conceal anything,

avvegna che si mova bruna bruna   31
sotto l'ombra perpetüa, che mai
raggiar non lascia sole ivi né luna.

   Coi piè ristetti e con li occhi passai   34
di là dal fiumicello, per mirare
la gran varïazion d'i freschi mai;

   e là m'apparve, sì com' elli appare   37
subitamente cosa che disvia
per maraviglia tutto altro pensare,

   una donna soletta che si gia   40
e cantando e scegliendo fior da fiore
ond' era pinta tutta la sua via.

   "Deh, bella donna, che a' raggi d'amore   43
ti scaldi, s'i' vo' credere a' sembianti
che soglion esser testimon del core,

   vegnati in voglia di trarreti avant,"   46
diss' io a lei, "verso questa rivera,
tanto ch'io possa intender che tu canti.

   Tu mi fai rimembrar dove e qual era   49
Proserpina nel tempo che perdette
la madre lei, ed ella primavera."

   Come si volge, con le piante strette   52
a terra e intra sé, donna che balli,
e piede innanzi piede a pena mette,

   volsesi in su i vermigli e in su i gialli   55
fioretti verso me, non altrimenti
che vergine che li occhi onesti avvalli;

   e fece i prieghi miei esser contenti,   58
sì appressando sé, che 'l dolce suono
veniva a me co' suoi intendimenti.

   Tosto che fu là dove l'erbe sono   61
bagnate già da l'onde del bel fiume,
di levar li occhi suoi mi fece dono.

although dark, dark is its current under
the everlasting shade that never
allows the sun or the moon to shine there.

31

I stopped with my feet, and with my eyes went on
across the little brook, gazing upon
the many forms of the blossoming hawthorn,

34

and there appeared to me there, as something may
suddenly appear that drives away
every other thought with the wonder of it,

37

a lady all alone, who was singing
as she went, and choosing flowers among
the flowers with which all of her path was painted.

40

"Ah, fair lady who are warmed by the rays
of love, if I trust appearances,
which often bear witness to the heart,

43

may it be your pleasure to come closer
alongside this stream," I said to her,
"so that I can hear what you are singing.

46

You make me remember Proserpina,
where she was and what she was like, that time
her mother lost her, and she was the Spring."

49

As a lady dancing turns with her feet
close to the ground and keeping together,
scarcely moving one foot in front of the other,

52

she turned above the vermilion and above
the yellow little flowers, not otherwise
than as a virgin veils her modest eyes,

55

and satisfied the prayer which I had made her,
coming closer to me until the sweet
sound reached me, and the meaning of it.

58

As soon as she had come to where the grass
was newly bathed by the waves of that lovely stream,
she made me the gift of raising her eyes.

61

Non credo che splendesse tanto lume   64
sotto le ciglia a Venere, trafitta
dal figlio fuor di tutto suo costume.

Ella ridea da l'altra riva dritta,   67
trattando più color con le sue mani,
che l'alta terra sanza seme gitta.

Tre passi ci facea il fiume lontani;   70
ma Elesponto, là 've passò Serse,
ancora freno a tutti orgogli umani,

più odio da Leandro non sofferse   73
per mareggiare intra Sesto e Abido,
che quel da me perch' allor non s'aperse.

"Voi siete nuovi, e forse perch' io rido,"   76
cominciò ella, "in questo luogo eletto
a l'umana natura per suo nido,

maravigliando tienvi alcun sospetto;   79
ma luce rende il salmo *Delectasti*,
che puote disnebbiar vostro intelletto.

E tu che se' dinanzi e mi pregasti,   82
dì s'altro vuoli udir; ch'i' venni presta
ad ogne tua question tanto che basti."

"L'acqua," diss' io, "e 'l suon de la foresta   85
impugnan dentro a me novella fede
di cosa ch'io udi' contraria a questa."

Ond' ella: "Io dicerò come procede   88
per sua cagion ciò ch'ammirar ti face,
e purgherò la nebbia che ti fiede.

Lo sommo Ben, che solo esso a sé piace,   91
fé l'uom buono e a bene, e questo loco
diede per arr' a lui d'etterna pace.

Per sua difalta qui dimorò poco;   94
per sua difalta in pianto e in affanno
cambiò onesto riso e dolce gioco.

I do not believe that such a light shone   64
from under the eyelids of Venus when
her son's arrow pierced her, against all his custom.

She smiled from the other bank, where she stood   67
arranging in her hands the many colors
which that high land scatters without seed.

Three paces away was how far the river   70
kept her, but the Hellespont where Xerxes
crossed—that curb to human pride always—

suffered no greater hatred from Leander   73
for its surging between Sestos and Abydos
than, at its not opening then, mine was.

"You are new here, and perhaps because   76
I am smiling," she began, "in this place
that was chosen to be the nest of humankind,

you are kept wondering by a doubt of some kind,   79
but the psalm 'Thou Lord hast made me glad' casts light
that may drive away the clouds from your mind.

And you who are in front and called me to you,   82
say what else you wish to hear, for I came ready
for all your questions, to satisfy you."

"The water," I said, "and the sound of the forest   85
contend in me with a belief I came to
lately, hearing something contrary to this."

At which she said, "I will tell you how what leaves you   88
wondering moves on by its own cause,
and clear away the cloud that troubles you.

The supreme Good, who pleases only Himself,   91
made man good, and for the sake of goodness, and gave this
place to him as a token of eternal peace.

Through his own fault he did not long remain here;   94
through his own fault he changed honest joy
and sweet play into tears and labor.

Perché 'l turbar che sotto da sé fanno   97
l'essalazion de l'acqua e de la terra,
che quanto posson dietro al calor vanno,

a l'uomo non facesse alcuna guerra,   100
questo monte salìo verso 'l ciel tanto,
e libero n'è d'indi ove si serra.

Or perché in circuito tutto quanto   103
l'aere si volge con la prima volta,
se non li è rotto il cerchio d'alcun canto,

in questa altezza ch'è tutta disciolta   106
ne l'aere vivo, tal moto percuote,
e fa sonar la selva perch' è folta;

e la percossa pianta tanto puote,   109
che de la sua virtute l'aura impregna
e quella poi, girando, intorno scuote;

e l'altra terra, secondo ch'è degna   112
per sé e per suo ciel, concepe e figlia
di diverse virtù diverse legna.

Non parrebbe di là poi maraviglia,   115
udito questo, quando alcuna pianta
sanza seme palese vi s'appiglia.

E saper dei che la campagna santa   118
dove tu se', d'ogne semenza è piena,
e frutto ha in sé che di là non si schianta.

L'acqua che vedi non surge di vena   121
che ristori vapor che gel converta,
come fiume ch'acquista e perde lena;

ma esce di fontana salda e certa,   124
che tanto dal voler di Dio riprende,
quant' ella versa da due parti aperta.

Da questa parte con virtù discende   127
che toglie altrui memoria del peccato;
da l'altra d'ogne ben fatto la rende.

So that the disturbances which the earth   97
and water breathe out down below it, as they
follow the heat however they may,

should do no harm to humans, this mountain   100
rose up to such a height toward Heaven,
and from the locked gate upward is free of them.

Now, since the whole of the air goes on circling   103
in a great circuit, with the first turning,
unless somewhere its revolving is broken,

that motion strikes upon this height that is   106
utterly free to the living air, and
makes the forest resound, dense as it is,

and the plant it strikes acquires such power   109
that with its virtue it impregnates the air,
which in its circling scatters it everywhere,

and the rest of the earth, wherever suitable   112
and the air is right for it, conceives and grows
various plants from various virtues.

Once this is known it would not seem to be   115
a marvel that any plant should take
root there from no seed that one can see.

And you should know that the holy ground   118
where you are is full of seed of every kind,
and bears fruit that is never picked back there.

The water that you see springs from no vein   121
refilled by vapor which the cold condenses,
like a river whose power comes and goes,

but flows out of a constant and sure fountain   124
that regains as much by the will of God
as it pours from openings on either side.

On that side it descends with the power   127
to take away the memory of sin,
and restores that of every good done, on the other.

Quinci Letè; così da l'altro lato   *130*
Eünoè si chiama, e non adopra
se quinci e quindi pria non è gustato:

a tutti altri sapori esto è di sopra.   *133*
E avvegna ch'assai possa esser sazia
la sete tua perch' io più non ti scuopra,

darotti un corollario ancor per grazia;   *136*
né credo che 'l mio dir ti sia men caro,
se oltre promession teco si spazia.

Quelli ch'anticamente poetaro   *139*
l'età de l'oro e suo stato felice,
forse in Parnaso esto loco sognaro.

Qui fu innocente l'umana radice;   *142*
qui primavera sempre e ogne frutto;
nettare è questo di che ciascun dice."

Io mi rivolsi 'n dietro allora tutto   *145*
a' miei poeti, e vidi che con riso
udito avëan l'ultimo costrutto;

poi a la bella donna torna' il viso.   *148*

Here it is called Lethe, and in the same way,   *130*
on that side, Eunoè, and it works only
when it has been tasted on this side and that,

and it tastes sweeter than any other,   *133*
and although your thirst might be completely
satisfied if I revealed no more,

I will add a corollary, as a favor,   *136*
and I do not think my words will be less dear
to you because they go beyond my promise.

Those who sang in ancient times of the age   *139*
of gold and of its happy state saw this place,
perhaps, in their dreams on Parnassus.

Here the root of humankind was innocent.   *142*
Here Spring and every fruit lasted forever;
when they told of nectar this is what each meant."

At that I turned around to my poets   *145*
and I saw that they had been listening
to this last interpretation, and were smiling.

Then I turned my face to the beautiful lady again.   *148*

CANTO XXIX

Cantando come donna innamorata,
continüò col fin di sue parole:
"Beati quorum tecta sunt peccata!"

E come ninfe che si givan sole   4
per le salvatiche ombre, disïando
qual di veder, qual di fuggir lo sole,

allor si mosse contra 'l fiume, andando   7
su per la riva; e io pari di lei,
picciol passo con picciol seguitando.

Non eran cento tra ' suoi passi e ' miei,   10
quando le ripe igualmente dier volta,
per modo ch'a levante mi rendei.

Né ancor fu così nostra via molta,   13
quando la donna tutta a me si torse,
dicendo: "Frate mio, guarda e ascolta."

Ed ecco un lustro sùbito trascorse   16
da tutte parti per la gran foresta,
tal che di balenar mi mise in forse.

Ma perché 'l balenar, come vien, resta,   19
e quel, durando, più e più splendeva,
nel mio pensier dicea: "Che cosa è questa?"

E una melodia dolce correva   22
per l'aere luminoso; onde buon zelo
mi fé riprender l'ardimento d'Eva,

che là dove ubidia la terra e 'l cielo,   25
femmina, sola e pur testé formata,
non sofferse di star sotto alcun velo;

sotto 'l qual se divota fosse stata,   28
avrei quelle ineffabili delizie
sentite prima e più lunga fïata.

Singing as a lady sings in love,
she continued, after saying the last word,
"Blessèd are they whose sins are covered,"

and like the nymphs who once wandered alone   4
through the shadows of the forest, one
longing to see, one avoiding the sun,

then she went, against the flow of the river,   7
walking along the bank, and I went with her,
following her small steps with my own small steps.

We had not taken a hundred steps between us   10
when the banks turned to the right as one,
so that I was facing the east again.

And we had not gone far in that direction   13
when the lady turned around toward me
saying, "My brother, look and listen."

And all at once there was a shining   16
that raced through the great forest on all sides,
making me wonder whether it was lightning,

but whereas lightning is gone as swiftly   19
as it comes, this stayed, shining brighter and brighter,
and in my mind I kept saying, "What can this be?"

And running through the luminous air was   22
a sweet melody, so that a good zeal
led me to blame Eve for her recklessness,

that there, where the earth and Heaven were obedient,   25
a woman, alone, and who had just been made,
could not bear to be veiled by anything.

If only she had stayed devoutly under   28
hers, I could have tasted these pleasures
beyond words earlier, and for longer.

Mentr' io m'andava tra tante primizie 31
de l'etterno piacer tutto sospeso,
e disïoso ancora a più letizie,

dinanzi a noi, tal quale un foco acceso, 34
ci si fé l'aere sotto i verdi rami;
e 'l dolce suon per canti era già inteso.

O sacrosante Vergini, se fami, 37
freddi o vigilie mai per voi soffersi,
cagion mi sprona ch'io mercé vi chiami.

Or convien che Elicona per me versi, 40
e Uranìe m'aiuti col suo coro
forti cose a pensar mettere in versi.

Poco più oltre, sette alberi d'oro 43
falsava nel parere il lungo tratto
del mezzo ch'era ancor tra noi e loro;

ma quand' i' fui sì presso di lor fatto, 46
che l'obietto comun, che 'l senso inganna,
non perdea per distanza alcun suo atto,

la virtù ch'a ragion discorso ammanna, 49
sì com' elli eran candelabri apprese,
e ne le voci del cantare "Osanna."

Di sopra fiammeggiava il bello arnese 52
più chiaro assai che luna per sereno
di mezza notte nel suo mezzo mese.

Io mi rivolsi d'ammirazion pieno 55
al buon Virgilio, ed esso mi rispuose
con vista carca di stupor non meno.

Indi rendei l'aspetto a l'alte cose 58
che si movieno incontr' a noi sì tardi,
che foran vinte da novelle spose.

La donna mi sgridò: "Perché pur ardi 61
sì ne l'affetto de le vive luci,
e ciò che vien di retro a lor non guardi?"

While I walked on among so many   31
first fruits of eternal happiness,
enraptured, and longing for still greater joys,

the air under the green boughs before us   34
came to be like a fire blazing
and we could hear that the sweet sound was singing.

Oh most holy virgins, if I have endured   37
fasting, cold, and vigils for you ever,
need drives me now to ask for the reward.

Now is the time for Helicon to brim over   40
and Urania to help me with her choir
to put into verse things hard to hold in thought.

A little farther, seven golden trees   43
appeared as an illusion the long space
gave rise to, which was still between us,

but when I had come so near to them that   46
the common object which deceives the sense
lost none of its features because of distance,

the faculty that nourishes the discourse   49
of reason saw that they were candlesticks,
and heard "Hosanna" in the singing voices.

Above us flamed the beautiful panoply,   52
far brighter than the moon in the clear sky
at midnight in the middle of the month.

Full of wonder, I turned around toward   55
the good Virgil, and he answered
with a look as amazed as my own.

Then I turned my face to the high things again   58
moving so slowly in our direction
that newlywed brides would have overtaken them.

The lady scolded me: "Why are you so   61
intent on the living lights that you pay no
attention to what there is behind them?"

Genti vid' io allor, come a lor duci,   64
venire appresso, vestite di bianco;
e tal candor di qua già mai non fuci.

L'acqua imprendëa dal sinistro fianco,   67
e rendea me la mia sinistra costa,
s'io riguardava in lei, come specchio anco.

Quand' io da la mia riva ebbi tal posta,   70
che solo il fiume mi facea distante,
per veder meglio ai passi diedi sosta,

e vidi le fiammelle andar davante,   73
lasciando dietro a sé l'aere dipinto,
e di tratti pennelli avean sembiante;

sì che lì sopra rimanea distinto   76
di sette liste, tutte in quei colori
onde fa l'arco il Sole e Delia il cinto.

Questi ostendali in dietro eran maggiori   79
che la mia vista; e, quanto a mio avviso,
diece passi distavan quei di fori.

Sotto così bel ciel com' io diviso,   82
ventiquattro seniori, a due a due,
coronati venien di fiordaliso.

Tutti cantavan: "*Benedicta* tue   85
ne le figlie d'Adamo, e benedette
sieno in etterno le bellezze tue!"

Poscia che i fiori e l'altre fresche erbette   88
a rimpetto di me da l'altra sponda
libere fuor da quelle genti elette,

sì come luce luce in ciel seconda,   91
vennero appresso lor quattro animali,
coronati ciascun di verde fronda.

Ognuno era pennuto di sei ali;   94
le penne piene d'occhi; e li occhi d'Argo,
se fosser vivi, sarebber cotali.

Then I saw people coming after them   64
as after their leaders; they were dressed in white,
and here there was never whiteness like that.

The water held my image on my left   67
and like a mirror showed me my own left
in a reflection, when I looked at it.

When I was at a point along the bank   70
where my distance from them was only
the river's width, I stood still, the better to see,

and I saw the flames moving ahead, leaving   73
the air painted behind them, and they
looked the way pennons do, streaming

so that overhead it was striped with seven   76
bands, in all the colors which the sun
makes his bow from, and Delia her girdle.

Those standards went back farther than I   79
could see, and to my mind there seemed to be
ten paces between the outer ones.

Under a sky as beautiful as I   82
have said came four and twenty elders, and they
walked two by two, wearing crowns of lilies.

All of them were singing, "Blessèd are you   85
among the daughters of Adam, and to
all eternity may your beauty be blessed."

After the flowers and other tender growth   88
opposite to me on the other shore
were without those elect people once more,

in the way star succeeds star in heaven   91
four animals came following them, each one
wearing green leaves made into a crown.

Each one of them was winged with six wings,   94
the feathers full of eyes, and the eyes of Argus,
if they were living, would be like those.

A descriver lor forme più non spargo 97
rime, lettor; ch'altra spesa mi strigne,
tanto ch'a questa non posso esser largo;

ma leggi Ezechïel, che li dipigne 100
come li vide da la fredda parte
venir con vento e con nube e con igne;

e quali i troverai ne le sue carte, 103
tali eran quivi, salvo ch'a le penne
Giovanni è meco e da lui si diparte.

Lo spazio dentro a lor quattro contenne 106
un carro, in su due rote, trïunfale,
ch'al collo d'un grifon tirato venne.

Esso tendeva in sù l'una e l'altra ale 109
tra la mezzana e le tre e tre liste,
sì ch'a nulla, fendendo, facea male.

Tanto salivan che non eran viste; 112
le membra d'oro avea quant' era uccello,
e bianche l'altre, di vermiglio miste.

Non che Roma di carro così bello 115
rallegrasse Affricano, o vero Augusto,
ma quel del Sol saria pover con ello;

quel del Sol che, svïando, fu combusto 118
per l'orazion de la Terra devota,
quando fu Giove arcanamente giusto.

Tre donne in giro da la destra rota 121
venian danzando; l'una tanto rossa
ch'a pena fora dentro al foco nota;

l'altr' era come se le carni e l'ossa 124
fossero state di smeraldo fatte;
la terza parea neve testé mossa;

e or parëan da la bianca tratte, 127
or da la rossa; e dal canto di questa
l'altre toglien l'andare e tarde e ratte.

I will not waste more rhymes describing their 97
forms, reader, for I am pressed by another
demand that does not leave me scope for this,

but read Ezekiel who portrays them as 100
he saw them, out of the cold places
coming with wind and cloud and fire,

and as in his pages you will find them, 103
so were they here, all except for the wings,
where John is with me and departs from him.

The space in the middle of these four contained 106
a two-wheeled triumphal chariot
with the neck of a griffin drawing it:

he stretched one wing and the other upward, between 109
the middle streamer and the two bands of three,
so that he did not cut or damage any.

They rose so high that they were out of sight. 112
The bird parts of him were made of gold
and the rest of him, mingled with red, was white.

Not only did Rome with so fine a chariot 115
never rejoice Africanus nor even Augustus,
but that of the sun would be poor beside it,

that of the sun which, leaving its track, was 118
burned up at the devout prayer of the earth
when Jove secretly acted with justice.

Beside the right wheel, dancing in a ring, 121
came three ladies: one of them so red
that in a fire she would not be noted;

another was as though her flesh and bone 124
were made of emeralds; the third one
seemed to be snow that only then had fallen.

And it seemed they were led now by the white, 127
now by the red, the others taking
their pace, slowing and quickening, from her song.

Da la sinistra quattro facean festa,   130
in porpore vestite, dietro al modo
d'una di lor ch'avea tre occhi in testa.

Appresso tutto il pertrattato nodo   133
vidi due vecchi in abito dispari,
ma pari in atto e onesto e sodo.

L'un si mostrava alcun de' famigliari   136
di quel sommo Ipocràte che natura
a li animali fé ch'ell' ha più cari;

mostrava l'altro la contraria cura   139
con una spada lucida e aguta,
tal che di qua dal rio mi fé paura.

Poi vidi quattro in umile paruta;   142
e di retro da tutti un vecchio solo
venir, dormendo, con la faccia arguta.

E questi sette col primaio stuolo   145
erano abitüati, ma di gigli
dintorno al capo non facëan brolo,

anzi di rose e d'altri fior vermigli;   148
giurato avria poco lontano aspetto
che tutti ardesser di sopra da' cigli.

E quando il carro a me fu a rimpetto,   151
un tuon s'udì, e quelle genti degne
parvero aver l'andar più interdetto,

fermandosi ivi con le prime insegne.   154

On the left there were four, making a festival,   130
dressed in purple, following the lead
of the one who had three eyes in her head.

Behind the whole knot that I have portrayed   133
I saw two old men, different in dress
but equally venerable and dignified.

One showed that he was among the descendants   136
of that supreme Hippocrates, whom nature
formed for those creatures who are dearest to her.

The other showed the opposite intent,   139
with a sword so sharp and shining that I,
on the other side of the river, was frightened.

Then I saw four of humble appearance   142
and behind all of them an old man alone
came in his sleep, with a sharp countenance.

And these seven were like the group who led,   145
in their garments, except that they had
no garlands of lilies around their heads

but instead roses and other red flowers.   148
One would have sworn, from a little distance,
that from the eyebrows up they were on fire.

And when the chariot was across from me   151
a sound of thunder was heard and that noble company
seemed forbidden to go any farther,

stopping there with the banners before them.   154

CANTO XXX

Quando il settentrïon del primo cielo,
che né occaso mai seppe né orto
né d'altra nebbia che di colpa velo,

e che faceva lì ciascuno accorto   4
di suo dover, come 'l più basso face
qual temon gira per venire a porto,

fermo s'affisse: la gente verace,   7
venuta prima tra 'l grifone ed esso,
al carro volse sé come a sua pace;

e un di loro, quasi da ciel messo,   10
"*Veni, sponsa, de Libano*" cantando
gridò tre volte, e tutti li altri appresso.

Quali i beati al novissimo bando   13
surgeran presti ognun di sua caverna,
la revestita voce alleluiando,

cotali in su la divina basterna   16
si levar cento, *ad vocem tanti senis*,
ministri e messaggier di vita etterna.

Tutti dicean: "*Benedictus qui venis!*"   19
e fior gittando e di sopra e dintorno,
"*Manibus, oh, date lilïa plenis!*"

Io vidi già nel cominciar del giorno   22
la parte orïental tutta rosata,
e l'altro ciel di bel sereno addorno;

e la faccia del sol nascere ombrata,   25
sì che per temperanza di vapori
l'occhio la sostenea lunga fïata:

così dentro una nuvola di fiori   28
che da le mani angeliche saliva
e ricadeva in giù dentro e di fori,

CANTO XXX

When the Wain of the first heaven,
which never knew setting nor rising
nor any mist except the veil of sin,

and made everyone there know what was   4
each one's duty, as the lower Wain does
for the one at the tiller, entering port,

stood still, the true company that had come   7
at first between the griffin and it,
turned, as to their peace, to the chariot,

and one of them, like a herald from Heaven,   10
singing, *"Come, bride, out of Lebanon,"*
shouted three times, and all the rest after him.

As the blessèd, when the last trumpet sounds,   13
will rise from the tomb, eagerly each one,
"Hallelujah" in each voice put on again,

so, over the holy hooded chariot,   16
at the voice of so great an elder, a hundred
messengers and ministers of eternal life

were, all of them, saying, *"Blessèd is He who comes,"*   19
scattering flowers upward and around them,
saying, *"Oh with full hands give lilies."*

I saw at the beginning of the day   22
it was all the color of roses to the east
and a clear sky made beautiful the rest,

and the face of the sun emerged shaded   25
so that, through the mists that tempered it
the eye could rest for a long time upon it.

So, in a cloud of flowers rising   28
from the angelic hands and again falling
into the chariot and around it,

sovra candido vel cinta d'uliva   31
donna m'apparve, sotto verde manto
vestita di color di fiamma viva.

E lo spirito mio, che già cotanto   34
tempo era stato ch'a la sua presenza
non era di stupor, tremando, affranto,

sanza de li occhi aver più conoscenza,   37
per occulta virtù che da lei mosse,
d'antico amor sentì la gran potenza.

Tosto che ne la vista mi percosse   40
l'alta virtù che già m'avea trafitto
prima ch'io fuor di püerizia fosse,

volsimi a la sinistra col respitto   43
col quale il fantolin corre a la mamma
quando ha paura o quando elli è afflitto,

per dicere a Virgilio: "Men che dramma   46
di sangue m'è rimaso che non tremi:
conosco i segni de l'antica fiamma."

Ma Virgilio n'avea lasciati scemi   49
di sé, Virgilio dolcissimo patre,
Virgilio a cui per mia salute die'mi;

né quantunque perdeo l'antica matre,   52
valse a le guance nette di rugiada
che, lagrimando, non tornasser atre.

"Dante, perché Virgilio se ne vada,   55
non pianger anco, non piangere ancora;
ché pianger ti conven per altra spada."

Quasi ammiraglio che in poppa e in prora   58
viene a veder la gente che ministra
per li altri legni, e a ben far l'incora;

in su la sponda del carro sinistra,   61
quando mi volsi al suon del nome mio,
che di necessità qui si registra,

wearing an olive wreath on a white veil,
a lady appeared to me, in a green mantle,
and her garments were the color of living flame.

31

And in my spirit, which for so long, by then,
had not been left helplessly undone
with awe and trembling in her presence,

34

without more knowledge from the eyes, but by
an unseen force that was coming from her, I
felt the old love in its great power.

37

And as soon as the high force beat upon my
sight, as it had pierced me before I
had yet emerged out of my childhood,

40

I turned to the left with the confidence that
a little child shows, running to its mother
when something has frightened it or troubled it,

43

to say to Virgil, "Not even one drop
of blood is left in me that is not trembling;
I recognize the signs of the old burning."

46

But Virgil had left us, he was no longer there
among us, Virgil, most tender father,
Virgil to whom I gave myself to save me,

49

nor did all that our ancient parent
had lost have any power to prevent
my dew-washed cheeks from running dark with tears.

52

"Dante, because Virgil leaves you, do
not weep yet, do not weep even yet, for you
still have another sword that you must weep for."

55

Like an admiral going from stern to bow
to see the men who are in service on
the other ships and to encourage them,

58

so at the left rail of the chariot
when I turned at the sound of my name
which of necessity is here noted,

61

vidi la donna che pria m'appario   64
velata sotto l'angelica festa,
drizzar li occhi ver' me di qua dal rio.

Tutto che 'l vel che le scendea di testa,   67
cerchiato de le fronde di Minerva,
non la lasciasse parer manifesta,

regalmente ne l'atto ancor proterva   70
continüò come colui che dice
e 'l più caldo parlar dietro reserva:

"Guardaci ben! Ben sem, ben sem Beatrice.   73
Come degnasti d'accedere al monte?
non sapei tu che qui è l'uom felice?"

Li occhi mi cadder giù nel chiaro fonte;   76
ma veggendomi in esso, i trassi a l'erba,
tanta vergogna mi gravò la fronte.

Così la madre al figlio par superba,   79
com' ella parve a me; perché d'amaro
sente il sapor de la pietade acerba.

Ella si tacque; e li angeli cantaro   82
di sùbito *"In te, Domine, speravi"*;
ma oltre *"pedes meos"* non passaro.

Sì come neve tra le vive travi   85
per lo dosso d'Italia si congela,
soffiata e stretta da li venti schiavi,

poi, liquefatta, in sé stessa trapela,   88
pur che la terra che perde ombra spiri,
sì che par foco fonder la candela;

così fui sanza lagrime e sospiri   91
anzi 'l cantar di quei che notan sempre
dietro a le note de li etterni giri;

ma poi che 'ntesi ne le dolci tempre   94
lor compatire a me, più che se detto
avesser: 'Donna, perché sì lo stempre?'

    I saw the lady, who first appeared to me   64
veiled beneath the angelic festivity,
turn her eyes to me, across the river.

    Although the veil descending from her head   67
with Minerva's leaves in a wreath around it
did not allow her to be seen distinctly,

    royal, and still severe in her bearing,   70
she went on, like someone who in speaking
holds back the hottest words to the end.

    "Look at me well; for I am, I am certainly   73
Beatrice. How did you dare approach the mountain?
Did you not know that here man is happy?"

    My eyes dropped down to the clear spring,   76
but seeing myself there, I drew them to
the grass, such shame weighing upon my brow.

    As a mother may seem harsh to her child,   79
she seemed to me, because the flavor
of raw pity when tasted is bitter.

    She was silent. And all at once the angels   82
sang, *"In you, Lord, I have put my hope,"* but
not beyond the verse that begins, *"My feet—"*

    As the snow freezes among the living   85
rafters, with the Slavonian wind blowing
and packing it, along the spine of Italy,

    then, melted, drips into itself, if the land   88
breathes as it loses its shadow, so that
it seems like a fire melting a candle,

    so was I, without tears or sighs, before   91
the singing of those who accord forever
with the notes of the eternal spheres,

    but when I heard how in their sweet tones they   94
sympathized with me, more than if they
had said, "Lady, why do you so undo him?"

lo gel che m'era intorno al cor ristretto,   97
spirito e acqua fessi, e con angoscia
de la bocca e de li occhi uscì del petto.

Ella, pur ferma in su la detta coscia   100
del carro stando, a le sustanze pie
volse le sue parole così poscia:

"Voi vigilate ne l'etterno die,   103
sì che notte né sonno a voi non fura
passo che faccia il secol per sue vie;

onde la mia risposta è con più cura   106
che m'intenda colui che di là piagne,
perché sia colpa e duol d'una misura.

Non pur per ovra de le rote magne,   109
che drizzan ciascun seme ad alcun fine
secondo che le stelle son compagne,

ma per larghezza di grazie divine,   112
che sì alti vapori hanno a lor piova,
che nostre viste là non van vicine,

questi fu tal ne la sua vita nova   115
virtüalmente, ch'ogne abito destro
fatto averebbe in lui mirabil prova.

Ma tanto più maligno e più silvestro   118
si fa 'l terren col mal seme e non cólto,
quant' elli ha più di buon vigor terrestro.

Alcun tempo il sostenni col mio volto: 121
mostrando li occhi giovanetti a lui,
meco il menava in dritta parte vòlto.

Sì tosto come in su la soglia fui   124
di mia seconda etade e mutai vita,
questi si tolse a me, e diessi altrui.

Quando di carne a spirto era salita,   127
e bellezza e virtù cresciuta m'era,
fu' io a lui men cara e men gradita;

the ice that had been clamped around my breast   97
turned to breath and water, and came forth
out of my breast through the eyes and mouth.

She, still standing without moving, on   100
the same side of the chariot, turned then
her words toward the compassionate angels:

"You keep watch in the eternal day   103
so that neither night nor sleep robs you
of one step that the world makes on its way,

therefore my answer is made with greater care   106
so that he may understand me, who is weeping there,
and fault and grief may be of the same measure.

Not only through the working of the great   109
wheels which direct each seed toward some end
depending on what stars accompany it,

but through the largesse of divine graces   112
which for their rain have vapors coming from
so high that our sight never comes near them,

such, potentially, was this man   115
in his new life, that every right disposition
would have come to marvelous proof in him,

but the more vigor there is in the ground,   118
the more rank and tangled grows the land
if the seed is bad and tilling left undone.

For a while I sustained him with my face,   121
drawing him, with the sight of my young eyes,
along with me, turned in the right direction.

As soon as I was on the doorsill   124
of my second age, and changed from one life to another
he took himself from me and gave himself to others.

When I had risen from flesh to spirit   127
and my beauty and virtue had become
greater, I was less dear and pleasing to him,

e volse i passi suoi per via non vera,   130
imagini di ben seguendo false,
che nulla promession rendono intera.

Né l'impetrare ispirazion mi valse,   133
con le quali e in sogno e altrimenti
lo rivocai: sì poco a lui ne calse!

Tanto giù cadde, che tutti argomenti   136
a la salute sua eran già corti,
fuor che mostrarli le perdute genti.

Per questo visitai l'uscio d'i morti,   139
e a colui che l'ha qua sù condotto,
li preghi miei, piangendo, furon porti.

Alto fato di Dio sarebbe rotto,   142
se Letè si passasse e tal vivanda
fosse gustata sanza alcuno scotto

di pentimento che lagrime spanda."   145

and he turned his steps in a way that was   130
not the true one, following false images
of good that never yield their full promises.

    Nor did it do me any good to summon   133
inspirations for him, with which I called him
in dreams and otherwise, so little he heeded them.

    So low he fell that every means which might   136
have saved him had become inadequate
other than showing him the lost people.

    For that I visited the door of the dead,   139
and to the one who has led him here
my prayers, spoken through my tears, were offered.

    The high decree of God would be broken   142
if Lethe were passed and such nourishment
were to be tasted without any payment

    in penitence that is poured out in tears."   145

"O tu che se' di là dal fiume sacro,"
volgendo suo parlare a me per punta,
che pur per taglio m'era paruto acro,

ricominciò, seguendo sanza cunta,   4
"dì, dì se questo è vero; a tanta accusa
tua confession conviene esser congiunta."

Era la mia virtù tanto confusa,   7
che la voce si mosse, e pria si spense
che da li organi suoi fosse dischiusa.

Poco sofferse; poi disse: "Che pense?   10
Rispondi a me; ché le memorie triste
in te non sono ancor da l'acqua offense."

Confusione e paura insieme miste   13
mi pinsero un tal "sì" fuor de la bocca,
al quale intender fuor mestier le viste.

Come balestro frange, quando scocca   16
da troppa tesa la sua corda e l'arco,
e con men foga l'asta il segno tocca,

sì scoppia' io sottesso grave carco,   19
fuori sgorgando lagrime e sospiri,
e la voce allentò per lo suo varco.

Ond' ella a me: "Per entro i mie' disiri,   22
che ti menavano ad amar lo bene
di là dal qual non è a che s'aspiri,

quai fossi attraversati o quai catene   25
trovasti, per che del passare innanzi
dovessiti così spogliar la spene?

E quali agevolezze o quali avanzi   28
ne la fronte de li altri si mostraro,
per che dovessi lor passeggiare anzi?"

"Oh you on that side of the sacred river,"
turning the point of her words toward me
when the edge itself had seemed sharp to me,

she began again, going on without pausing,   4
"say, say whether this is true: your confession
must be joined to such accusation."

What strength I had was so bewildered   7
that my voice stirred and was done before
it was set free of the organs that made it.

She scarcely waited, and then said, "What do you think?   10
Answer me, for the water has not
canceled the sad memories in you yet."

Bewilderment and fear mingled together   13
forced out of my mouth such a "yes" that
one would have had to see it to hear it.

As a crossbow, when it is drawn too far,   16
breaks both the cord and the bow so that
the shaft strikes the target with less power,

so I broke under that heavy burden,   19
with tears and sighs out of me pouring,
and my voice collapsed as it was leaving.

At that she said to me, "In your desires of me,   22
which to the love of that good were leading you
beyond which there is nothing to aspire to,

what ditches dug across the way, or chains   25
did you come to, that forced you to abandon
any hope that you had of going on,

and what attractions or advantages   28
were visible on the brows of the others
so that you had no choice but to loiter there?"

Dopo la tratta d'un sospiro amaro,   31
a pena ebbi la voce che rispuose,
e le labbra a fatica la formaro.

Piangendo dissi: "Le presenti cose   34
col falso lor piacer volser miei passi,
tosto che 'l vostro viso si nascose."

Ed ella: "Se tacessi o se negassi   37
ciò che confessi, non fora men nota
la colpa tua: da tal giudice sassi!

Ma quando scoppia de la propria gota   40
l'accusa del peccato, in nostra corte
rivolge sé contra 'l taglio la rota.

Tuttavia, perché mo vergogna porte   43
del tuo errore, e perché altra volta,
udendo le serene, sie più forte,

pon giù il seme del piangere e ascolta: 46
sì udirai come in contraria parte
mover dovieti mia carne sepolta.

Mai non t'appresentò natura o arte   49
piacer, quanto le belle membra in ch'io
rinchiusa fui, e che so' 'n terra sparte;

e se 'l sommo piacer sì ti fallio   52
per la mia morte, qual cosa mortale
dovea poi trarre te nel suo disio?

Ben ti dovevi, per lo primo strale   55
de le cose fallaci, levar suso
di retro a me che non era più tale.

Non ti dovea gravar le penne in giuso,   58
ad aspettar più colpo, o pargoletta
o altra novità con sì breve uso.

Novo augelletto due o tre aspetta;   61
ma dinanzi da li occhi d'i pennuti
rete si spiega indarno o si saetta."

After I had drawn a bitter sigh   31
I had scarcely any voice to answer,
and my lips formed one with great labor.

In tears I said, "Things of the moment   34
with their false pleasure turned my steps away
at once, after your face was hidden."

And she, "If you had said nothing or denied   37
what you confess, your guilt would be noted
nevertheless, by such a judge is it known!

But when the accusation of the sin   40
bursts from the cheeks of the accused, in our court
it turns the grindstone against the edge again.

All the same, so that now you may bear   43
the shame of your mistakes, and when you hear
the Sirens another time you may be stronger,

lay down the sowing of tears and listen   46
so you may hear how my flesh in the tomb
should have led you in the other direction.

Never did nature or art show you such   49
beauty as the lovely members in which
I was enclosed, and they are crumbled in earth.

And if the highest beauty, with my dying,   52
so failed you, what mortal thing after that
should have drawn you into desiring it?

Indeed at the first arrow of deceptive things   55
you should have risen and followed after
me, who was of that kind then no longer.

Your wings should not have been weighed down by any   58
girl or other vanity known so briefly,
and wait to be shot repeatedly.

Two or three times a fledgling bird will wait,   61
but in vain is the net spread or arrow shot
before the eyes of the bird when it has grown."

Quali fanciulli, vergognando, muti   64
con li occhi a terra stannosi, ascoltando
e sé riconoscendo e ripentuti,

tal mi stav' io; ed ella disse: "Quando   67
per udir se' dolente, alza la barba,
e prenderai più doglia riguardando."

Con men di resistenza si dibarba   70
robusto cerro, o vero al nostral vento
o vero a quel de la terra di Iarba,

ch'io non levai al suo comando il mento;   73
e quando per la barba il viso chiese,
ben conobbi il velen de l'argomento.

E come la mia faccia si distese,   76
posarsi quelle prime creature
da loro aspersïon l'occhio comprese;

e le mie luci, ancor poco sicure,   79
vider Beatrice volta in su la fiera
ch'è sola una persona in due nature.

Sotto 'l suo velo e oltre la rivera   82
vincer pariemi più sé stessa antica,
vincer che l'altre qui, quand' ella c'era.

Di penter sì mi punse ivi l'ortica,   85
che di tutte altre cose qual mi torse
più nel suo amor, più mi si fé nemica.

Tanta riconoscenza il cor mi morse,   88
ch'io caddi vinto; e quale allora femmi,
salsi colei che la cagion mi porse.

Poi, quando il cor virtù di fuor rendemmi,   91
la donna ch'io avea trovata sola
sopra me vidi, e dicea: "Tiemmi, tiemmi!"

Tratto m'avea nel fiume infin la gola,   94
e tirandosi me dietro sen giva
sovresso l'acqua lieve come scola.

As children stand feeling ashamed, without   64
a word, their eyes on the ground, listening,
admitting what they have done and repenting,

so I stood there, and she said, "Since what you   67
hear is painful, lift up your beard and you
will find that what you see is even more so."

With less resistance the massive oak is   70
uprooted, whether by wind out of our own
regions or that from the land of Iarbas;

I lifted my chin then at her command,   73
and when she summoned my face by the beard
I felt the full venom of the argument.

And when my face was raised, my eyes   76
came to see that those primal creatures
had paused in the scattering of flowers,

and my eyes, while they were still uncertain,   79
saw that Beatrice had turned toward the beast
that in two natures is one person.

Under her veil and across the stream, it seemed   82
to me she surpassed her former self even more
than she surpassed the others when she was here.

The nettle of remorse so stung me there   85
that whatever, among all others, had most
bent me to love it I hated worst.

Such recognition ate at my heart that   88
I fell, overcome, and what I became then
she knows who was the reason for it.

Then, when my heart gave my outward sense again   91
to me, I saw the lady I had found alone
above me, and she said, "Hold me! Hold me!"

She had drawn me into the river   94
up to my throat, and pulling me after her
she was moving, light as a shuttle, over the water.

Quando fui presso a la beata riva,   97
"*Asperges me*" sì dolcemente udissi,
che nol so rimembrar, non ch'io lo scriva.

La bella donna ne le braccia aprissi;   100
abbracciommi la testa e mi sommerse
ove convenne ch'io l'acqua inghiottissi.

Indi mi tolse, e bagnato m'offerse   103
dentro a la danza de le quattro belle;
e ciascuna del braccio mi coperse.

"Noi siam qui ninfe e nel ciel siamo stelle;   106
pria che Beatrice discendesse al mondo,
fummo ordinate a lei per sue ancelle.

Merrenti a li occhi suoi; ma nel giocondo   109
lume ch'è dentro aguzzeranno i tuoi
le tre di là, che miran più profondo."

Così cantando cominciaro; e poi   112
al petto del grifon seco menarmi,
ove Beatrice stava volta a noi.

Disser: "Fa che le viste non risparmi;   115
posto t'avem dinanzi a li smeraldi
ond' Amor già ti trasse le sue armi."

Mille disiri più che fiamma caldi   118
strinsermi li occhi a li occhi rilucenti,
che pur sopra 'l grifone stavan saldi.

Come in lo specchio il sol, non altrimenti   121
la doppia fiera dentro vi raggiava,
or con altri, or con altri reggimenti.

Pensa, lettor, s'io mi maravigliava,   124
quando vedea la cosa in sé star queta,
e ne l'idolo suo si trasmutava.

Mentre che piena di stupore e lieta   127
l'anima mia gustava di quel cibo
che, saziando di sé, di sé asseta,

When I was near the blessèd shore I heard   97
"*Purge me*" chanted so sweetly that it
cannot be written or even remembered.

The beautiful lady opened her arms,   100
embraced my head, and drew me under
so that I had to swallow the water.

Then she brought me out and, bathed now, led me   103
into the dance of the beautiful four,
and each of them held an arm over me.

"We are nymphs here and are stars in Heaven.   106
Before Beatrice went down into the world
we were ordained to be her handmaidens.

We will take you to her eyes. But in the happy   109
light within them, the three on the other
side will sharpen yours, for they see more deeply."

So they began to sing, and they drew me   112
with them to the breast of the griffin
where Beatrice stood, turned in our direction,

and said, "Be careful not to look away now.   115
We have brought you before the emeralds
from which Love shot his arrows once at you."

A thousand desires hotter than a flame   118
held my eyes on those shining eyes
that were fixed on the griffin the whole time.

Like the sun in a mirror, not otherwise,   121
the double beast was shining in her eyes
now with one nature, now with the other.

Think, reader, whether I marveled, seeing   124
the object remain still in itself, and
only the image of it changing.

While my soul, full of amazement and joy,   127
was tasting that nourishment which always
is enough, and for which one remains hungry,

sé dimostrando di più alto tribo   130
ne li atti, l'altre tre si fero avanti,
danzando al loro angelico caribo.

"Volgi, Beatrice, volgi li occhi santi,"   133
era la sua canzone, "al tuo fedele
che, per vederti, ha mossi passi tanti!

Per grazia fa noi grazia che disvele   136
a lui la bocca tua, sì che discerna
la seconda bellezza che tu cele."

O isplendor di viva luce etterna,   139
chi palido si fece sotto l'ombra
sì di Parnaso, o bevve in sua cisterna,

che non paresse aver la mente ingombra,   142
tentando a render te qual tu paresti
là dove armonizzando il ciel t'adombra,

quando ne l'aere aperto ti solvesti?   145

the other three, who by their bearing showed 130
their higher order, came dancing forward
to the angelic measure their feet followed.

"Turn, Beatrice, turn your holy eyes," 133
they were saying, "to your faithful one who
has traveled so many steps to see you.

Out of your grace, grace us by unveiling 136
your mouth to him, so that he may perceive
the second beauty which you are concealing."

Oh splendor of the living eternal light, 139
who has ever grown so pale in the shadow
of Parnassus, or has drunk from its well so

as not to have a mind that seems encumbered, 142
trying to render you as you appeared
there shaded by the harmonies of Heaven,

when you disclosed yourself to the open air? 145

Tant' eran li occhi miei fissi e attenti
a disbramarsi la decenne sete,
che li altri sensi m'eran tutti spenti.

Ed essi quinci e quindi avien parete   4
di non caler—così lo santo riso
a sé traéli con l'antica rete!—

quando per forza mi fu vòlto il viso   7
ver' la sinistra mia da quelle dee,
perch' io udi' da loro un "Troppo fiso!";

e la disposizion ch'a veder èe   10
ne li occhi pur testé dal sol percossi,
sanza la vista alquanto esser mi fée.

Ma poi ch'al poco il viso riformossi   13
(e dico 'al poco' per rispetto al molto
sensibile onde a forza mi rimossi),

vidi 'n sul braccio destro esser rivolto   16
lo glorïoso essercito, e tornarsi
col sole e con le sette fiamme al volto.

Come sotto li scudi per salvarsi   19
volgesi schiera, e sé gira col segno,
prima che possa tutta in sé mutarsi;

quella milizia del celeste regno   22
che procedeva, tutta trapassonne
pria che piegasse il carro il primo legno.

Indi a le rote si tornar le donne,   25
e 'l grifon mosse il benedetto carco
sì, che però nulla penna crollonne.

La bella donna che mi trasse al varco   28
e Stazio e io seguitavam la rota
che fé l'orbita sua con minore arco.

So fixed were my eyes, and so intent upon
satisfying a ten years' thirst, that every
other sense had been extinguished in me

and on one side and the other they had a wall   4
of not caring; thus the holy smile
drew them to itself with the old net,

when my face was perforce made to turn   7
to my left by those goddesses, as I
heard them saying, "Too fixedly,"

and the condition of sight that is in   10
eyes that have just been struck by the sun
left me for a time without vision.

But when my sight had found the less again   13
(I say "the less" with respect to the great
object from which I was forced to turn),

I saw that the glorious army had wheeled   16
around upon its right and, facing
the sun and the seven flames, it was returning.

As a troop, under its shields, wheels around   19
to save itself, turning with its standard
before the whole of it has come around,

that legion of the eternal   22
kingdom which led the way had all gone past
before the chariot turned around its pole.

Then the ladies stepped to the wheels again   25
and the griffin moved the blessèd burden
without disturbing any of its feathers.

The beautiful lady who had brought me through   28
the crossing, and Statius, and I, followed the wheel
that went around with the smaller arc of the two.

Sì passeggiando l'alta selva vòta,   31
colpa di quella ch'al serpente crese,
temprava i passi un'angelica nota.

Forse in tre voli tanto spazio prese   34
disfrenata saetta, quanto eramo
rimossi, quando Bëatrice scese.

Io senti' mormorare a tutti "Adamo";   37
poi cerchiaro una pianta dispogliata
di foglie e d'altra fronda in ciascun ramo.

La coma sua, che tanto si dilata   40
più quanto più è sù, fora da l'Indi
ne' boschi lor per altezza ammirata.

"Beato se', grifon, che non discindi   43
col becco d'esto legno dolce al gusto,
poscia che mal si torce il ventre quindi."

Così dintorno a l'albero robusto   46
gridaron li altri; e l'animal binato:
"Sì si conserva il seme d'ogne giusto."

E vòlto al temo ch'elli avea tirato,   49
trasselo al piè de la vedova frasca,
e quel di lei a lei lasciò legato.

Come le nostre piante, quando casca   52
giù la gran luce mischiata con quella
che raggia dietro a la celeste lasca,

turgide fansi, e poi si rinovella   55
di suo color ciascuna, pria che 'l sole
giunga li suoi corsier sotto altra stella;

men che di rose e più che di vïole   58
colore aprendo, s'innovò la pianta,
che prima avea le ramora sì sole.

Io non lo 'ntesi, né qui non si canta   61
l'inno che quella gente allor cantaro,
né la nota soffersi tutta quanta.

As we passed through the tall forest, empty   31
through her fault who believed a serpent, we
walked in time to an angelic music.

About three flights that an arrow would fly,   34
loosed from the string, was the distance we
had traveled when Beatrice stepped down.

I heard all of them murmur, "Adam,"   37
then they went around the tree that had been
stripped of its flowers and leaves on every limb.

Its branches, which spread farther out the higher   40
they rose, would have been marveled at
in the forests of India, for their height.

"Blessèd are you, griffin, who did not pick   43
from this tree, though it tastes sweet, with your beak,
for the belly writhes with pain because of it,"

so the others shouted around the massive   46
tree, and the twice-born animal said, "Thus
is preserved the seed of all righteousness."

And turning to the shaft he had drawn, he brought it   49
to the foot of the widowed trunk and left it
bound to the tree from which it had been made.

As plants with us, when the great light descends   52
upon them mixed with that shining behind
the Fishes in heaven, begin to swell

and then they become new again, each one   55
in its own color, before the sun
harnesses his steeds under other stars,

taking on color, less than roses but   58
more than violets, the tree once more
renewed itself, whose limbs had been so bare.

I did not understand, nor can I sing here   61
the hymns that company was singing there,
nor could I hear that music to the end.

S'io potessi ritrar come assonnaro   64
li occhi spietati udendo di Siringa,
li occhi a cui pur vegghiar costò sì caro;

come pintor che con essempro pinga,   67
disegnerei com' io m'addormentai;
ma qual vuol sia che l'assonnar ben finga.

Però trascorro a quando mi svegliai,   70
e dico ch'un splendor mi squarciò 'l velo
del sonno, e un chiamar: "Surgi: che fai?"

Quali a veder de' fioretti del melo   73
che del suo pome li angeli fa ghiotti
e perpetüe nozze fa nel cielo,

Pietro e Giovanni e Iacopo condotti   76
e vinti, ritornaro a la parola
da la qual furon maggior sonni rotti,

e videro scemata loro scuola   79
così di Moïsè come d'Elia,
e al maestro suo cangiata stola;

tal torna' io, e vidi quella pia   82
sovra me starsi che conducitrice
fu de' miei passi lungo 'l fiume pria.

E tutto in dubbio dissi: "Ov' è Beatrice?"   85
Ond' ella: "Vedi lei sotto la fronda
nova sedere in su la sua radice.

Vedi la compagnia che la circonda: 88
li altri dopo 'l grifon sen vanno suso
con più dolce canzone e più profonda."

E se più fu lo suo parlar diffuso,   91
non so, però che già ne li occhi m'era
quella ch'ad altro intender m'avea chiuso.

Sola sedeasi in su la terra vera,   94
come guardia lasciata lì del plaustro
che legar vidi a la biforme fera.

If I could depict how the pitiless eyes,   64
hearing of Syrinx, were lulled asleep,
those eyes whose watching had taken such toll,

as a painter who paints from a model   67
I would depict how I passed into sleep,
but let him truly paint falling asleep who will.

So I go on to when I woke, and I   70
say that a splendor broke the veil of my
sleep, and a call: "Stand up! What are you doing?"

As when they were brought to look at the apple tree   73
in bloom, whose fruit renders the angels greedy
and makes a perpetual marriage feast in Heaven,

Peter and John and James were overcome   76
and at that word came to themselves again
by which slumbers deeper than theirs were broken,

and they saw that their company had grown   79
smaller, with both Moses and Elias gone,
and their master in different raiment,

so I came back to myself and saw that   82
compassionate lady standing over me
who at first along the stream had led me.

And all doubtful, I said, "Where is Beatrice?"   85
To which she answered, "See, she is sitting there
on the root, with the new leaves over her.

See the company sitting around her.   88
The others have gone upward, following
the griffin, with sweeter and deeper song."

And I do not know whether she said more,   91
for in my eyes already was the one
who had closed in me every other attention.

She was sitting by herself on the bare ground,   94
left there as the chariot's guardian,
which I had seen the twice-born beast fasten.

In cerchio le facevan di sé claustro
le sette ninfe, con quei lumi in mano
che son sicuri d'Aquilone e d'Austro.

97

"Qui sarai tu poco tempo silvano;
e sarai meco sanza fine cive
di quella Roma onde Cristo è romano.

100

Però, in pro del mondo che mal vive,
al carro tieni or li occhi, e quel che vedi,
ritornato di là, fa che tu scrive."

103

Così Beatrice; e io, che tutto ai piedi
d'i suoi comandamenti era divoto,
la mente e li occhi ov' ella volle diedi.

106

Non scese mai con sì veloce moto
foco di spessa nube, quando piove
da quel confine che più va remoto,

109

com' io vidi calar l'uccel di Giove
per l'alber giù, rompendo de la scorza,
non che d'i fiori e de le foglie nove;

112

e ferì 'l carro di tutta sua forza;
ond' el piegò come nave in fortuna,
vinta da l'onda, or da poggia, or da orza.

115

Poscia vidi avventarsi ne la cuna
del trïunfal veiculo una volpe
che d'ogne pasto buon parea digiuna;

118

ma, riprendendo lei di laide colpe,
la donna mia la volse in tanta futa
quanto sofferser l'ossa sanza polpe.

121

Poscia per indi ond' era pria venuta,
l'aguglia vidi scender giù ne l'arca
del carro e lasciar lei di sé pennuta;

124

e qual esce di cuor che si rammarca,
tal voce uscì del cielo e cotal disse:
"O navicella mia, com' mal se' carca!"

127

The seven nymphs in a ring made of themselves
a cloister for her, with those lights in their hands
which are safe from the north and the south winds.

97

"Here you will be a forester for only
a little while, and without end will be with me
a citizen of that Rome of which Christ is Roman.

100

So, for the good of the world whose life is evil,
fix your eyes on the chariot, and when
you are back there again, write what you have seen."

103

So Beatrice said, and I who was wholly
devoted at the feet of her commands
gave over to her wishes my eyes and mind.

106

Never did fire with so swift a motion
drop out of a dense cloud, coming down
the whole distance from the farthest confine,

109

as I saw the bird of Jove descend upon
the tree, tearing not only the new
leaves and the flowers but the bark also,

112

and with its full force it struck the chariot
so that it shied like a vessel in a storm,
washed by the waves now to starboard, now to port.

115

Then I saw, leaping into the cradle
of the triumphal chariot, a fox
that seemed for long not to have eaten, or not well,

118

but my lady, reproving its ugly offenses,
drove it away again, fleeing as well
as its emaciated bones could manage.

121

Then, out of the same place it came from first
I saw the eagle plunge into the chariot's
body and leave it feathered with its own feathers.

124

And such a voice as comes from a grieving heart
came from Heaven, saying, "Oh my little boat
that has been given such an evil load!"

127

Poi parve a me che la terra s'aprisse 130
tr'ambo le ruote, e vidi uscirne un drago
che per lo carro sù la coda fisse;

e come vespa che ritragge l'ago, 133
a sé traendo la coda maligna,
trasse del fondo, e gissen vago vago.

Quel che rimase, come da gramigna 136
vivace terra, da la piuma, offerta
forse con intenzion sana e benigna,

si ricoperse, e funne ricoperta 139
e l'una e l'altra rota e 'l temo, in tanto
che più tiene un sospir la bocca aperta.

Trasformato così 'l dificio santo 142
mise fuor teste per le parti sue,
tre sovra 'l temo e una in ciascun canto.

Le prime eran cornute come bue, 145
ma le quattro un sol corno avean per fronte:
simile mostro visto ancor non fue.

Sicura, quasi rocca in alto monte, 148
seder sovresso una puttana sciolta
m'apparve con le ciglia intorno pronte;

e come perché non li fosse tolta, 151
vidi di costa a lei dritto un gigante;
e basciavansi insieme alcuna volta.

Ma perché l'occhio cupido e vagante 154
a me rivolse, quel feroce drudo
la flagellò dal capo infin le piante;

poi, di sospetto pieno e d'ira crudo, 157
disciolse il mostro, e trassel per la selva,
tanto che sol di lei mi fece scudo

a la puttana e a la nova belva. 160

Then it appeared to me that the earth opened 130
between the two wheels and I saw a dragon
come out and drive its tail up through the car,

and in the way a wasp withdraws its sting 133
so it pulled out its malicious tail, taking
part of the underside, and went away happy.

What was left was covered by the feathers 136
as living soil is covered by the wild grass,
perhaps offered out of good will and kindness;

first one wheel and then the other 139
and the shaft were covered over in less time
than a sigh will keep the lips open.

Thus transformed, out of the holy structure 142
heads grew from different parts of itself,
three over the shaft and one from each corner.

The first three had horns on them like oxen, 145
but the fourth had, on each forehead, only one horn.
A monster such as that had never been seen.

Secure as a stronghold on a high mountain 148
a whore appeared to me, loose in her gown,
sitting on it, brows raised, looking around.

And I saw a giant standing beside her 151
as though to make sure she was not taken from him,
and again and again they kissed each other.

But because she turned upon me her 154
lustful roving eye, that ferocious lover
beat her from her head to the soles of her feet,

then, full of suspicion and rough rage, he untied 157
the monster and through the forest dragged it
until the place itself had hidden

the whore and the strange wild creature from me. 160

CANTO XXXIII

"*Deus, venerunt gentes,*" alternando
or tre or quattro dolce salmodia,
le donne incominciaro, e lagrimando;

e Bëatrice, sospirosa e pia,   4
quelle ascoltava sì fatta, che poco
più a la croce si cambiò Maria.

Ma poi che l'altre vergini dier loco   7
a lei di dir, levata dritta in pè,
rispuose, colorata come foco:

"*Modicum, et non videbitis me;*   10
et iterum, sorelle mie dilette,
modicum, et vos videbitis me."

Poi le si mise innanzi tutte e sette,   13
e dopo sé, solo accennando, mosse
me e la donna e 'l savio che ristette.

Così sen giva; e non credo che fosse   16
lo decimo suo passo in terra posto,
quando con li occhi li occhi mi percosse;

e con tranquillo aspetto "Vien più tosto,"   19
mi disse, "tanto che, s'io parlo teco,
ad ascoltarmi tu sie ben disposto."

Sì com' io fui, com' io dovëa, seco,   22
dissemi: "Frate, perché non t'attenti
a domandarmi omai venendo meco?"

Come a color che troppo reverenti   25
dinanzi a suo maggior parlando sono,
che non traggon la voce viva ai denti,

avvenne a me, che sanza intero suono   28
incominciai: "Madonna, mia bisogna
voi conoscete, e ciò ch'ad essa è buono."

"Oh God, the heathen have come," the ladies were
singing in alternation, now three, now four,
beginning a sweet psalmody, and weeping,

and Beatrice, sighing and pitying,   4
listened to them, and overcome by it so
that Mary at the Cross was scarcely more so.

But after the other virgins gave her   7
place to speak, she rose onto her feet
and was the color of fire as she answered,

"A little while and you will not see me,"   10
and again, "my belovèd sisters,
"a little while and you will see me."

Then she put all seven in front of her,   13
and behind her, simply beckoning, she put
me, and the lady, and the sage who remained there.

So she went on, and I do not believe   16
that she had set a tenth step on the ground
before she struck upon my eyes with her own,

and with a tranquil look, "Come more quickly,"   19
she said to me, "so that if I speak to you
you will be well placed to listen to me."

Once I was with her, as I was meant to be,   22
she said to me, "Brother, why do you not
venture to question me, now while you come with me?"

As those who are too reverent, speaking   25
in the presence of persons greater than they are,
cannot bring the living voice to their teeth,

so it happened to me, and with only part   28
of a sound I began, "My lady, you know
what my need is, and what is good for it."

Ed ella a me: "Da tema e da vergogna   31
voglio che tu omai ti disviluppe,
sì che non parli più com' om che sogna.

Sappi che 'l vaso che 'l serpente ruppe,   34
fu e non è; ma chi n'ha colpa, creda
che vendetta di Dio non teme suppe.

Non sarà tutto tempo sanza reda   37
l'aguglia che lasciò le penne al carro,
per che divenne mostro e poscia preda;

ch'io veggio certamente, e però il narro,   40
a darne tempo già stelle propinque,
secure d'ogn' intoppo e d'ogne sbarro,

nel quale un cinquecento diece e cinque,   43
messo di Dio, anciderà la fuia
con quel gigante che con lei delinque.

E forse che la mia narrazion buia,   46
qual Temi e Sfinge, men ti persuade,
perch' a lor modo lo 'ntelletto attuia;

ma tosto fier li fatti le Naiade,   49
che solveranno questo enigma forte
sanza danno di pecore o di biade.

Tu nota; e sì come da me son porte,   52
così queste parole segna a' vivi
del viver ch'è un correre a la morte.

E aggi a mente, quando tu le scrivi,   55
di non celar qual hai vista la pianta
ch'è or due volte dirubata quivi.

Qualunque ruba quella o quella schianta,   58
con bestemmia di fatto offende a Dio,
che solo a l'uso suo la creò santa.

Per morder quella, in pena e in disio   61
cinquemilia anni e più l'anima prima
bramò colui che 'l morso in sé punio.

And she to me, "From here on I would have you   31
disengage yourself from fear and shame
so that you no longer speak like a man in a dream.

Know that the vessel which the serpent broke   34
was and is not; but let the one at fault believe
that God's vengeance cannot be frightened off.

Not for all time will the eagle be without   37
an heir, who left the feathers on the chariot
which became a monster and a prey,

for I see clearly and so tell of it: there are   40
stars near us already, bringing us,
undeterred by obstacle or barrier,

a time when a five hundred, ten, and five   43
whom God will send, will slaughter the whore
and the giant who offends with her.

And it may be that my somber story,   46
like Themis and the Sphinx, is harder to
believe because it darkens your mind as they do,

but events, before long, will be the Naiads   49
that will solve this hard enigma without
flocks or harvests being paid for it.

Take note of my words just as I say them,   52
and teach them to those who are living lives
that are races they are running toward death.

And when you come to write it, bear in mind   55
not to keep back what you have seen of the tree
and how, twice over here, it has been ruined.

Whoever robs it, or whoever harms it   58
with an act of blasphemy, offends God,
who for His own sole use made it sacred.

For a bite of it, in craving and torment   61
five thousand years and more the first soul longed
for Him who in Himself punished that taste.

Dorme lo 'ngegno tuo, se non estima   64
per singular cagione essere eccelsa
lei tanto e sì travolta ne la cima.

    E se stati non fossero acqua d'Elsa   67
li pensier vani intorno a la tua mente,
e 'l piacer loro un Piramo a la gelsa,

        per tante circostanze solamente   70
la giustizia di Dio, ne l'interdetto,
conosceresti a l'arbor moralmente.

    Ma perch' io veggio te ne lo 'ntelletto   73
fatto di pietra e, impetrato, tinto,
sì che t'abbaglia il lume del mio detto,

        voglio anco, e se non scritto, almen dipinto, 76
che 'l te ne porti dentro a te per quello
che si reca il bordon di palma cinto."

    E io: "Sì come cera da suggello,   79
che la figura impressa non trasmuta,
segnato è or da voi lo mio cervello.

    Ma perché tanto sovra mia veduta   82
vostra parola disïata vola,
che più la perde quanto più s'aiuta?"

    "Perché conoschi," disse, "quella scuola   85
c'hai seguitata, e veggi sua dottrina
come può seguitar la mia parola;

    e veggi vostra via da la divina   88
distar cotanto, quanto si discorda
da terra il ciel che più alto festina."

    Ond' io rispuosi lei: "Non mi ricorda   91
ch'i' stranïasse me già mai da voi,
né honne coscïenza che rimorda."

    "E se tu ricordar non te ne puoi,"   94
sorridendo rispuose, "or ti rammenta
come bevesti di Letè ancoi;

Your intelligence is asleep if it does not 64
think there is a singular reason for its height
and for its reversal at the top,

and if thoughts turning in your mind had not 67
been the water of Elsa, and your delight
in them a Pyramus to the mulberry,

from such circumstances alone 70
the justice of God would have been known
morally, in the forbidding of the tree.

But since I see that your mind has been turned 73
to stone, and has acquired a stony hue
so that the light of my speech dazzles you,

I would have you also carry it away 76
within you, painted even if not written,
as palm wreathes the pilgrim's staff, and for the same reason."

And I, "As wax under the seal, which does not 79
alter the figure that is stamped into it,
you are imprinted now upon my brain.

But why is it that, longed for as they are, 82
your words fly above my sight so far
that the harder it peers, the more it loses them?"

"So you may know," she said, "that school which you 85
have followed, and see whether it can follow
with its doctrines the things that I say,

and may see that your way is as far away 88
from the divine as the earth is from that
heaven which turns at the greatest height."

Then I answered her, "I do not remember 91
ever having been estranged from you, nor
is it something I feel the bite of conscience for."

"And if you cannot remember it," she 94
said, smiling, "bear in mind that this
is the day on which you drank from Lethe.

e se dal fummo foco s'argomenta,   97
cotesta oblivïon chiaro conchiude
colpa ne la tua voglia altrove attenta.

Veramente oramai saranno nude   100
le mie parole, quanto converrassi
quelle scovrire a la tua vista rude."

E più corusco e con più lenti passi   103
teneva il sole il cerchio di merigge,
che qua e là, come li aspetti, fassi,

quando s'affisser, sì come s'afigge   106
chi va dinanzi a gente per iscorta
se trova novitate o sue vestigge,

le sette donne al fin d'un'ombra smorta,   109
qual sotto foglie verdi e rami nigri
sovra suoi freddi rivi l'alpe porta.

Dinanzi ad esse Ëufratès e Tigri   112
veder mi parve uscir d'una fontana,
e, quasi amici, dipartirsi pigri.

"O luce, o gloria de la gente umana,   115
che acqua è questa che qui si dispiega
da un principio e sé da sé lontana?"

Per cotal priego detto mi fu: "Priega   118
Matelda che 'l ti dica." E qui rispuose,
come fa chi da colpa si dislega,

la bella donna: "Questo e altre cose   121
dette li son per me; e son sicura
che l'acqua di Letè non gliel nascose."

E Bëatrice: "Forse maggior cura,   124
che spesse volte la memoria priva,
fatt' ha la mente sua ne li occhi oscura.

Ma vedi Eünoè che là diriva: 127
menalo ad esso, e come tu se' usa,
la tramortita sua virtù ravviva."

And if from smoke you can argue a fire,   97
this forgetfulness proves clearly that your
will was doing wrong when it turned elsewhere.

Truly from now on my words will be   100
as simple as they will have to be
if they are to be clear to your rude vision."

Now, shining brighter and with slower pace,   103
the sun held to the noon meridian
that moves back and forth with the angle of vision,

when, as one who goes ahead, escorting   106
others, comes to a stop at finding
something strange, or the remains of it,

the seven ladies stopped at the margin   109
of light shadow such as that which the mountains
cast on cold streams under green leaves and dark boughs.

I saw before them, it seemed to me,   112
the Euphrates and Tigris rising from
one fountain and, like friends, parting slowly.

"Oh light, oh glory of humankind, what is   115
this water that from one beginning flows
and takes away, out of itself, itself?"

When I asked her this she said to me, "Inquire   118
that of Matelda," and that beautiful lady
answered, as someone who wished to be

freed of blame, "I have told him that,   121
and other things, and I am sure that
the water of Lethe did not hide it from him."

And Beatrice, "It may be that some greater   124
concern, which can make one not remember
sometimes, has darkened the eyes of his mind.

But see Eunoè flowing away there;   127
lead him to it and revive, as you are
used to doing, this weakened power of his."

Come anima gentil, che non fa scusa,
ma fa sua voglia de la voglia altrui
tosto che è per segno fuor dischiusa;

130

    così, poi che da essa preso fui,
la bella donna mossesi, e a Stazio
donnescamente disse: "Vien con lui."

133

    S'io avessi, lettor, più lungo spazio
da scrivere, i' pur cantere' in parte
lo dolce ber che mai non m'avria sazio;

136

    ma perché piene son tutte le carte
ordite a questa cantica seconda,
non mi lascia più ir lo fren de l'arte.

139

    Io ritornai da la santissima onda
rifatto sì come piante novelle
rinovellate di novella fronda,

142

    puro e disposto a salire a le stelle.

145

As a gentle soul, with no excuses,   130
makes of another's will her own
once an outward sign has made it known,

so when she had laid her hand on me   133
the beautiful lady moved on, and gracefully,
in the way of ladies, said to Statius, "Come with him."

Reader, if I had more space to write   136
I would sing something at least about that
sweet drink which I could have drunk forever,

but since all the pages that were laid upon   139
the loom for this second cantica have been
filled, the curb of art lets me go no farther.

From the most sacred waters I returned   142
remade in the way that trees are new,
made new again, when their leaves are new,

pure and ready to ascend to the stars.   145

NOTES

9–12   Calliope (sometimes spelled Caliope) is the Muse of epic poetry, chief of
the nine Muses, and the mother of Orpheus. The allusion here is to the
Pierides, the nine daughters of Pierus, king of Macedonia, who chal-
lenged the Muses to a singing contest. They sang in pride, of a battle in
which the giants were said to have defeated and routed the gods. But the
Muses chose Calliope to sing on their behalf, and she sang of springtime
and planting, Ceres and Proserpine, the annual resurrection of Proser-
pine from Hades. The Pierides were defeated, in the opinion of the
nymphs judging the contest, and were turned into magpies.

19   Venus: The morning star.

23   Not the Southern Cross. Dante knew that all the stars of the Southern
Hemisphere could be seen from the Equator, and it is doubtful whether
he knew of the Southern Cross at all. These stars are symbolic and his
own invention, and they represent the four "cardinal virtues": Justice,
Prudence, Fortitude, Temperance.

30   The Wain: The Big Dipper, Ursa Major.

31   The old man is Cato—Marcus Porcius Cato Uticensis, known as Cato the Younger. Dante refers to him as an old man, but he was only forty-eight or -nine when he died. But in Dante's time old age officially began at forty-six. Cato was a stoic, a supporter of Cicero, firmly opposed to the autocratic actions of Caesar, Pompey, and Crassus. In the civil war between Pompey and Caesar he was on the losing side and he decided to die rather than be taken captive by Caesar. He sat up most of the night reading Plato's *Phaedo* on the immortality of the soul, then ended his own life.

74   Utica: Next to Carthage the most important city in North Africa, not far from modern Tunis. There Cato took his life.

77   Virgil, in Limbo, is outside the jurisdiction of Minos.

79   Marcia: Cato's second wife.

88   The *mal fiume*, the "evil river," is Acheron.

131–133   The lines allude directly to Ulysses' fatal voyage recounted in *Inferno* 26, and the words "as pleased another" echo Ulysses' own words there.

CANTO II

46   First verse of Psalm 113.

63   Pilgrim. C. S. Singleton notes that this is the first use of the word in the poem. The journey through Hell is not a pilgrimage, which assumes hope of some kind.

76   Casella, a musician of Florence or Pistoia, is said to have set some, perhaps many, of Dante's poems to music; and in several sources Dante is said to have known him well, and to have loved to visit him to rest from his studies and listen to his music. And he did so, according to Benvenuto, "when he was excited by love."

101   The Tiber flows into the sea near Ostia, the port of Rome.

112   First line of Dante's Canzone II.

CANTO III

27   Virgil died at Brundisium, the present Brindisi, near Apulia, in 19 B.C., on his way back from Greece. Augustus ordered his body to be taken from Brindisi to Naples.

49   Lerice, seaport in Liguria, fortified in Dante's time. Turbia, village near the coast of France above Monaco. That coast, with steep cliffs rising from the sea, was virtually impassable in Dante's time.

112   Manfred, a natural son of Emperor Frederick II of Sicily, and Bianca, daughter of Count Bonifazio Lanzia. He was born in Sicily about 1232. This was the great court where poetry and the arts flourished, the tradition of the troubadours was cherished, and the first sonnets were written. Manfred was greatly taken with Arab civilization and had many Saracens among his followers, which did not endear him to the Church.

Upon the death of Frederick, Manfred was appointed regent, and he was the choice of the Sicilian nobles to succeed Frederick. The Pope interfered with Manfred's succession, and though Manfred was crowned, two Popes excommunicated him and offered the crown first to Louis IX of France, who refused it, and then to Charles of Anjou, who brought an army to Italy to claim it. Pope Urban IV proclaimed a crusade against Manfred, a papal habit of the time for which the rhetoric was kept warm. The armies met in February 1266 near Benevento. Manfred's was outnumbered but fought bravely until the Apulian barons, perhaps as part of a plan to betray Manfred, deserted the field. Manfred, with a small faithful remnant, charged and was killed. His surviving followers requested his body for honorable burial. Charles said he would have granted that if Manfred had not been excommunicated. He was buried in unconsecrated ground at the end of a bridge over the Calore, near the battlefield. Passing soldiers each put stones on his grave, leaving a great cairn. Later Clement IV is said to have commanded to have his body dug up and thrown out without any burial along the banks of the river Verde.

113 Empress Costanza, 1154–98, mother of Frederick II.

115 Constance, daughter of Manfred and Beatrice of Savoy. (Named for the Empress Constance, from whom Manfred was proud to be descended). She married Pedro III of Aragon, and four of her sons became kings.

124 Cosenza: town in northern Calabria a few miles from the coast.

CANTO IV

25 San Leo: A mountain town in the district of Montefeltro, on a steep hill.
   Noli: In Liguria, a town above the gulf of Genoa, approachable in Dante's day only by a notoriously steep descent from the mountains behind it.

26 Bismantova: In Dante's time, a fortified village on a steep mountain and a crag, near Canossa. Nothing is left of it now but the sheer crescent of rock on which it stood.

61 Castor and Pollux: The Twins, the sign of Gemini. One version of the classical myth relates that Jupiter, in the form of a swan, descended upon Leda, who gave birth to two eggs. From one of them Helen emerged, from the other, the twins Castor and Pollux. When the twins died, Jupiter set them among the stars as the constellation Gemini.

123 Belacqua: Evidently a friend of Dante's, but almost nothing is known of him now. He was said by early commentators to have been a maker of musical instruments, with a reputation for laziness.

CANTO V

24 *Miserere:* The fiftieth psalm in Latin, the fifty-first in the King James Version: "Have mercy upon me, O God." One of the Seven Penitential Psalms, praying for forgiveness and the cleansing of sin.

67   Jacopo del Cassero, a nobleman of Fano, murdered by the order of the marquis of Este.

68–69 The March of Ancona, between Romagna and Naples.
       Carlo: The Kingdom of Charles of Anjou.

75   Antenori: The Paduans, said to be descendants of Antenor of Troy, who in medieval legend was believed to have betrayed Troy to the Greeks.

77   He of Este: Azzo III d'Este, marquis of Este.

79   La Mira: Town between Padua and Venice.

80   Oriaco: A village between Padua and Venice. La Mira is beside the Brenta Canal, Oriaco close to lagoons.

88   Montefeltro here is a family name rather than a geographical identification. Buonconte was a leader of the Ghibellines in the war between Florence and Arezzo (1287). He was killed at the battle of Campaldino (June 11, 1289), at which the Guelphs defeated the Ghibellines, but his body was not found after the battle.

89   Giovanna: Buonconte's widow.

94   Casentino: In Tuscany, the region of the headwaters of the Arno.

95   Archiano: A torrent descending from above Camaldoli, eventually reaching the Arno.

96   The Hermitage: the monastery of Camaldoli.

116   Pratomagno: A mountain ridge.

122   The Arno. The term "royal" rivers meant those that flow into the sea directly, rather than into another river.

130   Not much is known with any certainty about Pia. She was a lady of Siena, perhaps a daughter of Buonincontro Guastelloni. She married Paganello (also known as Nello) de Pannocheschi, of Castello della Pietra in the Sienese Maremma, who is believed to have had her put to death in 1295. According to some accounts, no one knows where or how she was killed. Benvenuto and others say that Paganello had her thrown out of a window of his castle in the Maremma. There was a local legend that identified the place and called it the Salto della Contessa. Paganello is said to have had her killed in order to be able to marry Guy de Montfort's widow.

CANTO VI

13   "The Aretine" refers to Benincasa da Laterina, a judge from the upper valley of the Arno who sentenced to death a brother or uncle of Ghino di Tacco, a notorious highwayman. Tacco murdered him in revenge while Benincasa was in Rome, in the papal audit office.

15   The reference is to Guccio de Tarlati. Stories of his death differ. According to one he was drowned when his horse bolted as he was pursuing Guelph exiles from Arezzo. Another says that he was drowned while trying to escape, perhaps after the battle of Campaldino.

16 Federigo Novello, one of the Conti Guidi. He was killed near Bibbiena, it is said, in an encounter with the Guelph Bostoli party of Arezzo.

18 Marzucco, a judge in Pisa, from an ancient family. What his "fortitude" related to is no longer certain.

19 Orso degli Alberti della Cerbaia. Pietro di Dante says that he was "foully murdered by his friends and relatives." His murder is believed to have been a sequel in a feud between the fathers of two cousins who had killed each other.

22 Pier de la Broccia. Pierre de la Brosse, from Touraine, a chamberlain and at one time a favorite of Philip III of France. He joined others in accusing the queen, Marie of Brabant, of poisoning the heir to the throne, and he was arrested and hanged in 1278.

23 Brabant: Former duchy of the Netherlands, now a province of Belgium.

74 Sordello: One of the Italian poets who wrote in Provençal, continuing the tradition and conventions of the troubadours. He was born in Goito, near Mantua, around the year 1200. Some time around 1227 he had a liaison with Cunizza, a sister of Ezzelino III of Romano, a very powerful and ambitious man. Cunizza was married to Count Riccardo di San Bonifacio, but at her brother's request Sordello abducted her from her husband, for political reasons, and then had to flee to Provence. He spent the latter part of his life in the service of Charles d'Anjou.

Lament

I mean to mourn Blacatz with this light song
sad and grieving at heart and with good reason
for in him I have lost lord and dear friend
and all things precious in his death have gone
so mortal is the loss my hope is done
and never can come back but in one fashion
let someone take his heart for the nobles to dine upon
who have no heart they will have enough heart then

Let him eat first who has most need of this
the emperor of Rome who wants to seize
Milan by force though he is in their eyes
beaten and ruined for all his German allies
and let the King of France then eat a piece
and get Castille back lost through his foolishness
though he eats only as his mother wishes
he is renowned for doing as she pleases

Let the king of England who is faint of heart
eat the heart heartily and turn brave and stalwart
and take back the land for which he lives dishonored
which the French king seized knowing his indolent heart
and the king of Castille should eat enough heart
for two with his two kingdoms and not enough heart

for one but if he wants to eat he must keep it
a secret or his mother will beat him if she finds out

I want the king of Aragon to eat some of this
heart and relieve part of the shame he has
from Marseilles and Milan because otherwise
he has no honor whatever he says or does
then take the heart to the king of Navarre who is
a better count than king as the saying goes
a pity God ever raised to that high office
someone whose small heart would bring it down in disgrace

The count of Toulouse needs a good meal of it
to remember his land and how he came by it
for unless he gets another heart to regain it
the one we know as we know will never do it
and the count of Provence should eat it with the thought
that a man is worthless who loses his estate
and even if he tries to defend it
he should eat some heart for the burden will be great

The nobles wish me ill for what I have said well
let them know whose care for me is small
I care for them as little

Belh Restaur as long as your favor is with me
I never notice who else does not befriend me

—Sordel
(the name in Occitan, the language in which he wrote, for Sordello)

88–89   Justinian, emperor of Constantinople, 527–67, brought about the compilation and codification that became the body of Roman law.

97   Albert of Austria, elected emperor but never crowned. Pope Boniface VIII recognized him, as a political move, but five years later he was assassinated by his own nephew.

106   The Montecchi—the Montagues—were a family that became synonymous with the imperial party. Their aspirations included the conquest of all Lombardy.

107   The Monaldi were a Guelph family of Orvieto; the Filippeschi, a Ghibelline family of Orvieto.

111   Santafior. Santafiore: Town in the territory of Siena.

125   Marcellus: Roman consul bitterly opposed to Julius Caesar.

CANTO VII

6　Octavian: The first Roman emperor, Augustus, born 63 B.C., died A.D. 14. Augustus was a title conferred upon him by the Roman senate during Virgil's lifetime.

94　Rudolf I, emperor 1273–1291.

97　The "other" is Ottokar, who in life was Rudolf's enemy.

98–99　The Moldau rises in Bohemia, turns north through Prague, and enters the Elbe, which flows to the North Sea.

101　Wenceslas II, son of Ottokar, son-in-law of Rudolf. He was king of Bohemia 1278–1305.

104　Henry I, king of Navarre 1270–74.

109　Philip IV, the Fair, king of France 1285–1314.

112–114　Pedro III, king of Aragon 1276–1285.

113　Charles I, king of Naples and Sicily 1266–85, very powerful in his time and much praised.

119　James II, the Just. King of Sicily 1285–95 and king of Aragon 1291–1327. Frederick II, king of Sicily 1296–1337.

131　Henry III of England, king 1216–72. (See Sordello's elegy for Blacatz.)　'

133–136　William VII, surnamed "Spadalunga" or "Longsword," marquis of Montferrat 1254–94. Soon after he came to power he brought under his rule the independent cities of Lombardy. He was at first an ally of Charles of Anjou, until the latter tried to seize Lombardy. William's power grew with alliances. His son-in-law was the emperor of Constantinople, and William's rule grew to include Tortina, Vercelli, and Pavia in the 1280s. In 1290 he marched against Alessandria to put down a rising, but was taken prisoner, put into an iron cage, and displayed in it for seventeen months, until his death. The war went on after he had died, and Montferrat and the Canovese were overrun.

CANTO VIII

13　*Te lucis ante.* The hymn attributed to Ambrose: "Before the ending of the day . . ."

28–30　Singleton points out that these are the only green angels in Dante, and that green is the color of hope.

53　Nino Visconti of Pisa. His grandfather was Ugolino della Gherardesca. After 1285 Nino and his grandfather shared high office in Pisa. Ugolino betrayed Nino, who fled to Florence in 1288.

71　Giovanna was the daughter of Nino Visconti of Pisa and Beatrice d'Este. As a child, because of her ancestry, she was given the guardianship of Volterra by Pope Boniface VIII, but political factions stripped her of her power and her possessions. She married Rizzardo da Camino, lord of

Treviso, but after his death in 1312 she became poor again, and a grant was provided to take care of her.

73   Beatrice, daughter of Obizzo II of Este. She was married to Nino Visconti of Pisa and had a daughter, Giovanna. Later she was married to Galeazzo Visconti of Milan. It seems that she had been betrothed, before this second marriage, to Alberto Scotto of Piacenza, but Matteo Visconti of Milan wanted an alliance with the house of Este and arranged for her to marry his son Galeazzo. Two years later the Torriani, with the help of Alberto Scotto, drove the Visconti from Milan. After Galeazzo's death in 1328 Beatrice returned to Milan, where she died.

79–80   The device of the Visconti of Milan was a blue viper swallowing a red Saracen. Nino's device was a cock.

81   Nino was a judge in Gallura, Sardinia.

116   Val di Magra: The river Magra flows through Luningiana, the territory of the Malaspina family, where the castle of Villafranca stood, the home of Federigo I, marquis of Villafranca, Corrado's father.

118   Corrado II, "Il Giovano," marquis of Villafranca, died around 1294.

119   Corrado I, "L'Antico," grandfather of Corrado II.

CANTO IX

9   Aurora, goddess of the dawn, loved Tithonus, and through her intercession he was made immortal. But she forgot to request eternal youth for him, and he withered into age, until at last she changed him into a grasshopper.

In Virgil's Georgics and Aeneid, Aurora the dawn is described rising at the end of night from the bed she shares with Tithonus. But there has been learned controversy debating whether this passage may refer, instead, to the moonrise.

15   Allusion to the legend of Philomela and Procne. Singleton's account of it is based on Ovid, Metamorphoses VI, which Dante would have known. According to that version, Procne was married to Theseus and bore a son. She lived far from her sister, Philomela, and wanted to see her. Tereus left for Athens to fetch Philomela. On the way back he raped her and then, to prevent her telling about it, he cut out her tongue and abandoned her. When he got back he told Procne that her sister was dead. Philomela contrived to weave her story into a piece of cloth and got her sister to see it and learn what happened. Procne, to avenge herself on Tereus, killed her son and served the child's flesh to Tereus, who ate it without knowing what it was. When Procne told him what he had done he tried to kill both sisters with an ax, but in answer to the sisters' prayers they were all changed into birds—Procne into a nightingale, Philomela into a swallow, and Tereus, in one version, into a hoopoe, and in another, into a hawk.

22–24   Ganymede was the most beautiful of mortals, and according to one legend he was carried up from Mount Ida by an eagle, to become an immortal, Jupiter's cupbearer. His brother, Assaracus, was an ancestor of Aeneas.

39   Achilles' mother hid him on the island of Skyros, disguised as a woman. Ulysses, disguised as a merchant, visited the island, accompanied by Diomedes, and offered for sale women's dresses, and weapons among them. Achilles' enthusiasm for the weapons revealed who he was, and Ulysses persuaded him to join the forces of the Greeks.

62   *"li occhi suoi belli"*: In the legend of St. Lucy, when a noble suitor admires her eyes she plucks them out. She is rewarded with still more beautiful eyes. She is the patron saint of eyes.

136–138   The temple of Saturn, in Rome, containing the Roman treasure, was built on Tarpeia, the Tarpeian Rock. When Julius Caesar, in 49 B.C., broke into the treasury, Marcellus tried to defend it, on behalf of Pompey. He was pushed aside, the door was opened, and the rock echoed the terrible sound of the doors opening.

140   *Te Deum laudamus:* A famous medieval hymn, ascribed to Ambrose and to Augustine but probably composed by Nicetas in the fifth century. It was often sung at the induction of someone into a religious order.

CANTO X

32   Policletus, famous Greek sculptor, active around 452–412 BC. Said to have been peerless at carving figures of humans, as Phidias was at making images of deities.

55–69   King David, "the humble psalmist," dancing before the Ark of the Covenant (2 Kings 6:2–17).

57   This is an allusion to Uzzah, in whose house the ark had been kept for twenty years. He and his brother went with the ark when David oversaw its removal to Jerusalem. One of the oxen stumbled as they were going, and Uzzah reached out to steady the ark, which was in danger of falling. This, according to the story (II Kings 6:3–7) was an act of such presumption and profanation that Uzzah was struck dead on the spot.

73–96   Emperor Trajan ruled from A.D. 98–117. In the legend, as he was setting out for the wars a poor widow stopped him and requested redress for the death of her son. The emperor tried to put her off but she persuaded him to do as she asked.

75   Gregory I—Saint Gregory, Gregory the Great—pope 590–614. Medieval legend has it that through his intercession Emperor Trajan was restored to life so that he might repent.

CANTO XI

58   Omberto Aldobrandeschi, lord of Campagnatico, killed in 1259 in an attack by the forces of Siena.

59   Guiglielmo Aldobrandesco, count of Santafiore, also an enemy of the Sienese and an ally of the Guelphs of Florence.

79 Oderisi da Gubbio, a miniature painter who, according to Vasari, was a friend of Giotto and was employed, along with Franco of Bologna (mentioned in l.83) by Pope Boniface VIII to illuminate manuscripts in the papal library.

80 Gubbio: Town in the Appenines in northern Umbria.

94 Cenni di Peppo, known as Giovanni Cimabue, great painter of Florence, master of Giotto. He developed Italian painting in a direction that diverged from the Byzantine tradition into a new one of its own. He was born about 1240 and died after 1302.

95 Giotto di Bondona, great Florentine painter, born around 1266, a year or two after Dante. Died in Florence, 1337.

97–98 The glory of eloquence in the vulgar tongue has passed from Guido Guinizzelli (whom Dante will call his father in canto 26) to Guido Cavalcanti, Dante's friend.

109 Provenzan Salvani, Sienese Ghibelline, born about 1220. After a victory in 1260 he became virtual dictator of Siena, and advocated the destruction of Florence. He was captured in a battle with the Florentines in 1269 and beheaded.

112–113 This refers to the battle of Montaperti (September 4, 1260), when the Florentines were disastrously defeated.

133–138 The commentary known as the *Ottimo Commento* tells that King Charles had imprisoned a friend of Provenzan's, captured at the battle of Tagliacozzo, and was demanding 10,000 gold florins for his release, to be paid in a short time or else he would be executed. Provenzan, then lord of Siena, and normally extremely haughty, had a bench set in the marketplace in Siena and sat there in plain clothes humbly asking help of the Sienese, forcing no one. It is said that they were moved to pity by his humility and the friend was ransomed before his term.

CANTO XII

25–27 Lucifer.

28–30 Briareus, one of the giants who fought against Olympus.

31 Thymbraeus: An epithet for Apollo.
  Pallas: The goddess Athena.

34–36 Nimrod, legendary builder of the Tower of Babel in the plain of Shinar.

37–39 Niobe, wife of the king of Thebes, was proud of her many children, and compared herself boastfully with Latona, who had only two, Apollo and Diana. Latona persuaded Apollo and Diana to kill Niobe's seven sons and seven daughters with arrows. Niobe was turned to marble and carried away to her native mountain, but tears continued to run down her stone cheeks.

40–42 Saul, first king of Israel. Several turns in his story present him as an image of pride. He killed himself on the mountain of Gilboa, in Samaria.

43–45   Arachne was proud of her skill as a weaver and challenged Minerva to a contest. Arachne wove a cloth depicting the loves of the gods, but Minerva destroyed it. Arachne hanged herself, but the goddess undid the knot and saved her, turning the rope into a web and Arachne into a spider.

46–48   Rehoboam, king of Israel. The people rose against his harshness, only two tribes remaining loyal to him. The rebellious tribes stoned his messenger to death, and Rehoboam fled to take refuge in Jerusalem.

50–51   Alcmaeon, son of the seer Amphiaraus and Eriphyle. Amphiaraus knew that he would be killed if he went in the army against Thebes, and he hid. His wife, bribed by Polynices with the necklace of Harmonia, gave away his hiding place, so that he had to go with the army, and was killed. Before he left he enjoined Alcmaeon to kill Eriphyle in punishment for betraying him, and Alcmaeon killed his own mother.

52–54   Sennacherib, king of Assyria 765–681 B.C. He sent an army against Hezekiah, king of Judah, which was annihilated in one night by an angel of the Lord. Sennacherib escaped but later was murdered by two of his sons.

55–57   Tomyris, or Thamyris, a queen of the Scythians, defeated Cyrus and killed him in 529 B.C. She had his head cut off and thrown into a skin bag full of human blood, and jeered at it because he had treacherously killed her son.

58–60   Holofernes, king of the Assyrians, killed by Judith, who cut off his head.

101   The Rubaconte was a bridge in Florence now known as the Ponte alle Grazie. It was named for Messer Rubaconte da Mandello of Milan, who, in 1237, had the bridge built. While he was *podestà* of Florence he had the streets paved.

104–105   The reference to the safety of the records related to a scandal in Florence after 1295 which involved the destruction of records. The "measures" refers to another scandal at the same time in which an overseer of salt removed a stave from a salt measure to augment his profits.

CANTO XIII

29   "They have no wine": Mary's words to Jesus about the wedding feast at Cana.

50–51   The Litany of the Saints.

70–72   Falcons captured in the woods when they were well grown, and therefore hard to domesticate, had their eyelids stitched shut to force them to be still, for training.

109   Sapia (there is an etymological wordplay on the word *"savia,"* which means wise, or well-behaved). A lady of Siena, born around 1210, married in 1230, aunt of Provenzan Salvani.

116   Colle: Town in the Val d'Elsa, Tuscany, site of a battle on June 17, 1269.

123   In a fable, the blackbird is said to fear foul weather and to hide from it.

When good weather returns, it comes out and makes fun of the other birds and says, "Lord, I am not afraid of you, for the winter is over."

127 Pier Pettinaio, the comb seller or comb maker. Born in Campi northeast of Siena. He was a Franciscan hermit, locally famous for piety and miracles. It was said that he would never sell a comb that had any defects. He died in 1289 when, according to documents, he was 109 years old, and was buried in Siena in a fine tomb, at public expense. In 1957 F. Ageno published a bibliography of studies on Pier Pettinaio.

152 Talamone: Small seaport on the Tyrrhenian Sea, its harbor the mouth of a creek with a tendency to silt up. In 1303 the town of Siena bought the harbor of Talamone, but the cost of dredging it and the unhealthiness of the marshes led them to abandon their plans there.

153 The Diana: A river which the Sienese believed ran under their city. They spent large sums looking for it. They named the river for Diana because of a tradition that a statue of the goddess had once stood in the marketplace of Siena.

CANTO XIV

42 Circe: Sorceress who could turn men into swine. Ulysses was kept on her island, and escaped, on his way home to Ithaca.

46 Botoli: Inhabitants of Arezzo. Botoli are small dogs. In Dante's time the standard of Arezzo bore the motto "A small dog often can hold down a boar"—a statement whose inaccuracy apparently did not trouble them.

58 The soul here addressed is Rinieri de Paolucci da Calboli, *podestà* of Faenza in 1247, of Parma in 1252, of Ravenna in 1265, the year Dante was born. His grandson, Fulcieri da Calboli, is the one referred to: a vicious, corrupt, cruel man, *podestà* of Florence in 1303. He was a bitter enemy of the Ghibelline Whites and arrested many of the party's leaders, accusing them of plotting to betray Florence. He tortured those he arrested to extort confession. One died under torture; he beheaded the others.

81 Guido del Duca: From Bertinoro; his family came, it seems, from Ravenna. In 1199 he was a judge in Rimini. In 1218 the Guelphs seized Bertinoro and drove out the Ghibellines there, and Guido del Duca and his family returned to Ravenna. When Guido died, his friend Arrigo Mainardi of Bertinoro had the bench where they had sat sawn in two, saying that no one was alive any longer who was his equal in nobility and honor.

92 The ancient province of Romagna.

97 Lizio da Valbona, nobleman of Romagna. His castle, Valbona, was in the valley of the Bidente.

   Arrigo Mainardi, gentleman of Bertinoro, known for courtesy and generosity.

98 Pier Traversaro, of a powerful Ravenna family; he was *podestà* of that city several times.

   Guido di Carpigna: *Podestà* of Ravenna in 1251.

Carpigna, now Carpegna: Town in Romagna in the district of Montefeltro.

100   Fabbro: A nobleman of Bologna, said to be a man of judgment. He was *podestà* of several cities in northern Italy.

101   Bernardo di Fosco: A man of humble origin who rose to be *podestà* of Siena. Helped defend Faenza against Emperor Frederick II in 1240.

104   Guido da Prata: Man of importance in Ravenna, died c. 1245.

105   Ugolin d'Azzo: Wealthy member of a powerful Tuscan family, died 1293.

106   Federigo Tignoso: Nobleman of Rimini, known for his wealth and hospitality. He was known to have surrounded himself with admirable people.

107   Traversara: A Ghibelline family of Ravenna.
        Anastagi: A noble Ghibelline family of Ravenna.

115   Bagnacavallo: Town in Romagna.

116   Castrocaro: Once a castle, now a village in Romagna, near Forli.
        Conio: Castle in Romagna near Imola; nothing remains of it.

118   Pagani: Ghibelline noble family of Faenza.

118–119   Reference to Maghinardo Pagano da Susinana, lord of Faenza in 1290, of Forli in 1291, of Imola in 1296.

121   Ugolin de' Fantolin: Gentleman of Faenza, said to be courageous, virtuous, and noble. *Podestà* of Faenza 1253.

139   Aglauros: Daughter of Cecrops, king of Athens. She is said to have been turned into a stone by Mercury because she had tried to prevent him, out of envy, from coming to visit her sister Herse, with whom he was in love.

CANTO XV

38   The Fifth Beatitude.

87–92   Luke 2:40–48.

94–105   Pisistratus was a tyrant of Athens. A young man who was in love with his daughter came up to her on the street and kissed her. Pisistratus' wife demanded that the young man should be executed for this, but Pisistratus answered, "If we kill those who love us, what shall we do to those who hate us?"

106–114   The stoning of St. Stephen, the "first martyr" (Acts 7:54–59).

109–110   Ovid, *Metamorphoses* IV: the story of Pyramus and Thisbe.

CANTO XVI

17–19   The words are from the Agnus Dei, which prays first for mercy and then for peace.

46   Doubt remains as to the identity of this Marco of Lombardy, early commentators suggesting several possibilities.

115   A general description of Lombardy, the greater part of northern Italy.

124 Currado da Palazzo, a Guelph of Brescia, vicar for Charles of Anjou in Florence, 1276, and *podestà* of Piacenza, 1288. Benvenuto says that in battle, while bearing a standard, he had both his hands cut off, but went on holding the standard with the stumps of his arms.

Gherardo da Cammino, landowner near Belluno and Cadore. Dante regarded him as an epitome of nobility.

125 Guido da Castel, another prime example of nobility in Dante's view.

140 Gaia, Gherardo da Cammino's daughter. Some early commentators speak well of her; others tell of her loose and abandoned ways. Dante seems to have used her as a contrast to her father, citing her as an example of degeneracy.

CANTO XVII

19-20 Procne, wife of Tereus and sister of Philomela. See note to canto 9, l.15.

26-30 From Esther 3:5. Haman, prime minister of Ahasuerus, was indignant at the Jew Mordecai's refusal to bow to him. He persuaded Ahasuerus to order the execution of all the Jews in the Persian Empire. The extermination failed and Esther and Mordecai intervened, so that in the end Haman was hanged on the gallows that had been set up for Mordecai.

34-39 Amata, wife of Latinus, mother of Lavinia, understood that Lavinia's betrothed, Turnus, had been killed in battle. The account was not true; but Amata, certain that Lavinia would then marry Aeneas, which Amata did not want her to do, hanged herself in rage and despair.

CANTO XVIII

82 Pietola: Modern Pietole, a village some three miles south of Mantua, thought to be the ancient Andes, where Virgil was born.

91-93 The Ismenus and the Asopus are small rivers of Boeotia. The former flows past Thebes, where Bacchus was born to Semele. The reference is to the Bacchic orgies.

101-102 Caesar besieged Marseilles on his way to Lerida. He left part of his army at Marseilles under Brutus to finish the siege.

118 The Abbot, as far as is known, was Gherardo II, who died in 1187.

119 Frederick Barbarossa.

120 In 1162 Emperor Frederick Barbarossa destroyed Milan, razed the walls to the ground, and according to Villani had the site plowed and sown with salt.

121-126 Reference to Alberto della Scala, who died as an old man in 1301. His illegitimate son became abbot of San Zeno and Alberto's three legitimate sons succeeded Alberto, one after another. One of them was Can Grande, who was Dante's host and protector in Verona.

134 The people of Israel leaving Egypt.

135 Numbers 14:1-39: Except for Joshua and Caleb, none of the Israelites

who had left Egypt would see the Promised Land, but only those who had been born in the desert.

136–138 Refers to those followers of Aeneas who, in order to evade the rigors of the voyage, stayed behind with Acestis in Sicily.

CANTO XIX

4–6 Geomancy: Divination by means of lines or points made at random and then construed in relation to configurations in the stars. One such configuration was called *Fortuna major*. It included some of the last stars in Aquarius and some of the first in Pisces.

99–114 Adrian V, elected pope July 11, 1276, died thirty-eight days later, before he was crowned.

100 Siestri and Chiavari: Two towns east of Genoa.

100–101 The river is the Lavagna, which flows between the two towns.

142 Alagia de' Fieschi, niece of Adrian V, wife of Dante's friend Moroello Malaspina. Adrian says that the niece is good as long as she does not follow the example of other women of her house.

CANTO XX

10 The ancient she-wolf represents greed.

25–27 Gaius Fabritius Luscinus, a Roman hero, consul in 282 B.C., a model of frugality, probity, integrity.

31–33 Nicholas, bishop of Myra in Lycia, Asia Minor; said to have been present at the Council of Nicaea. Venerated as a saint in both Greek and Roman churches, patron saint of Russia, of virgins, sailors, travelers, merchants, thieves. Santa Claus: The legend here referred to tells of Nicholas keeping a destitute fellow citizen from selling his three daughters into prostitution by throwing purses full of gold pieces in at their windows on three successive nights, providing dowries for them.

43–45 The speaker is Hugh Capet, king of France 987–996, the first of the Capetian line of kings.

46 The four cities represent Flanders. At the end of the thirteenth century Flanders was coveted by Philip the Fair of France and Edward I of England. Guy de Dampierre, count of Flanders, caught between them, was held prisoner by the French king and died in prison. In 1302 the Flemish rose against the French and defeated them at Courtrai, where the French losses among the nobility were extremely heavy. This is the vengeance that Dante foretells.

49–60 Dante appears to have followed a common tradition and confused Hugh Capet with his father, Hugh the Great, who died in 956, and to have confused in the same way the succession which made Hugh Capet king. Hugh the Great was descended from the counts of Paris, but it was commonly believed in Dante's time that he had been the son, or nephew, of a butcher.

50–51 The kings of the Capetian line, whose names were Philip or Louis.

54 Here, apparently, Charles of Lorraine, whom Hugh Capet kept in prison until he died there, because he was the last remaining heir of the Carolingian line and so had a claim upon the throne, seems to have been confused with Childeric III, the last of the Merovingians, who was deposed by Pepin the Short in 752 and confined to a monastery, where, Villani says, he became a monk, and where he died in 755.

61 In 843 the Carolingian Empire was divided and Provence, which bore with it the title of king, went to Lothair. Later it was part of the kingdom of Arles, and returned to the empire in 1033, though the counts of Provence continued to claim independence. In 1246 Beatrice, heir of Raymond Berenger IV of Provence, married Charles of Anjou, the brother of King Louis IX of France, and Provence became a dependency of the French royal house.

67 Charles of Anjou was invited by Urban IV to accept the crown of Naples and Sicily. He entered Italy in 1065 and defeated the Hohenstaufen power there.

68 Conradin, son of the Emperor Conrad IV, was the last of the Hohenstaufen line.

73 Charles entered Italy with a small force, counting on the army of Charles II of Naples, and the full support of Pope Boniface VIII.

79 Charles II, king of Naples.

80–81 Beatrice, daughter of Charles II, was married to Azzo VIII, marquis of Este, in return, it was believed, for a large sum of money.

85–87 Hugh is prophesying the outrageous actions of Philip the Fair, which included the imprisonment, for a brief period, of the Pope himself, in Anagni, the town in Latium where Boniface VIII was born.

91 The new Pilate is Philip the Fair.

92–93 Reference to the persecution and deliberate destruction, by Philip the Fair, of the Knights Templar, a campaign prompted by jealousy, anxiety, and greed, and carried out with treachery and great cruelty, including the burning alive of the Grand Master of the Templars, Jacques de Molay.

103 Pygmalion, brother of Dido, whose husband he murdered out of greed.

106 Midas, who asked the god Bacchus for the gift of being able to turn everything he touched into gold, and the wish was granted. He was finally relieved of it, but later, having declared that Pan played the flute and lyre better than Apollo, was punished by having to wear ass's ears.

109–111 Achan, son of Carmi, took for himself some of the spoils of Jericho (Joshua 7:1). The Israelites were defeated, Achan confessed, and at Joshua's orders he and his whole family were stoned to death.

112 Ananias and his wife, Sapphira, disciples in Jerusalem, sold their possessions for the Church, but kept back part of the proceeds. Peter condemned their hypocrisy and they fell dead at his feet (Acts 5:1–11).

113   Heliodorus, treasurer of the king of Syria. He was commanded to remove the treasure from the temple in Jerusalem, and according to the account in 3 Machabees 25–27, he was attacked by a horse with "a terrible rider," which struck him with its forefeet, and by two men, "bright and glorious," who struck him, and he was covered with great darkness.

115   Polymestor, a king of Thrace to whom Priam entrusted his son Polydorus and a great deal of money. Polymestor killed the boy for the sake of the money and threw the body into the sea.

116–117   Marcus Licinius Crassus, known as Dives, "the Wealthy," who was a triumvir with Pompey and Caesar in 60 B.C. He was famous for his passion for money.

130–132   Delos: According to legend it was raised from the sea depths by Neptune but was a floating island until Jupiter anchored it with chains of adamant, so that Latona might have a place to hide from the anger of Juno. There Latona gave birth to Apollo and Diana.

CANTO XXI

7–9   Luke 24:13–16.

25–27   Lachesis, the second of the three Fates, on whose distaff the wool placed by Clotho, the first of the Fates, is spun.

50–51   Iris, the rainbow.

67   Publius Papinius Statius, Roman poet, c. A.D. 45–96, author of the *Thebaid*. Dante mistakenly believed that Statius was born in Toulouse, but the poet was a native of Naples. Statius' conversion to Christianity appears to be Dante's invention.

82–84   Titus, Roman emperor A.D. 79–81. He captured Jerusalem in A.D. 70.

93   Statius' second labor, the *Achilleid*, was never finished.

CANTO XXII

13   Decimus Junius Juvenalis, Roman satiric poet.

42   Among the prodigals and avaricious in the fourth circle of Hell.

56   Jocasta's "twofold sorrow" is the chief subject of the *Thebaid*. Jocasta was the wife of Laius, the King of Thebes. Later she married Oedipus, her own son, without knowing who he was. With Oedipus she became the mother of two boys, Eteocles and Polynices, and two girls, Antigone and Ismene. Eteocles and Polynices killed each other in combat, and their death was Jocasta's twofold sorrow.

58   Clio, the Muse of history.

63   Peter was a fisherman.

65   Mount Parnassus (present-day Liákoura) is a mountain over eight thousand feet high, 83 miles northwest of Athens. It was sacred to Apollo and the Muses. South of the mountain, above Delphi, is the Castalian spring.

70–72   Dante is quoting, with alterations, a famous "prophetic" passage from Virgil's *Eclogue IV*:

> The great line of the centuries begins again. Now the Virgin returns, the reign of Saturn returns; now a new progeny decends from high heaven.

Dante replaces "the Virgin" (Virgo) with "Justice" and sees the reign of Saturn as the golden age.

83   The emperor Domitian (Titus Flavius Domitianus Augustus), born Rome A.D. 51, emperor in 81, assassinated in 96. According to Tertullian and Eusebius he was a persecutor of the Christians.

88–89   "The rivers of Thebes" refers to Statius' composition of the *Thebaid*.

97   Terence (Publius Terentius Afer), Roman comic playwright.

98   Gaius Caecilius Statius: Roman comic poet earlier than Terence.
Titus Maccius Plautus: Roman comic poet.
Varius: Lucius Varius Rufus, Roman poet, friend of Virgil and of Horace.

100   Aulus Persius Flaccus, Roman satiric poet.

101–2   Homer.

105   The Muses.

106   Euripides: Greek playwright.
Antiphon: Greek tragic poet; according to Plutarch one of the greatest, but only a few fragments survive.

107   Simonides: Greek lyric poet.
Agathon: Greek tragic poet; nothing of his has survived.

110   Antigone: Daughter of Oedipus and Jocasta.
Deiphyle: Daughter of Adrastus, king of Argos, and sister of Argia, who was the wife of Polynices.

111   Ismene: sister of Antigone.

112   Hypsipyle, daughter of Thoas, king of Lemnos. She led Adrastus and his company to the fountain of Langia near Nemea in the Peloponnese and while she was away she left the child Archemorus, son of Lycurgus, king of Nemea, lying on the grass. A serpent killed the child, and Lycurgus wanted to put her to death, but her two sons arrived and prevented it.

113   Manto, the daughter of Tiresias mentioned in the *Thebaid*.
Thetis: One of the Nereids, mother of Achilles.

114   Deidamia: Daughter of the king of Skyros. Thetis left Achilles, disguised as a woman, with Skyros, to try to keep him from going to Troy.

CANTO XXIII

10   Psalm 50: "O Lord, open my lips and my mouth shall proclaim your praise."

25   Erysichthon, son of King Triopas of Thessaly, cut down trees in a grove

sacred to Ceres and was punished with a hunger so fierce that he ate his own flesh.

28–30 From Flavius Josephus, *The Jewish War, book 6.* When Titus laid siege to Jerusalem a Jewish woman named Mary was driven by hunger to kill and eat her infant son.

32–33 According to a belief current in Dante's time, the Italian word for "man"—"*omo*"—was visible in the human face: the eyes as *o*'s and the brows and nose forming an *m*, at least in the uncial script.

48 Forese Donati, a friend of Dante's and a fellow poet. They wrote sonnets sparring with each other, in the convention of the *tenzone,* or dialogue in alternating stanzas, but not always with good humor. In two of the sonnets Dante speaks of Forese's gluttony, as other commentators did.

74 Matthew 27:46: "Jesus cried out with a loud voice, saying 'Eli, Eli, lama sabacthani,' that is "My God, my God, why hast thou forsaken me?"

85 Apparently an abbreviation of Giovanella; Forese's wife was named Anella.

94 The Barbagia: A mountainous region in central Sardinia whose inhabitants were said to be descendants of prisoners left there by the Vandals. In the Middle Ages they were notorious for their lax mores. It was said that the woman exposed their breasts.

96 The Barbagia Dante is alluding to here is Florence.

CANTO XXIV

10 Piccarda is Forese's sister, whom Dante will meet in the heaven of the moon.

20 Bonagiunta da Lucca, a notary and poet, known for his facility with words and his love of wine.

20–24 The Pope is Martin IV, born in Montpincé in Brie. He was chancellor of France in 1260, became Pope in 1280, died in 1285. According to one account, his death was caused by eating too many eels from Lake Bolsena. The eels from the lake were customarily kept in milk and then stewed in wine.

24 Vernaccia: a white wine from Vernaccio (now Vernazza).

29 Ubaldin da la Pila, member of a powerful Ghibelline family, the Ubaldini. He held positions of power and was well known for his gluttony.

30 Bonifazio de' Fieschi of Genoa, archbishop of Ravenna, 1274–95, a very wealthy man with a famous collection of plate and embroideries.

31–33 Messer Marchese, known as a great drinker of wine.

56 Giacomo da Lentini, from Sicily, was known as "the Notary" and belonged to a school of poets at the court of Emperor Frederick II and his son Manfred. Many of his *canzone* and sonnets, which are marked by the influence of Provençal poetry, survive.

Fra Guittone d'Arezzo. Early Italian poet, b. 1230.

64   Cranes.

82   Corso Donati and his followers were involved in a violent power struggle for the control of Florence in 1301, which turned into a prolonged massacre of the Whites. In 1308, after a later surge of ambition, intrigue, and violence, he fled Florence and was overtaken and captured by Catalan horsemen. Rather than be returned to Florence and executed, he let himself fall from his horse and was dragged by a stirrup. One of the Catalans speared him through the throat, another struck him in the side, and he died soon afterward.

121–123   Centaurs. Their mother, Nephele, was said to have been "formed in the clouds." The representation of them as gluttonous, drunken, and debauched comes in part at least from Ovid's account of the wedding of Pirithoüs and Hippodamia.

124–126   From Judges 7:4–8: The winnowing of the soldiers who were to go with Gideon, one of the judges of Israel; he delivered the Jews from the Midianites. He was to take only the three hundred who lapped water with one hand rather than kneeling to drink.

126   Midian: Region of northwest Arabia, east of the gulf of Aquaba.

CANTO XXV

22–23   Meleager, son of Oeneus, the king of Calydon, sailed with Jason and the Argonauts and led the warriors who killed the Calydonian boar. He gave the boar skin to Atalanta, his beloved, but his mother's brothers took it away from her, and he killed them for that. Seven days after Meleager's birth, his mother had heard from the Fates that he would live as long as the piece of wood then on the fire went on burning. She took the wood out of the fire, put out the flame, and hid the log, but after Meleager killed her brothers she brought it out again and threw it into the flames, and as it burned up Meleager died.

79   The time of death, when the Fate reaches the end of the thread. Lachesis: one of the three Fates. She is the measurer.

128   Luke 1:34: "But Mary said to the angel, 'How shall this happen, since I do not know man?' "

130–132   Helice, or Callisto, daughter of Lycaon, the king of Arcadia, was one of Diana's nymphs, but when Diana learned that Jupiter had seduced her, she sent the nymph away; and the nymph gave birth to Arcas.

CANTO XXVI

40   In Genesis 19:1–28, the two cities Sodom and Gomorrah were destroyed by fire from heaven as punishment for their evil ways. Here, those who shout their names represent sinners "against nature" and circle the mountain in the opposite direction from the others.

41–42   Pasiphaë had herself enclosed in a wooden cow built for her by

Daedalus, in order to copulate with a bull, and she brought forth the Minotaur.

43   The Riphaean Mountains, a mythological range that marked the northern rim of the world. Classical writers used the name for a mountain range in the north of Scythia.

77–78   The sin is sodomy, and the allusion is to one of Julius Caesar's triumphs at which the crowd is said to have shouted "Queen," because of an account of his having engaged in sodomy with King Nicomedes of Bithynia.

82   Hermaphroditus, the original of the word, was the son of Hermes and Aphrodite and had inherited the beauty of both parents. A nymph of the fountain of Salmacis was in love with him, and one day as he was bathing she embraced him and prayed to the gods to be united to him forever. The gods granted her request and the two became one but kept the traits of both sexes.

92   Guido Guinizzelli, the leader of a school of poets from Bologna, was the most celebrated Italian poet before Dante.

> I have seen the bright star of the morning
> that appears before the break of day
> take the form of a human figure shining
> above all others, as it seems to me.
>
> A countenance of snow colored with scarlet,
> eyes shining and full of love and joy—
> I cannot believe the world has in it
> a Christian girl so full of good and beauty.
>
> And from the love of her I am overtaken
> by so violent an attack of sighing
> that I do not dare say a word before her.
>
> If only she could know of my desire
> without my speaking she might show compassion
> and so reward me for my suffering.
>
> —Guido Guinizzelli (1235–76)

108   Lethe, the river of oblivion.

115   Arnaut Daniel, great troubadour, active around the end of the twelfth century. He came from a noble family of Riberac near Perigord and spent much time at the court of Richard Coeur-de-Lion. His reply here, in Provençal in the original, is a distinct echo of Daniel's most personal and one of his most powerful poems, which is thought to be the first sestina.

Canso

> Into a light and joyful song
> I shape the words and polish them

so that they will be right and true
when I have finished with the file,
for it is love direct from her
who judges and awards the prize
that smooths and turns to gold my singing.

Serving devoutly as I do
the noblest lady in the world
daily betters and refines me.
From sole to crown I am hers only
and when the cold wind starts to blow
the rain of love within my heart
warms me in the worst of winters.

A thousand masses I attend
and offer, and burn oil and candles
that God may turn her in my favor
against whom I have no defense.
I love the sight of her gold hair
and graceful body, fresh and slender,
more than if all Lucerne were given me.

So fares my heart with love of her
that I may lose it from pure longing
if in true love there can be losing,
because her heart has flooded mine
utterly and the flood remains.
She has played so well that she owns
both the workman and the tavern.

I would not have the Roman Empire
nor be named to succeed Saint Peter
if it meant that I could not see her
who has kindled and cleft my heart,
and unless with a kiss she heals me
before the New Year, from this pain,
she has killed and to Hell consigned me.

And still nothing that I endure
turns me from my true love of her
which drives me out into the desert
to make these words into a song.
Love is harder than field labor
and Moncli's love for Audierna
not by an egg surpasses mine.

I am Arnaut who gather the wind
and ride an ox to hunt the hare
and I swim against the tide.

—Arnaut Daniel, Provençal, active 1180–1210

120   "The Limousin" is the troubadour Giraud de Borneil, from Excideuil near Limoges.

CANTO XXVII

3   The river Ebro in Spain.

23   Geryon, the monster on whose back Dante rode in *Inferno* 22.

37–39   Pyramus and Thisbe were lovers in Babylon. They lived in adjoining houses, and because their parents did not approve of their love and would not allow them to marry, they conversed through a hole in the wall between them. They arranged to meet at the tomb of Ninus. Thisbe arrived first and found a lioness who had just killed an ox and was eating it. Thisbe ran off, dropping a piece of her clothing, which the lioness covered with blood. Pyramus arrived, found the bloodstained garment, believed that Thisbe had been killed, and stabbed himself, falling at the foot of a mulberry tree, whose white berries at once turned red. Thisbe came back, found him dying, and killed herself beside him.

94   Cytherea: A name for Venus. It comes from the island of Cythera (modern Cerigo) off the southeast coast of the Peloponnesus. She is said to have risen from the sea off the shore of this island. Venus is the morning star.

100–108   In the Old Testament, Laban's daughters were Leah and Rachel. Jacob served Laban for a period of years and married first Leah and then Rachel. The two later became allegorical figures representing the active life (Leah) and the contemplative life (Rachel).

CANTO XXVIII

49–51   Proserpina, daughter of Ceres by Jupiter, was gathering flowers in a meadow in Sicily when Pluto suddenly appeared and carried her away to Hades to be queen there.

64–66   Venus, kissing her son Cupid, was accidentally wounded by one of his arrows and fell in love with Adonis.

71   Xerxes, king of Persia, led his vast army to attack Greece in 480 B.C., crossing the Hellespont on a bridge. He was defeated at sea; his fleet scattered at Salamis, and he was forced to retreat.

73–74   Leander, a young man of Abydos, swam across the Hellespont every night to visit Hero, the priestess of Venus at Sestos, on the other side.

80   Psalm 91:5–6.

130–131   On the one side is Lethe, the river of oblivion; on the other, Eunoè, a name which Dante apparently based on the word Protonoe, found in Uguccione da Pisa's *Magnae derivationes,* where the meaning of Protonoe is given as "first mind, that is, the divine mind."

CANTO XXIX

78 Delia is a name for Diana, goddess of the moon, born on the island of Delos.

92 The four animals are in Ezekiel 10:4–14 and in Revelations 4:6–8.

108 The griffin represents the double nature of Christ, human and divine.

116 Publius Cornelius Scipio Armilianus Africanus Numantianus, known as Scipio the Younger.

122 The three "theological" virtues: faith, hope, and charity.

131 In deep red, or "purple": the cardinal virtues.

136 Saint Luke was a physician and thus a descendant of Hippocrates, the most famous physician of the ancient world. Here, in the procession of the books of the New Testament, he represents the Acts of the Apostles.

143 The old man is John, who was often depicted asleep, as he had been when he had his great vision, and it was believed that he continued to sleep in Ephesus until the Day of Judgment.

145 The procession of colors represents, again, the "theological virtues": white for faith, green for hope, red for charity.

CANTO XXX

1 The seven candlesticks represent the sevenfold spirit of God.

11–12 Song of Solomon 4:18: "Come from Lebanon . . ."

21 A line freighted with allusions. It is translated from a famous line of elegy and farewell from Virgil's *Aeneid* (book 6, 967–886), *Manibus, oh, date lilia plenis* and serves as both a welcome from the angels and a farewell to Virgil.

43–51 The farewell to Virgil and his disappearance is a moment of great symbolic and personal significance. It is formalized by numerological designs: Virgil is named five times, first once, then three times in one tercet, then again once. The echo, several commentators have pointed out, recalls in turn lines of Virgil's in *Georgic* IV, 525–527, where Orpheus' voice, calling the lost Eurydice, is echoed down the stream.

55 Here Dante is named for the only time in the poem.

68 The olive was sacred to Minerva (Athena to the Greeks), goddess of wisdom.

83–84 Psalm 30:2–9.

121–123 Beatrice is speaking of the time about which Dante had written in his *La Vita Nuova*, as he would have seen it himself.

CANTO XXXI

11   The water of Lethe.

36   Among the losses inevitable in translation is the distinction, which Dante
     uses, between the formal, respectful second-person pronoun *voi* and the
     familiar *tu,* a distinction not available in English, where even the now all
     but obsolete *"thou"* and *"ye"* do not draw the same division, or do not do
     it consistently. Dante uses the respectful *voi* in speaking to Beatrice until
     his final words to her in *Paradise* 31, thus dramatically presenting the rev-
     erence of his attitude toward her, and continuing the formal manner of
     addressing the beloved in early Italian and in Provençal poetry.

59   The beloved of Dante's *Rime* 87 and 89 is referred to as a *pargolette,* a girl.

72   Iarbas, or Hiarbas, was a king of the Gaetulians in North Africa and a
     suitor of Dido at the time when she founded Carthage.

92   The lady is Matelda, and her name is mentioned only once, near the end
     (119) of canto 33. In the allegory she represents natural justice, but who
     her original was in the world of historic time—if indeed there was such a
     person at all—remains unknown. Her role here is to administer the
     waters of the two streams, Lethe and Eunoè, to all the souls who arrive
     at the summit of the mountain.

98   Psalm 50:9: "Purge me with hyssop and I shall be clean."

101–102   Drinking the water of Lethe removes the memory of sin, and drinking
     the water of Eunoè restores the memory of every good action.

104   The cardinal virtues (see canto 29, l.131).

111   The three on the other side are the theological virtues.

132   *Caribo:* a kind of dance music. Provençal *Garip.*

138   The second beauty is the mouth. The eyes are the first.

141   Castalia, the spring on Mount Parnassus.

CANTO XXXII

8   The three theological virtues, faith, hope, and charity.

37–39   In its first allegorical meaning, this is the Tree of the Knowledge of Good
     and Evil. It also signifies, as Beatrice announces, divine justice, or law,
     and stands for the Church. Singleton is insistent that it does not mean the
     Empire. The Church is represented by the chariot, and the Empire
     by the eagle, as the griffin represents Christ. The stripping of the leaves is
     the consequence of Adam's sin.

49–51   According to legend, the Cross was made from the wood of the forbid-
     den tree in Eden. Seth, in the legend, planted a shoot from the Tree of
     Knowledge on Adam's grave. By the time of Solomon it was a big tree.
     Solomon cut it down and used the wood, some say for his palaces and
     others say for a bridge across a pool. The Queen of Sheba, who had been
     miraculously informed that the Savior of the world would hang on this

wood in the future, refused to step on it, and warned Solomon against doing so. In order to prevent the prophecy from coming to pass, Solomon had the beam buried deep in the earth. The Pool of Bethesda welled up from the spot, its healing properties rising from the wood. Shortly before the Passion of Christ the wood itself rose to the surface and was used for the Cross.

55 See Numbers 17:8: The flowering of Aaron's rod.

58 The color, between red and violet, signifies the sacrifice of the crucifixion.

64–66 Io's guardian, Argus, had a hundred eyes. Mercury, with the song of the nymph Syrinx, put all hundred of them to sleep and then killed him.

72 It is Matelda who is calling.

76–81 Peter and James and John come to represent the theological virtues, faith, hope, and charity.

99 Aquilone, the north wind.

109–117 The early persecutions of the Christian Church.

118–123 The early heresies. Beatrice, as wisdom, drives the fox away.

124–129 The Church's acquisition of wealth through the "Donation of Constantine."

130–135 The dragon is probably the devil, here perhaps in the form of Mohammedanism.

136–141 Further acquisition of worldly wealth by the Church.

142–147 Further distortions of the Church, taking forms that represent the deadly sins.

148–160 The whore and the giant continue to represent deformations of the Church, following images taken from Revelation. By this point the allegory is close to Dante's own time, and the giant may represent Philip the Fair and others of the hated royal house of France. The removal of the chariot evidently refers to the removal of the papacy to Avignon in 1305, under Clement V, even though that occurred after the "ideal date" of Dante's vision.

CANTO XXXIII

11 From this point on Beatrice represents divine wisdom, and the seven virtues are her handmaidens.

43–44 The numerology here is still not clear after centuries of commentary. It appears to refer to a succession of kings, and to an epoch in the ages of Christianity. The use of numerology in prophetic and mystical writing was much in fashion in Dante's time.

47 Themis, daughter of Uranus (Heaven) and Gaea (Earth), a prophetic deity, thought to have been Apollo's predecessor at Delphi.
   The Sphinx was a female monster who sat on a rock near Thebes and asked a riddle of every Theban who passed, killing all those who could not answer. The riddle: What has four feet, two feet, three feet, but only

one voice? The number of its feet change and it is weakest when it has most feet. Oedipus said it was a man, on all fours in infancy, erect in maturity, walking with a cane in age. When the Sphinx heard the answer she flung herself down and was killed.

49 Naiads: nymphs of fountains and streams. Apparently a mistaken reading of Ovid made Dante think that the Naiads had solved the riddle posed by Themis, after the Sphinx's riddle had been guessed.

68 Elsa: A river in Tuscany that flows into the Arno near Empoli. Sections of the river contain carbonic acid and subcarbonate of lime and are able to petrify objects that remain in the water.

69 In the story of Pyramus and Thisbe (see note to canto 27:37–39), when Pyramus stabbed himself the fruit of the mulberry tree above him turned from white to red.

112 The Euphrates, a river that rises in Turkey, joins the Tigris, a river that rises in Turkestan, and flows into the Persian Gulf. These are two of the four rivers that water the Earthly Paradise. Singleton has commented upon Dante's use of only two rivers rising from a single fountain.

A NOTE ON THE TYPE

This book was set in Monotype Dante, a typeface designed by Giovanni Mardersteig (1892–1977). Conceived as a private type for the Officina Bodoni in Verona, Italy, Dante was originally cut only for hand composition by Charles Malin, the famous Parisian punch cutter, between 1946 and 1952. Its first use was in an edition of Boccaccio's *Trattatello in laude di Dante* that appeared in 1954. The Monotype Corporation's version of Dante followed in 1957. Although modeled on the Aldine type used for Pietro Cardinal Bembo's treatise *De Aetna* in 1495, Dante is a thoroughly modern interpretation of the venerable face.

Composed by Creative Graphics,
Allentown, Pennsylvania

Printed and bound by Quebecor,
Fairfield, Pennsylvania

Designed by Cassandra J. Pappas